Controlling and Analyzing Costs in Food Service Operations

Controlling and Analyzing Costs in Food Service Operations

JAMES KEISER
The Pennsylvania State University

ELMER KALLIO

JOHN WILEY & SONS

New York • Chichester • Brisbane • Toronto

Library of Congress Cataloging in Publication Data:

Keiser, James, 1928-
    Controlling and analyzing costs in food service
operations.

    1. Food service—Cost control. I. Kallio,
Elmer, joint author. II. Title.

TX911.3.C65K44   658.1'552   73-20156
ISBN 0-471-46710-3

Printed in the United States of America

20 19 18 17 16 15 14 13 12 11

preface

This textbook is designed primarily for cost control courses in schools of food service and hospitality management. The control of cost has become increasingly important in food management and undoubtedly will be receiving more attention in academic instruction; progressive thinking in this area is discussed here. Although the book was written as a text, it contains specific information to help operators combat their rising costs and to increase their productivity. It contains both theoretical material and suggestions for practical application and will be equally useful to food service students, to the commercial operator who wants to increase his profit, and to the institutional operator who wants to provide the best food service with the resources available to him.

In addition to covering such traditional areas of control as purchasing, receiving, storing, issuing, preparing, costing, and menu planning, the book emphasizes labor control and the use of financial management techniques for control purposes. We have concentrated on the control function as it relates to costs, instead of trying to cover the entire spectrum of food management. This approach has helped us to provide a thorough analysis of an aspect of food management that is too often neglected.

We trust that the student, the instructor, the commercial food service manager, and the institution operator will find this book a valuable contribution and a continuing resource.

University Park, Pa., 1972   *James R. Keiser*

acknowledgments

Regrettably, the pronoun must change here from "we" to "I." Coauthor Elmer Kallio died unexpectedly at a time when most of the first draft of this book had reached completion. His contribution both to its conception and to its final form was, of course, immense. Elmer's colleagues at Laventhol Krekstein Horwath and Horwath cooperated wholeheartedly throughout the subsequent revisions, and I am extremely grateful to all of them. In particular, I appreciate the help of David A. Arnold, J. Peter Kline, Peter Keim, and Robert A. Bressler.

I also deeply appreciate the help of my friends and colleagues in the Department of Food Service and Housing Administration at the Pennsylvania State University, including Professors Sara Clemen, Thomas Powers, and Leo Renaghan and my graduate assistant Mark Chaplin.

In addition, I thank Cordelia W. Swinton, Librarian of the Pennsylvania State University's College of Human Development, for furnishing me with a variety of helpful materials, and her husband, John, of Penn State's English Department, who reviewed the manuscript and offered numerous suggestions concerning stylistic matters.

Most of all I am grateful to my wife, Josephine, as I know Elmer Kallio was to his wife, Leona. They always encouraged us in our work and cheerfully endured the trials that accompanied the preparation of this book.

J.R.K.

contents

x   **Contents**

chapter 5   *Receiving*   63

chapter 6   *Storage, Issuing and Inventory*   73

chapter 7   *Preparation and Control*   93

chapter 1

The Problem of Labor Costs

Traditionally in food service operations, labor costs have been second in importance to food costs. However, the situation has changed dramatically in the last decade. Labor is becoming the major cost item and usually the major problem. There is every indication that labor costs will continue to rise. The constant demand by labor organizations in other industries will automatically force wage increases in the food service industry. Minimum wage laws in the food industry, as in other industries, will continue to increase the wages of both union and nonunion workers. The shortage of skilled help will encourage competent people to demand a premium for their services. Workers, generally, are demanding shorter hours and higher salaries. These demands are unusually hard on services that cannot operate on a regular nine-to-five, five-day week basis. Many industries have been able to increase their productivity an average of 2 to 4 percent or more a year, but the food service industry as a whole is far behind. For example, one study recently estimated that service industry operations increased production less than 1 percent per year; the food area, specifically, is probably lower. In many places, a waiter serves the same number of covers that he served 25 years ago, and a baker prepares the same number of pies as he did 40 years ago. Wages in the food industry generally are below those in other industries for positions requiring comparable intelligence and effort.

For a long time, many food service operators and managers thought that very little could be done about high labor costs, other than to raise menu prices to compensate for them. Food preparations needed a certain number of people to staff the different positions, and the fluctuations from high peaks to low valleys of activity resulted in inefficient use of labor. However, the cost-price squeeze and the drawbacks to passing high labor costs on to the consumer have forced the industry to search for ways and means to lower labor costs, increase employee productivity, and provide a satisfactory wage level that will retain competent and skilled employees in the industry.

The public often fails to appreciate the cost of the labor in the food service industry and compares it to the household where the cook receives no wages. Since the public associates a restaurant with the home dining room and the family food budget, it becomes a problem of educating the patrons to the fact that the cost of wages must be included in the menu price. With the current low percentage of profit in food service operations, there is little room for abnormal labor costs.

PAYROLL DETERMINANTS

Payroll is the result of two factors: the time required for performing the job, and the rate of pay for doing the job. If either factor is too high, the payroll cost will be too high. If someone takes four hours to do a job that could be done in two, or if he is paid $5.00 per hour instead of $2.50 (the amount which should be paid for that type of job), the labor cost, in each case, will be twice what it should be. In the food service industry, the problem is usually one of either decreasing the time requirement or raising productivity, rather than paying excessive wages. An unduly high wage cost results, however, when highly skilled people consistently do the work that lower-paid workers could perform. A chef should not spend time pre-preparing vegetables. A highly trained waitress should not nor mally have to bus dishes, a job that a bus boy with little training can do, probably with less effort.

ACTUAL LABOR COSTS

There is a false impression among some people that low wages result in low labor costs. On the contrary, with low wages you often get what you pay for in low-productive personnel. An operation is much better off by paying a fair wage to three good workers than to pay substandard rates to four people doing the same amount of work. It is surprising that many operators do not know when their employees are actually costing them profits. Assume that an employee is paid $2.50 per hour. Beyond this base pay, the employee might represent additional cost to his employer, as shown in Table 1.

The employee is paid $2.50 an hour, but the actual cost to the employer can be calculated to be close to three times this, or $7.17 per hour for productive time. It has been estimated that the average food service worker is actually doing productive work about 50 percent of the time that he is on duty. (This compares with about 80 percent for general

TABLE 1

BASE RATE PAID TO EMPLOYEE PER HOUR	$2.50
Other employer-paid costs on hourly basis (in cents)	
Vacation (one week)	0.05
Social Security (employer's share)	0.147
Workmen's Compensation	0.05
Unemployment Compensation	0.078
Time off for sickness (7 days)	0.05
Holiday pay (7 days)	0.05
Coffee or relief breaks (2 at 15 minutes)	0.18
Meal break time (½ hour)	0.18
Medical and hospital insurance	0.10
Meals (two, each costing employer 80¢)	0.20
TOTAL EFFECTIVE HOURLY COST	$3.585
TOTAL PRODUCTIVE HOURLY COST (50% productivity)	$7.17

industry productivity.) The figures above do not include such employee costs as employee payroll preparation, bookkeeping, uniforms, supervision, pilferage, maintaining employee facilities, overtime, bonuses, recreation activities, local employer wage taxes, life insurance, or other employee benefits. As the figures show, employees who are paid low hourly rates are expensive regardless of their low wages.

PRODUCTIVITY

Probably the most important element in labor cost is the productivity of employees. A high wage rate can be justified by the employees' productivity, but the food service industry has generally lagged behind other industries in improving productivity. In many instances, workers are using the same methods and the same type of equipment to produce the same amounts as they did years ago. If the food service industry is to prosper, offer better service to its patrons, and provide adequately for its employees, then productivity must be improved through the application of new and creative methods.

The study of productivity is complicated. Many of the different factors in productivity are inherent in the food service industry, while others have actually been developed by the industry, in many cases to its own disadvantage. In any case, comparatively little has been done by the industry to combat this stranglehold on profits and benefits.

KITCHEN VERSUS FACTORY

A commercial kitchen has been compared to a factory, since it produces goods for quantity consumption. If industrial factories have been able to increase their production efficiency, why can't kitchens, using the same methods and theories, show the same gains?

Unfortunately, the kitchen has several inherent differences. A factory usually has long production runs of uniform items. In a kitchen, many different items are prepared, often in small amounts and with frequent variations. If its goods cannot be sold immediately, a factory can produce for inventory. Food generally must be sold when produced and, unless it is frozen, food cannot be held for long periods. Nor is it in the nature of the food service business to sell its excess production by offering lower prices or having sales to move unsold items. Instead of producing at a constant steady rate, the kitchen must be ready to serve peak loads at meal times. At certain periods of the day there is relatively little activity in the kitchen, and its personnel and facilities are not fully utilized.

There are estimated to be over one-half million operations providing food in the United States. The variety and differences in these many individual operations preclude standardization of output or quality. A major problem in combating low productivity is trying to determine what a fair output per worker is. By its nature, a service industry requires a great deal of personnel time and effort. Obviously, it is also much easier to regulate a machine that will control production volume—a common practice in general industry—than it is to deal with individual employee speeds and temperaments.

COST SOLVING APPROACHES

There have been several approaches aimed at solving these problems, which will be discussed in detail throughout this book. One is the use of a food system using pre-prepared convenience foods. These foods can be produced under factory conditions for inventory regardless of immediate consumption requirements. In normal restaurant operations with a wide choice of items, comparatively few foods are produced in quantities large enough to require specialized labor and equipment. Convenience items are produced in large quantities allowing this specialization.

Another approach is to serve a limited menu. Specialty operations are becoming very popular; they appeal to the customer and help the operator to reduce labor requirements and costs. It is inevitable that even operators who pride themselves on preparing their own food items, and who like to provide variety, will utilize more convenience foods and will begin to limit their menu offerings somewhat. Menus containing an excessive number of items create higher food and labor costs, and also cause severe problems in maintaining quality in each of the many items.

Physical factors involved in productivity include layout, equipment, and working conditions. Too often, production facilities have taken second place to merchandising considerations in planning commercial operations. Too often, supply companies have installed superfluous equipment that actually impedes efficiency. Layouts are often unnecessarily large, requiring miles of extra walking and extra employees as well; or they may be too small, crowded, or confused, requiring extra help to relieve the tension. Frequently, operators plan their kitchens without first considering the expected menu, types of service, periods of service, and most efficient labor utilization.

The most vital asset of any food service organization is its employees. Their psychological needs are vital to productivity. Unfortunately, they are often treated as a commodity, like the food they prepare and serve. Too little thought is given to incentives that encourage workers to produce more and raise morale. Attendance is often taken for granted. An employee is criticized if his attendance is poor but is not rewarded for faithfulness. To increase morale and cut absenteeism, some employers are now giving bonuses for good attendance. These bonuses may come in the form of additional money or extra wages paid out for unused sick time. Since employees often feel that sick time is something they have "coming to them," they tend to take advantage of it whether or not they are actually ill. If they are not really sick, most workers prefer extra money. Moreover, their continued presence on the job causes less confusion, and production remains at a higher level.

The food service industry is notorious for its lack of profit-sharing plans. These have been found to be readily adaptable even to nonprofit organizations (where a cost saving approach can be utilized). Certainly, there should be some reward for exemplary service. People will exert themselves more when they feel that they are directly sharing in the endeavor. Psychological motivation can take psychological, rather than purely financial, forms. Many operations develop a feeling of cooperation and esprit de corps while actually paying employees less than competing organizations. This feeling is usually created by having the employee feel that someone is interested in him and that he is vital to the operation. Fairness is all important. Employees regard inequalities and partiality within the organization as more demoralizing than differences in material benefits among organizations.

MANAGEMENT AND PRODUCTIVITY

The quality of management has an important influence on employee productivity. Management functions of screening, hiring, orienting, training, and supervising all relate to productivity. Too often, management hires the first person available and immediately throws him at the job. This practice usually results in poor productivity and high turnover rates.

Management often fails to plan the production activities of its employees in advance but merely instructs someone to do something as the need arises. With the constantly changing variety of items produced, food service operations should require a high degree of supervision. Industry finds that one supervisor for ten employees is often a desirable ratio, but in food service, the ratio is often 1 to 30.

PRODUCTIVITY STANDARDS

A major problem in the food service industry is the determination of proper productivity standards. These standards are relatively easy to establish in general industry where output rates are steady. Where the jobs are repetitive, time study analysis can be undertaken and a standard production rate determined. If output does not have to be distributed immediately, but can be held for inventory, long and steady production runs are possible, which are conducive to the establishment of work standards. The inherent diversity of the food service industry makes the standardization of jobs or general production standards very difficult to achieve. Physical layout, pricing, service, and menu choice will all affect the productivity of employees differently in different operations. The volume of many commercial operations, that fluctuates with the busy and slow periods, may make some hourly based standards unrealistic. Therefore, productivity standards must be developed for each individual operation that take into consideration the circumstances under which the food service operates.

In analyzing productivity, it is sometimes helpful to classify employees as "variable," "semivariable," or "fixed." Variable employees are those who vary closely with volume of activity such as waitresses and bus boys: if business increases, the number of waitresses is increased, but if business is slow, fewer waitresses are needed. Cooks, pantry girls, cooks' helpers, and dishwashers might be semivariable employees: business would have to increase or decrease considerably before changes are made in the cook staff. A cashier is usually thought to be in the "fixed" category: even if business should decrease temporarily, it would probably still be necessary to retain a cashier. Productivity standards are considerably more helpful in regulating the number of "variable" employees than they are in regulating the "fixed" ones.

Sometimes it is desirable to consider the productivity standards for a particular department or section, rather than for the individual positions within it. Food service organizations are frequently divided into four major divisions: preparation, service, sanitation, and administration. Sections within the preparation division could include chefs, cooks, vegetable preparers, salad makers, bakers and butchers.

The total number of customers served per man-hour or man-day helps to gauge productivity and could help management to decide whether the section is over or understaffed. The service section can include captains, hostesses, waiters, waitresses, and bus boys. These "variable" employees can generally be changed to accommodate changes in volume. Sanitation employees include dishwashers, potwashers, porters, and janitors. These workers often fall into the "semivariable" category. Administration includes management, office help, store room help, receiving clerks, and cashiers. It is usually not feasible to increase or decrease the number of people in administration temporarily, so they would fall into the "fixed" category.

A SYSTEM FOR EMPLOYEE CONTROL AND PRODUCTIVITY

Unfortunately, the most efficient utilization of employees often comes as matter of pure chance in food service operations. Most employees are hired and assigned to jobs where it is hoped that they will produce. Little thought is given by many operators to the broader overall picture of productivity and efficiency. This lack of concern has caused two of the major problems facing the industry today: low productivity and comparatively low wages for employees. In an attempt to relieve these interrelated problems and to combat increasing labor costs, managers and experts have been trying to devise systems that will help control employees and direct them toward their greatest productivity. A number of systems, called "Personnel Staff Control," "Staff Planning," or "Professional Staff Planning," have been developed. Each system has the same goal: getting the greatest production from employees—not by undue exertion on their part (the work itself may even become easier) but by better organization of work, better planning of jobs, tighter scheduling of employees, and more thorough reviews of employee productivity.

A system or method for employee control and productivity might employ seven steps.

1. Personnel policies.
2. Job analysis.
3. Work simplification.
4. Work production standards.
5. Forecasting workload.
6. Scheduling.
7. Control reports.

To be most effective, the system must be reinforced by strong supervision with good personnel administrative policies, up-to-date management policies, and modern techniques. The productivity of employees depends partly on such personnel practices as recruiting, hiring, orienting, training, supervising and evaluating, together with the operation's compensation and termination policies. Management affects productivity with its kitchen layout, the equipment it provides, the type of food service it runs, the standards it expects, its scheduling, and its interest in and concern for its employees.

A job analysis usually contributes to the development of a job description and a job specification. The job specification lists such qualifications necessary to hold the job as the educational, physical, mental, and age requirements. The job description lists the tasks and duties that are performed in the job. It is extremely helpful in training and orienting new employees. The job analysis is very important for the control system. Management must take the entire work load, determine which divisions should do which jobs, and how much each position should be expected to accomplish. A job analysis eliminates questions of who does what, and permits less chance of someone being overworked or underworked in relation to others.

Work simplification involves studying and analyzing a job to find the easiest and most productive way to perform it. It might involve changes in the layout, introduction of labor saving equipment, introduction of pre-processed food, or changes in other methods currently being followed. Whether the employees are producing a maximum output commensurate with their labor input and whether an easier way of performing the work may be available is part of work simplification.

Work production standards provide a gauge that measures what to expect from an employee or position. The work production standards can be measured either in dollars of sales per day per employee or position, or in units or covers produced or served each day, or hour, per employee.

The work-load forecast is based on a forecast of the sales expected each day. Management calculates the number and the kinds of meals that it expects to sell. Dividing the forecasted volume of sales by work production standards (or the normal workload per each type of employee) should provide a basis for determining the number of each type of employee the operation requires.

In institutional type food service operations that have a definite census, the forecasting of volume is very easy. In commercial operations where volume may fluctuate considerably, the problem is much more difficult. For commercial operations, an individual or a committee may be assigned the task of forecasting sales for subsequent days or meals. Besides being necessary for personnel requirements, the forecasting of activity is very necessary for food purchasing and production planning.

Too often, scheduling is done routinely. The same number of employees report in and leave at the same time every day. Some food authorities suggest that up to one-third of all labor time may be either wasted or severely limited by poor scheduling alone. Scheduling in the food service field is complicated by the fact that meals are usually served during three peak periods during the day, and that production and service must be geared for these three periods, rather than for steady production throughout the day. In our model control system, the volume in covers was forecasted, and the number of employees required was determined by work production standards. Scheduling ensures that the proper number of employees will be actually on hand for the volume of work required at the times needed.

Control reports are definitely the responsibility of management. The system will not succeed unless management checks its results carefully. The control reports indicate how accurate the forecasting has been and whether the operation has been over or understaffed for the level of activity. These reports must be current, and management must take action on them immediately for optimum effectiveness.

In summary, the system provides for the proper utilization of the employee, for the analyzing of jobs to determine who should do what, for eliminating overlapping responsibilities, and for covering all necessary tasks. The jobs are then analyzed to find the easiest and most efficient ways of performing them. (There is not one best way to perform any job, but there is always a better way, and management must always be looking for that better way.) Production standards or goals must be established to provide a basis for determining a fair day's work. The volume of activity and consequent work loads are then forecasted. By knowing the production expected from each job position and the total amount of work expected, the number of people necessary for each job can be determined. Knowing whether a position is "fixed" or "variable" is very important here. Once the number of employees required for the different times is determined, it becomes necessary to schedule them for those times. This may involve changing regular hours. By means of control reports, management can constantly review the system and the results reported. It must make sure that there is no excess labor to increase labor costs or, conversely, too little labor, which would result in poor service and perhaps increases in other costs.

The system is very simple and logical, and it is based on common sense principles. When operating properly, it can provide an alternative to random and potentially wasteful personnel utilization practices. The system can definitely increase productivity, lower labor costs, and help boost employee satisfaction and morale.

chapter 2

Analyzing Labor Costs

PURPOSE

The cost of labor is a major consideration in food service operations. Progressive operators must know how to analyze and control this cost if they are to maintain the profit margins they desire. Nonprofit operations like hospitals and schools must also analyze their labor costs so that they can convert any savings into the best possible food service for their patrons.

In analyzing employee labor costs, an operator should keep in mind that there are different classes of employees who are affected differently by changes in sales volume. These classes are sometimes labeled "fixed," "semivariable," and "variable." A fixed employee is an employee who is necessary to the operation regardless of the volume of business. Whether business is heavy or light, the operation will still need a manager's secretary, a cashier, or a porter, for example. The only way to effect a lower unit-labor cost on these fixed positions is to increase the sales volume. Dishwashers might be considered semivariable workers, since there is usually a significant change in volume before fewer or additional dishwashers are required.

Waitresses and preparation personnel are variable personnel in most operations. Their numbers fluctuate according to changes in sales volume. Some operators have chosen to turn these variable employees into fixed employees by keeping a constant number of waitresses on duty regardless of the forecasted volume. This practice may help explain why up to a third of all labor time in the food service industry may be wasted due to poor scheduling.

Labor cost analysis has two major functions: one is determining whether labor costs are excessive or insufficient; the other is determining where these inadequacies occur. Necessary corrective measures may then follow.

LABOR COST AS A PERCENTAGE OF SALES

The first labor cost analysis simply compared the amount paid for labor with sales dollar volume. This led to the calculating of labor cost as a percentage of sales, a very simple and frequently used approach. The statement that labor costs are 30 percent of sales refers to the total cost of labor as 30 percent of the sales dollar volume. If sales were $100,000, labor costs would then be $30,000 or 30 percent.

$$\frac{\text{Cost of labor } (\$30,000)}{\text{Sales } (\$100,000)} = \frac{\text{Labor cost}}{\text{percentage } (30\%)}$$

Calculating labor cost simply as a percentage of sales is very common and helpful, but it is limited in scope. If the percentage is calculated over a particular period, such as a week or month, daily discrepancies often balance out. During this period the labor cost might have been too high at certain times and too low at other times, but the overall percentage for the period might be acceptable. A single overall percentage, without a careful breakdown, makes it difficult to pinpoint profit drains.

A change in menu pricing will also change the labor cost percentage. If menu prices were increased 10 percent on the $100,000 volume, and if the number of covers served remained the same, a new volume of $110,000 would result. If the labor cost remained at $30,000, the new labor percentage would be 27.3 percent instead of 30 percent. This new figure would seem to indicate an improvement in labor productivity, when actually, productivity and efficiency remained the same. Conversely, when employees are given wage increases, the labor cost percentage rises even though the efficiency and productivity may remain at the same level. Operations, like hospitals, institutions, and American Plan hotels that serve food without receiving payments directly for it, often assign an arbitrary dollar value for food sales. The resulting percentage is only as accurate as the arbitrary value. The inclusion of sick or vacation pay will distort a labor percentage figure as calculated over a short period.

It is very difficult to compare the labor percentages of apparently similar operations accurately. The labor cost of an operation depends on such factors as the menu (that is, choice of food and its selling price), the amount of convenience foods used, the layout, the equipment, the labor market in the area, and the services provided. Seemingly similar operations may produce vastly different percentages.

To refine and increase the usefulness of a labor cost percentage, many operations calculate percentages for different labor categories. These categories usually are administration and general labor costs, preparation labor costs, dining room service labor costs, and sanitation (including dishwashing) labor costs. The labor costs for each of these groupings may be calculated as a percentage of sales or as a percentage of the total labor cost. If total sales were $100,000, total labor costs $30,000, and preparation labor costs $12,000, then preparation costs would be 12 percent of total sales and 40 percent of total labor costs.

$$\frac{12,000}{100,000} = 12\% \text{ of sales}$$

$$\frac{12,000}{30,000} = 40\% \text{ of total labor costs}$$

With sanitation labor costs at $3000, service labor costs at $9,000, and supervision at $6,000, percentages of category labor cost to total labor cost are:

Preparation	$12,000	40%
Sanitation	3,000	10
Service	9,000	30
Supervision	6,000	20
Total labor cost	$30,000	100%

It is possible to break the groupings down even further. If desired, the labor cost percentage for customer service could be obtained separately for waitresses, bus boys, and captains. The preparation personnel could be divided into the various cooks, bakers, salad makers, and pantry workers. (The breakdown could conceivably proceed until each employee was considered separately.)

The value of calculating labor costs as a percentage of sales is enhanced when percentage figures are available for past weeks and months. These can be correlated with future sales forecasts and used in employee scheduling and as a guide to control future labor costs. It must not be assumed, however, that since labor costs have always been a certain percentage of sales, this percentage is the best one for the operation.

Despite their limitations, labor cost percentages are helpful in determining whether labor costs are within desired limits, and they can help to pinpoint where labor costs may be excessive. At best, however, the percentage figure shows the relationship between costs and sales and is not, itself, a positive control.

When relying on a labor cost percentage, the operator must remember to maintain his standards for customer service. It is possible to reduce a labor percentage figure by providing unsatisfactory service to the customer. But this practice creates a long range problem of business survival. An unduly low percentage thus is not necessarily desirable, since it can indicate that there are not enough employees on hand to render the appropriate service. The percentage may also vary for different levels of sales volume. For low volumes, the necessary number of fixed employees may cause a higher percentage than that calculated during a higher volume of business. For an operation with few employees, the addition or elimination of one employee may have a marked effect on the percentage figure; it may even make a standard percentage difficult to maintain.

WORK PRODUCTION STANDARDS

The establishment of work production standards and detailed job analyses comprises the next logical development in the attempt to analyze labor costs in food service operations.

Work production standards are simply the amount of work that a worker with a certain type of job is expected to accomplish. These standards can then be compared with the average amount of work that a person on that job actually performs. Work production standards can be used to better pinpoint the area in which the labor costs are not normal; in some cases they will indicate the individuals or the particular jobs that cause the discrepancies. Work production standards are, then, goals that are established for each type of job. They often provide an upper limit which, if surpassed, may mean that the employee is being overworked and that the quality of service is therefore compromised. They may also establish a lower limit suggesting the minimal fair day's output.

Work production standards are most useful with variable type employees or when the number of employees varies with the sales volume. They are less helpful in analyzing the contributions of the semivariable or fixed-type employees, since it may not be feasible to increase or decrease their numbers even though the sales volume may change.

Generally, production standards are based either on dollar sales generated during an employee's time period or on units served or produced during the period. A waitress may be rated on the dollar volume of business she handles, or she might be rated in the number of covers she handles. A coffee shop waitress might be expected to handle 45 to 60 covers in a two-meal period, while a waitress in a more formal dining room could be expected to handle only 25 to 30 covers. The coffee shop waitress might be expected, for example, to produce sales of $90 to $120, while the dining room waitress might reasonably produce sales of $120 to $180, depending upon the menu prices and meal period. Unit production standards can be expressed in covers served by waitress, dishes washed per dishwasher, covers prepared per cook, and patrons serviced by a cashier. The production standards may be measured on an hourly, daily, or weekly basis. An hourly analysis usually pinpoints hourly output per work-unit. However, activity usually fluctuates between the peak meal periods during the day. Hourly analysis thus becomes less meaningful in the food service industry than in general industry. In food service the production standard, "man days," is often used. A "man day" is determined by dividing the total number of hours spent in each job category by eight. If 100 hours of the waitress' time are used during a day, the number of "man days" would be 12.5.

Analysis on a daily basis is most appropriate to the food service field. It provides production standards (daily covers or dollar sales) for each day's activities and permits fast corrective action. Weekly analysis is not as helpful as daily analysis, but it can be a guide and certainly takes less effort to compute. The analysis can be computed on a monthly basis, but by the end of the month it is too late to correct the month's discrepancies. Also, there is more chance of high and low cost days canceling each other out and giving a satisfactory figure, even though individual days were unsatisfactory.

Obviously, to employ work production standards effectively and to secure all of their benefits, it is necessary to forecast the volume accurately and to schedule personnel accordingly. It is useless to determine how much a worker should produce if this standard is not then divided into the total production expectation to determine how many workers of each type should be on hand. If 600 covers are forecast for a period, and a waitress is expected to handle between 45 and 60 covers, then 10 or 11 waitresses should be scheduled. As scheduling of employees is done on a daily basis, it is obvious that labor costs will not be controlled effectively unless daily production standards are established.

DETERMINING WORK PRODUCTION STANDARDS

The first problem, and one of the hardest problems in using work production standards, is the establishment of those standards. Because of the diversity and individuality of food service operations, it is usually not feasible to use standards developed by other food operations. The menu, production methods, layout, equipment, service, pricing, and the type of patron will contribute to differences in work production standards among various operations. In setting standards, the past productivity records of the better employees should be used. If a satisfactory dishwasher averages a production range of 135 to 270 covers per day, over a specified period (say, a month) it can be assumed that the proper production standards are somewhere within this range. The low of 135 may have been too low and the high of 270 might have required undue effort and thus be unreasonably high. If a number of observations show him to be consistently busy handling between 190 and 220 covers, this may be considered a fair work load. There may be times when circumstances (special events or poor weather, for example) force him to exceed or fall below these standards, but at least management has a fairly sound basis for determining the amount of dishwashing help it needs after forecasting its volume.

Larger operations, like chain restaurants, in which all units are very similar, may employ more sophisticated techniques, like time studies and job breakdowns, for setting their standards. However, despite the many similarities in operations, differences in the local work force and in the character of the customers affect the work production standards differently in the various units.

Operations that have used work production standards over long periods have found that their standards can often be revised upward. Since management and supervisors begin to look at jobs more critically when setting and maintaining the standards, they tend to discover new ways of doing the work better, faster, and easier. Some operators have been able to introduce a "competitive spirit," pitting their employees against the standards. Some of the chain restaurants have recognized the value of this approach and pay special monthly bonuses to workers in the units that produce the lowest monthly payroll cost and the lowest food cost. However, care must be taken to see that quality standards have been maintained in the wake of these lower costs—an unduly low cost may be cause for investigation.

Work production standards and labor cost percentages are often involved in advanced scheduling. One method of scheduling in advance requires an operator to forecast the volume of anticipated business in dollar sales for the following week (or for any other convenient period). This figure is then multiplied by the desired labor cost percentage to provide a budgeted labor cost. The payroll for the period should not exceed that dollar amount. An example: 1000 covers are forecasted for a certain period at a check average of $2 or $2000 in sales. If a 35 percent payroll figure is desired, the dollar cost of labor scheduled should not exceed $700 or $2000 multiplied by 35 percent. (There can be variations, usually centering on whether to use the total labor cost percentage or a figure which excludes some fixed employees and better reflects the volume for variable employees.)

Another system for scheduling in advance requires an operator to set an expected dollar return per hour of labor expended. If, for example, $8 in sales is desired for every labor hour and forecasted sales are $2000, the number of hours scheduled should not exceed 250 or $2000 divided by 8.

Labor cost percentages and work production standards both help to analyze and control costs, but each shows different measurements, so one may supplement the other.

One advantage of work production standards over labor cost percentages is that the labor cost percentage shows only the relationship between labor costs and sales, and it varies with changes in either. The standards provide a definite standard or goal to achieve, and it is easy to determine how close each job comes to the predetermined standard. With the standards, it is a simple matter for management to see if there is an excess, or a deficiency, of workers in the variable job categories. The work production standard can also relate to the overall quality of service, since it can establish whether personnel had adequate time for their work. Whether to use a work standard based on covers served or on dollar sales per job is up to the individual operator. Some feel the number of covers served is a more objective standard while others feel dollar sales per-man-day is a criterion more related to profit, the main goal of the business. Adjustments in menu selling prices will require changes in a standard based on dollar sales.

EXAMPLES OF TYPICAL ANALYSES OF PAYROLL

To illustrate the preceding discussion a number of examples are presented which show some typical methods and standards used to analyze payroll costs.

Figure 1 is a format that is very simple to prepare on a weekly basis. It requires a minimum of information: the number of full time employees, the number of covers served, the total sales, and the weekly payroll by classification. It divides employees into the four major classes and computes, weekly for each class, the number of covers served, the sales for each employee of a certain class, and the ratio of payroll costs to food sales. These three indexes can indicate whether payroll costs are excessive and where discrepancies occur. They may also be expanded to show details for different groupings of employees within the respective major classes.

Used on a weekly basis, the form cannot reveal daily discrepancies. However, the form does reveal unfavorable trends, and even on a weekly basis, this usually allows time enough for corrections.

Figure 2 was designed for a different type of operation and is somewhat more detailed than Figure 1. The example is prepared on a weekly basis but the format could also be used on a daily or monthly basis. Unlike Figure 1, which indicates covers per employee classification per week, Figure 2 indicates the covers per man-day of time per job type during the week—a more specific approach. It also provides a total labor cost percentage—percentages for each of the four major employee classifications, and also percentages for each type job. (These percentage calculations can be eliminated if desired.)

In utilizing this control, the manager would first look at the total labor

ANALYSIS OF WEEKLY PAYROLL

Week Ending_____

	Number of Employees	Weekly Payroll Cost	Number of Covers per Employee	Sales per Employee	Ratio of Payroll to Food Sales
Administrative					
Manager	1	$200.00			
Bookkeeper	1	100.00			
Cashier	2	180.00			
Total	4	$480.00	760	$1,600	7.5%
Preparation					
Cooks—					
Cook's helper	4	$500.00			
Baker	1	125.00			
Pantry	2	160.00			
Total	7	$785.00	434	$ 914	12.3%
Service					
Hostess	1	$ 80.00			
Waitresses	10	420.00			
Bus Boy	2	150.00			
Total	13	$650.00	234	$ 492	10.2%
Cleaning					
Dishwashers	2	$170.00			
Porter	1	85.00			
Total	3	$255.00	1,013	$2,133	4.0%
Grand Total	27	$2,170.00	113	$ 237	34.0%
Statistics					
Food sales		$6,400.00			
Covers served		3,040			
Average check		$2.10			

Figure 1

cost percentage (33.3 percent) and total covers per man-day (17.8). These figures provide an indication of overall productivity and a comparison of labor costs to sales. He would then look at the figures for the various classifications, concentrating on the Preparation and Service categories, since they have both the largest number of employees and the most variable-type employees.

Figure 3 can be used both as a forecast for scheduling personnel and as a report of labor costs during the period. First, an average hourly wage

Number of Employees	Position	Salary or Hourly Wage (H)	Total Amount	Man-Hours	Man-Days	Covers Man-Day	Ratio of Payroll to Sales (%)
	Administrative and General						
1	Manager	200.00	200.00	44	5.5	374.0	2.31
1	Office	125.00	125.00	40	5.0	598.4	1.44
1.5	Cashier (H)	2.50	130.00	52	6.5	460.3	1.50
1	Storeroom (H)	2.25	101.25	45	5.6	534.3	1.17
4	Total		556.25	181	22.6	132.9	6.43
	Preparation						
1	Chef	175.00	175.00	48	6.0	498.7	2.02
2	Cooks (H)	3.00	390.00	130	16.3	183.6	4.51
2	Pantry (H)	2.75	269.50	98	12.3	243.3	3.11
1	Pastry (H)	2.75	115.50	42	5.3	564.5	1.33
1	Utility (H)	2.00	88.00	44	5.5	544.0	1.01
7	Total		1,038.00	362	45.4	66.0	12.01
	Service						
1.5	Hostess (H)	2.50	150.00	60	7.5	398.9	1.73
10	Waitresses (H)	1.35	540.00	400	50.0	59.8	6.25
3	Bus Boys (H)	1.10	115.50	105	13.1	228.4	1.33
14	Total		805.50	565	70.6	42.4	9.32
	Sanitation						
4.5	Dishwashers (H)	2.00	400.00	200	25.0	119.7	4.63
1	Porter (H)	2.00	80.00	40	5.0	598.4	.92
5	Total		480.00	240	30.0	99.7	5.55
30	**Totals**		2,879.75	1,348	168.5	17.8	33.3

Statistics

Food Sales	8,639.25
Food Covers	2,992.00
Average Check	2.89

Figure 2

is calculated (the total wages for the last payroll period divided by the number of hours worked in the period). Multiplying the average hourly rate ($3) by the number of hours (B) will give labor costs (C). Dividing sales (A) into the labor cost (C) will give the labor cost percentage (D). Dividing the number of hours (B) into sales (A) provides the sales per man-hour (E). If this form is prepared before the actual period begins, management can subsequently see if labor costs are in line with the projected volume. After the period, actual figures rather than projected ones are used, and management can see how labor costs actually compared with sales and productivity as shown by sales per man-hour.

Some modifications in the form include figures by work shifts rather

SALES AND LABOR FORECAST AND REPORT

Week Ending _6/1_   Average Hourly Rate _$3.00_

Date	6/1	6/2	6/3	6/4	6/5	6/6	6/7
Day of Week	mon.	Tues.	Wed.	Thur.	Fri.	Sat.	Sun.
(A) Sales							
Today	$550	$585	$600	$575	$650	$850	$700
Week-to-Date	—	1,135	1,735	2,310	2,960	3,810	4,510
Month-to-Date	—	1,135	1,735	2,310	2,960	3,810	4,510
(B) Hours							
Today	60	63	65	63	70	80	75
Week-to-Date	60	123	188	251	321	401	476
Month-to-Date	60	123	188	251	321	401	476
(C) Labor Cost ($)							
Today	$180.	$189.	$195.	$189.	$210.	$240.	$215.
Week-to-Date	—	369	564	753	963	1,203	1,418
Month-to-Date	—	369	564	753	963	1,203	1,418
(D) Labor Cost (%)							
Today	32.7	32.3	32.5	32.9	32.3	28.2	30.7
Week-to-Date	32.7	32.5	32.5	32.6	32.5	31.6	31.4
Month-to-Date	32.7	32.5	32.5	32.6	32.5	31.6	31.4
(E) Sales/Man-Hour							
Today	$9.17	$9.29	$9.23	$9.13	$9.29	$10.63	$9.33
Week-to-Date	9.17	9.23	9.23	9.20	9.22	9.50	9.47
Month-to-Date	9.17	9.23	9.23	9.20	9.22	9.50	9.47

Figure 3

than total daily ones and breakdown by various classes of employees. Management's own compensation may or may not be included in the average hourly wage but it is important that a consistent policy be followed regarding its inclusion.

In Figure 3 the format is used as a forecast report. Management wants the scheduled labor percentage to be not higher than 33 percent. To maintain this percentage with anticipated sales, no more than the number of hours indicated on the Hours Today blank can be actually scheduled. The average hourly rate of $3 was determined by dividing the payroll for the previous period by the number of hours worked. If this is thought to be too high, a goal figure for the hourly rate could be used instead.

Since this is the first week of the month, the week to date figures and month to date figures are identical.

WEEKLY ANALYSIS OF EMPLOYEE PRODUCTIVITY

Week Ending *June 6*

Positions	Payroll	Hours	Sales/Hour	Sales Goal per Hour	Sales/Hour Last Week
Administrative and General					
Manager	$ 200.00	44	196.35	200.00	198.64
Office	125.00	40	215.98	225.00	217.46
Cashier	130.00	52	166.14	170.00	169.45
Storeroom	101.25	45	191.98	200.00	197.24
Total	$ 556.25	181	47.73	50.00	48.18
Preparation					
Chef	$ 175.00	48	179.98	185.00	183.78
Cooks	390.00	130	66.46	72.00	70.41
Pantry	269.50	98	88.16	94.00	92.10
Pastry	115.50	42	205.70	215.00	208.00
Utility	88.00	44	196.35	200.00	194.23
Total	$1038.00	362	23.86	25.00	24.05
Service					
Hostess	$ 150.00	60	143.99	150.00	146.11
Waitresses	540.00	400	21.60	25.00	23.14
Bus boys	115.50	105	82.28	85.00	80.18
Total	$ 805.50	565	15.29	17.50	16.75
Sanitation					
Dishwashers	$400.00	200	43.20	46.00	45.22
Porter	80.00	40	215.98	225.00	217.54
Total	$ 480.00	240	36.00	40.00	38.19
Grand total	$2,879.75	1,348	6.41	7.00	6.69

Figure 4

Figure 4 shows sales per man-hour and also compares them with a sales goal per man-hour and the sales per man-hour during the previous week.

The Sales/Hour figure is calculated by dividing the number of hours worked into the dollar sales for the period. The Sales Goal per Hour figure represents the amount of sales desired for each hour worked in the various categories. The Sale per Hour Last Week figure represents the Sales/Hour of the previous week and permits a comparison of the two weeks.

Figure 5 is a simple form that can be of assistance to a hospital dietary

DIETARY DEPARTMENT

Monthly Performance Standard

Positions	Man-Hours	Man-Days	Number of Covers Served per Man-Day
Administration and General			
Administrator	184	23	977
Dietitian (diet aide)	192	24	937
Receiving and storeroom	184	23	977
Total Administration	560	70	321
Preparation			
Cooks	704	88	255
Potwashers	356	44½	505
Vegetable cleaners	188	23½	957
Pantry	344	43	523
Pastry	176	22	1,022
Total Preparation	1,768	221	102
Service			
Tray girls	2,776	347	65
Servers	584	73	308
Total Service	3,360	420	54
General			
Warewashing	1,856	232	97
Porter	208	26	865
Total General	2,064	258	87
Grand Total	7,752	969	23

	MONTH	WEEK
Total Meals Served	22,480	5,190

Figure 5

department by relating the number of covers served per eight-hour man-day. The hospital food administrator can readily see how the dietary department is staffed for the current patient load. In the example, a monthly evaluation is made, but the analysis could be made on a daily basis.

A daily analysis is desirable but, because of the amount of paperwork involved and the fact that hospital dietary workers usually work the same number of hours regardless of changes in the patient census, a monthly analysis may be acceptable.

BAR CHARTS

Bar charts are a great help in analyzing the use of labor in food service establishments. Not only do they present the information in a form which may be readily analyzed, they also provide a unique visual presentation which makes the information easier to absorb. Bar charts can help determine how busy employees are, how well they are scheduled in relation to work loads, and whether or not too many employees have been hired.

Through the use of bar charts, management quite often discovers, for example, that employees are arriving for work before they are actually needed (as when dishwashers come on duty at 7 A.M. but the dishes do not arrive at the dishroom in any quantity until 9 A.M.). Management may find that there are too many employees on hand for the volume of activity at one time during the day and that there are too few at another time. Employees may have originally been properly scheduled, but conditions or work loads may have changed while the working hours remained the same. Under changing conditions, alert management will reschedule its employees.

How well employees are scheduled (as demonstrated by bar charts) can also be used as a criterion to help evaluate supervisory personnel, sometimes for possible merit salary increases.

Preparing Bar Charts. Bar charts are easy to prepare. Charts appear as graphs with the working hours of the operation plotted along the top. Names of employees or the various jobs are listed along the side of the form. The hours that each employee or job classification is on duty are then drawn across the appropriate time intervals. These lines need not necessarily be solid, as different shadings can be used to indicate the nature of the work and the nature of the time off: serving, production, or sanitation, on the one hand; lunch break, or rest period, on the other. Different shadings might also be used to indicate how busy the employee actually is. The chart can also show information about the volume of activity by superimposing a graph on the chart or by listing the appropriate figures.

Figure 6 shows the activity in one hotel kitchen. This graph was plotted by observing the kitchen activity and evaluating it on a scale ranging from 0 to 100 percent. Plotting points using such specific measurements as covers served per hour is not practical in ths preparation department. To measure preparation activity in this operation, it is neces-

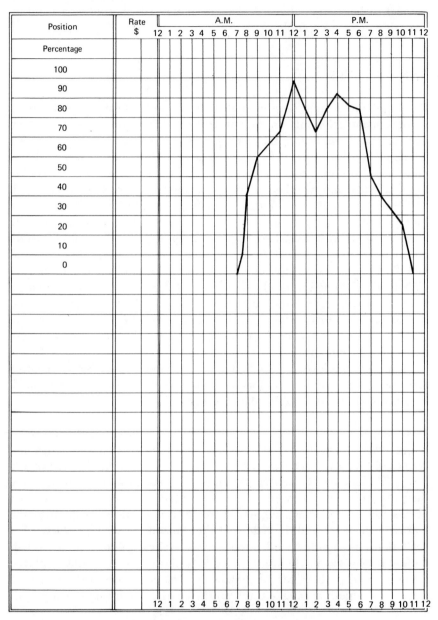

Position	Rate $	A.M.	P.M.
Percentage		12 1 2 3 4 5 6 7 8 9 10 11	12 1 2 3 4 5 6 7 8 9 10 11 12
100			
90			
80			
70			
60			
50			
40			
30			
20			
10			
0			

Figure 6   Kitchen production—level of activity.

sary to actually observe the activity and subjectively estimate the various levels of activity on a scale of 100. In this operation, pre-preparation and preparation activities reach a peak just before noon and hold rather steady until about 6 P.M. Eight people were scheduled for the production unit, four on a seven-to-three shift and four on a three-to-eight shift, as shown in Figure 7. This scheduling did not coincide with the activity.

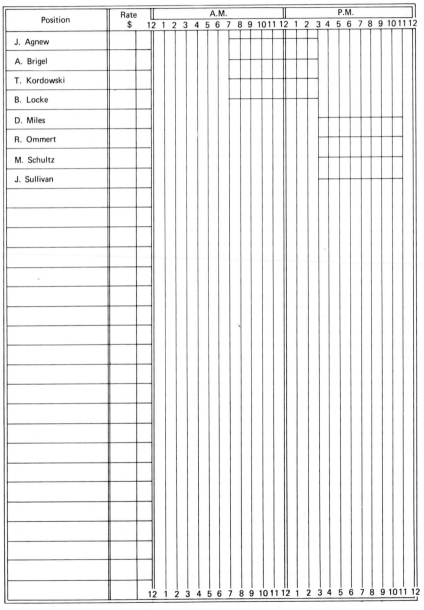

Figure 7   Kitchen production—original scheduling.

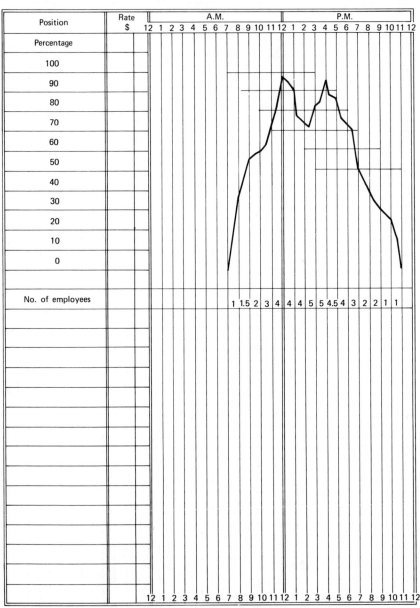

Figure 8   Kitchen production—rescheduling to production.

By rescheduling according to the bar chart shown in Figure 8, it was possible to eliminate two workers yet have the same number of employees on hand for the key periods necessary to complete the work adequately. In addition, the person preparing the graphs was able to notice ways in which the work peaks could be leveled somewhat and some work eliminated. There were also benefits in not having a complete change of shifts at one time. Since people tend to slow down as they approach the end of their work day, and since it usually takes a little time to get started, there was less work being performed at change-over time. With personnel starting and stopping at different times, this problem was largely eliminated.

Another method, utilizing bar charts to determine how hard employees are working and whether the number of scheduled hours is reasonable, was developed by a hospital food supervisor. The various positions and the on-duty hours are shown by the charts. The supervisor made ratings of the level of activity in each position over a specified period of time using a scale of one to six. A "one" on the scale indicated that the employee was working much too slowly or was under utilized; a "six" indicated that the employee was forced to work harder than he should. A rating of "four" was considered the proper level of activity for the job. The ratings for all positions were totaled for each hourly period and divided by four (as shown in Figure 9). The resulting figure suggested the optimum number of people that should be on duty during any specific hour. By indicating times of surplus labor, the supervisor was better able to coordinate labor hours with production needs and to make a sizeable reduction in the labor required.

Figure 10 shows the bar chart scheduling of a small hospital.

Figure 11 shows the charting for a fast-service, short-order operation. Further analysis is made at the bottom of the chart by customer number, sales, labor costs, and the labor cost percentage (broken down into two-hour periods). The first and last periods are somewhat distorted by the incorporation of opening and closing labor costs.

Figure 12 demonstrates another application of bar charts. In this figure, the work hours of four dishwashers are shown on bar charts. The level of activity of each is determined visually and is indicated by a different shading. This helps indicate where there may be excess labor. By different scheduling it was shown that the work load could be handled by three people instead of four and that one of the three was available for other work between 3 p.m. and 5:30 p.m. Not only were savings in payroll achieved, but it was also found that the morale of the dishwashers increased with more consistent work levels replacing alternating periods of activity and idleness.

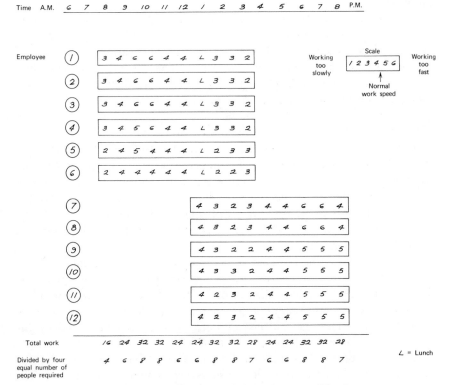

Figure 9   Evaluation of tray room workload.

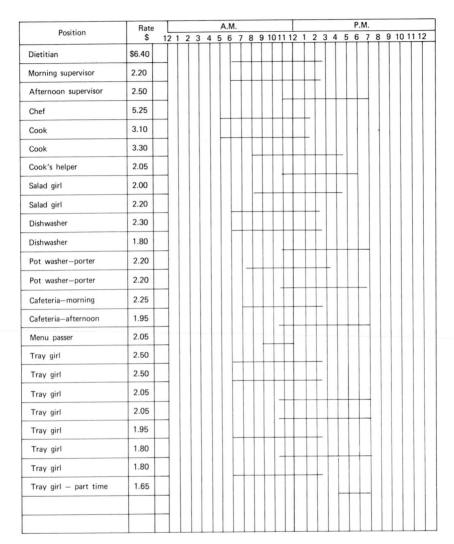

Figure 10   Typical daily staffing schedule.

Job no.	Position	Hours Worked	Hourly Rate	Daily Pay	A.M. / P.M. (6 7 8 9 10 11 12 1 2 3 4 5 6 7 8 9 10 11 12)	Hours
1	Chief cook	9	$2.85	$25.65	————————————	8:30-6
2	Day cook	8	2.50	20.00	————————	6:30-3
3	Eve. cook	8	2.50	20.00	————————	3-11:30
4	Utility	8	2.20	17.60	————————	7:30-4
5	Utility cook	8	2.35	18.80	————————	3-11:30
		41		$102.05		
10	Waitress counter	8	1.35	10.80	————————	6:30-3
11	" "	8	1.25	10.00	————————	7-3:30
12	" "	6	1.35	10.80	————————	8-2:30
13	" "	8	1.25	10.00	————————	11-7:30
14	" "	7.5	1.25	9.37	————————	3:30-11:30
15		6	1.25	7.50	————————	4:30-11
		43.5		$58.47		

Covers								Totals
Covers by periods	33	41	66	42	21	59	34	26	322
Sales by periods	$38.28	$47.56	$102.30	$65.10	$32.55	$128.62	$74.12	$56.68	$545.21
Labor costs	$18.21	$23.00	$25.90	$24.83	$23.24	$20.05	$15.23	$17.81	$168.27
Labor cost percentage (%)	47.6	48.3	25.3	38.1	71.3	15.6	20.5	31.4	30.9

Figure 11   Daily labor analysis chart.

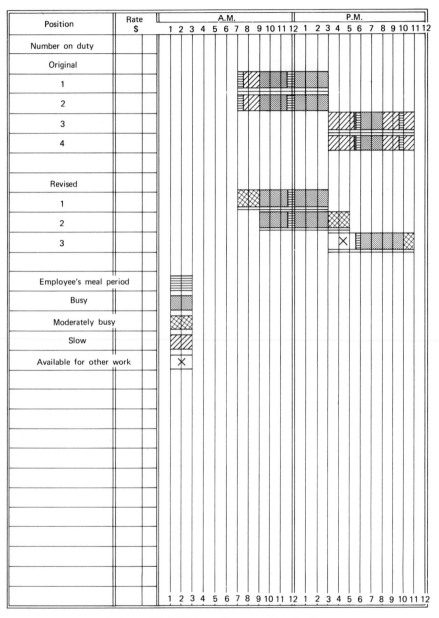

Figure 12   Dishwashers work schedule.

chapter 3

Controlling Labor Costs

Chapters 2 and 3 are closely related: Chapter 2 discusses techniques for determining whether, or where, labor costs are excessive; and Chapter 3 discusses ways to keep these costs as low as possible. However, labor cost control does not consist only of a one-time correcting of problems as revealed by the techniques of Chapter 2. It is also a continuous process. The better the routine cost control procedures, the less chance that corrective action will be necessary.

The labor costs of an operation result from many factors. Some labor costs arising from such factors as layout design, equipment, and union restrictions are built into the operation from its beginning. Others result from management decisions concerning such other aspects of the operation as the menu selection, the use of convenience foods, the prices to be charged, and the amount of employee training required. Still others are frequently caused by lack of direct control over the workers and poor labor practices generally. All factors are important, and the neglect of any one can cause costs to rise.

STAFFING AND SCHEDULING

The terms "staffing" and "scheduling" are sometimes used interchangeably, but they refer to separate functions. Staffing entails the determination of the appropriate number of workers needed for the operation for the work that has to be accomplished. This determination can be worked out rather objectively in advance by using work production standards and job analyses. Scheduling entails having the proper number of workers on duty, as determined by the staffing needs. Scheduling presents special problems since the volume of activity, and consequently the labor need, varies during the working day.

Of great help in staffing is the use of a "Job Number Control List." This list requires that each job be analyzed, described, formalized, and numbered with the payroll or time card number, for example. When a new employee is hired, he must be hired for a specifically numbered and classified job, not just to work where needed. Those who use a Job Number Control List system must plan the duties and responsibilities of each job in advance. Overlapping of jobs is decreased; control is increased, since no one is added to the payroll on a permanent basis unless to a definite numbered position and need. (Too often, employees are hired for a temporary need but remain after that need is over.) Having jobs listed on the job control form does not mean that every number has to be filled. Ten cook positions may be listed but if business warrants only eight, only eight have to be employed.

Work production standards are very helpful in determining the number required in each position. Figure 1 shows a sample job control form for the dining room department of a table service restaurant. Not all the positions would be filled unless business had reached its maximum. The dining room service positions are numbered in the 100s. Positions in preparation could be numbered in the 200s, sanitation in the 300s, and administration in the 400s. Positions are further classified with hostesses and cashiers being listed from 100 to 109, waitresses 110 to 149, and bus boys 150 to 170. This system allows for easy identification. The use of a job control list will also help eliminate dissatisfaction about scheduled hours. The worker is hired for a definite job having specified hours. He may eventually move into another job number that has more desirable hours for him.

Scheduling is the assigning of employees to specific working hours and work days. One goal in scheduling is having enough staff for the handling of busy meal periods without having excess help in the slower periods between meals. Advance preparation can help achieve this goal. Employees should do as much advance work as possible during the slow periods so that they will not have to perform it during the peak meal periods. The menu can be changed for large volume days to eliminate time consuming food items. For example, a fine restaurant in a university town finds itself swamped after football games. It discards its regular diversified menu and serves only roast beef, which requires little effort in the kitchen during the serving period. Some operations use convenience foods to reduce the labor demand during their busiest periods. This practice may provide a more expensive food cost but it does not require expensive and inefficient temporary help; thus, the payroll and overall costs may be kept low. In some locations it is possible to find part-time help to supplement peak periods. A hospital may hire full time tray girls to cover two meals and part time girls for the third meal. Split shifts can be very useful if employees can be found who will work the staggered hours. However many employees do not like the "off" time in-between and double transportation costs can be a problem.

JOB NUMBER CONTROL LIST

Predetermined Job Numbers	Classification	Hours
Dining Room Service		
101	Hostess	8:00 A.M.–5:00 P.M.
102	Evening hostess	4:30 P.M.–11:00 P.M.
103	Assistant hostess	Variable
104	Relief hostess and relief cashiers	Variable
105	Cashier	8:00 A.M.–5:00 P.M.
106	Evening cashier	4:00 P.M.–12:00 P.M.
110	Waitress	7:30 A.M.–4:30 P.M.
111	Waitress	7:30 A.M.–4:30 P.M.
112	Waitress	7:30 A.M.–4:30 P.M.
113	Waitress	11:00 A.M.–7:30 P.M.
114	Waitress	11:00 A.M.–7:30 P.M.
115	Waitress	11:00 A.M.–7:30 P.M.
116	Waitress	11:00 A.M.–7:30 P.M.
117	Evening waitress	4:30 P.M.–12:00 P.M.
118	Evening waitress	4:30 P.M.–12:00 P.M.
119	Evening waitress	4:30 P.M.–12:00 P.M.
120	Evening waitress	4:30 P.M.–12:00 P.M.
121	Evening waitress	4:30 P.M.–12:00 P.M.
122	Relief waitress	Variable
123	Relief waitress	Variable
124	Relief waitress	Variable
125	Relief waitress	Variable
126	Relief waitress	Variable
150	Busboy	8:00 A.M.–5:00 P.M.
151	Busboy	8:00 A.M.–5:00 P.M.
152	Busboy	8:00 A.M.–5:00 P.M.
153	Busboy	5:00 P.M.–12:00 P.M.
154	Busboy	5:00 P.M.–12:00 P.M.
155	Busboy P.T.	5:00 P.M.–9.00 P.M.
156	Relief busboy	
157	Relief busboy	

Figure 1

Care should be taken to see that employees are not scheduled before they are needed. It is a rare food service operation where all employees are needed at the same time; staggered times of starting and stopping may do much to increase productivity. Some operations with a five-day work week schedule a six day work week during busy periods and pay overtime. During slow periods, some employees welcome voluntary time off which helps lower labor costs. The adoption of the ten-hour day, four-day week may help some operations cover three meals with some of their employees.

Scheduling and staffing are so important that large organizations have staff planners or operation analysts who devote much of their time to it. By using Job Control Lists and seeing that the work schedules conform to the times when help is most needed, the small operator can go far in equalizing the advantages of the specialists.

TURNOVER

A major problem in the food industry, and one which has a direct effect on costs and productivity, is turnover of employees. ("Turnover" occurs when employees leave the operation and are replaced by new ones.) In the food service industry, turnover is far above that of general industry. One figure sometimes quoted is 10.4 percent per month or about 125 percent per year. Despite these high percentages, many individual operations have low turnover rates, proving that high turnover is not necessarily inherent in the food industry and that it can be solved. Estimates of the cost of replacing a rank and file employee range from $200 to $800. This cost includes finding a new worker, hiring and training him, initial lack of efficiency and the increased supervision requirement, increased breakage, additional unemployment and social security tax payments, and additional record keeping. There is also the intangible nonmonetary cost of poorer service to the patron, resulting in possible dissatistfaction and loss of patronage. The greatest turnover usually occurs within the first two weeks of employment and any long term benefit of training and supervision is wasted. The following list discusses some of the major causes of turnover among food service employees.

1. Poor selection, hiring and orientation. (Management hires the first "body" to apply without adequately checking his qualifications or references.)
2. New employees placed in jobs that are not compatible with their capabilities. (A person will become bored if the work is not challenging or interesting to him or he will become frustrated if the job is too difficult for him.)
3. Inadequate information about the job or its requirements. (The new employee may find the job vastly different from what he had imagined. The use of job descriptions and job specifications can

be very helpful in preventing this. The new employee should be fully informed concerning the job.)

4. Inadequate or poor supervision causing a potentially good worker to give up during the "breaking in period." (A new worker needs help, guidance, and assurance.)

5. Lack of a proper wage rate structure. (New employees should not be hired at a higher rate than that being paid to present workers in similar positions. A violation of this rule leads to resentment and and employee turnover. A definite wage rate policy is necessary.)

6. Lack of a training program. (The more highly trained an employee is, the more likely he is to stay on the job. An operation with a continuous training program will retain employees for a longer period of time. Training an employee gives him a feeling of status and professionalism besides increasing his efficiency, productivity, and loyalty.)

7. Lack of a grievance outlet. (If an employee has a grievance, there should be a procedure whereby he can express it without future prejudice. A grievance may be real or imagined and may smolder then flare beyond rational importance. Misunderstanding should be cleared up before they become major problems.)

8. Poor working conditions. (Substandard working conditions and inadequate facilities can contribute to a high turnover rate. Proper restrooms and washroom facilities are most important to the food industry and help to increase morale and sanitation standards.)

9. Lack of advancement. (Ambitious new employees like to see a path by which they can advance. The bus boy who can reasonably expect to become a waiter, and then the head waiter, or the scullery boy who can conceivably become a chef, will be less likely to leave their place of employment.)

10. Lack of financial incentive. (A worker likes to earn as much as possible and will gravitate toward the highest wage. Higher wages alone will not retain employees. If an adequate wage is already being earned, then other considerations, both psychological and material, become more important when considering a change of jobs. Fringe benefits are important to those seeking employment. Some food industry employers give the employees their meals, uniforms, health and life insurance, and provide, in addition, profit sharing contributions, pensions, vacations, and other smaller benefits.)

11. Apparent lack of supervisory interest. (Sensitive, good supervisors and department heads and good employee relations will materially

lower employee turnover. Incentive plans of recognition, awards, sports teams, picnics, company activities, comfortable working conditions, and pleasant surroundings all contribute to a satisfied employee. In fact, all of the ten previously mentioned causes of high turnover rates are closely tied to the lack of the human factor.)

Turnover, then, may be lowered by good personnel administration and by reducing the causes of high turnover where possible. To combat turnover, it is very important to know what is causing it. Termination interviews are often used for this purpose. The departing employee is interviewed by management to determine the reason for his leaving (even if he is being fired). Quite often the reason for leaving may not be the one first mentioned; unfavorable situations such as poor working conditions or an unfair or incompetent supervisor may be brought to light only reticently. Larger organizations have regular report forms for the termination interview and summarize the prevalent reasons for turnover regularly. Since the departing employee may have strong feelings for leaving, some managers prefer to send him a letter the following week containing a form for him to fill in the reasons for his departure, and a stamped self-addressed envelope to return it, theorizing that the employee may be more objective about his departure at a later time.

Figure 2 shows a termination interview report. These should be periodically summarized to determine whether there are trends or curable situations causing terminations.

To control turnover, it is necessary to establish the current turnover rate for comparison purposes. There are a number of different formulas that may be used to compute the turnover rate, but whichever one is chosen, it is important that the same formula be used each time. One formula for determining a monthly turnover rate divides the number of separations during the month by the total number of workers on the payroll in the pay period ending nearest the fifteenth of the same month:

$$T \text{ (Separation rate)} = \frac{S \text{ (number of separations)}}{M \text{ (midmonth work force)}} \times 100$$

If 50 employees were on the payroll at midmonth, and six were terminated during the month, the separation rate would be 12.0 percent.

$$T = \frac{6}{50} = 12.0$$

If more refined information is desired, the same formula could be used to determine the quit rate, discharge rate, or layoff rate. And, instead of using the arbitrary midmonth employment figure, one could substitute the average monthly work force figure obtained by adding the number of

Name:	Date:	Dept.	Shift	Date hired
Address:	Sex	Marital Status	Age	Dependents
Present job	Previous training and experience			
Supervisor's name	Type of separation Quit □ Discharge □ Lay-off □ Mil. □ Misc. □ sep. sep.			
Reason for separation—employee's statement:				
Reason for separation—supervisor's statement:				
Indirect causes or conditions contributing to this separation—foreman's statement and his suggestions for correcting these conditions:				
Reason for separation—interviewer's statement:				
Final action taken:				
Would you rehire? Yes □ No □				
	Signature of Interviewer			

Figure 2. Termination Interview Report.

employees at the beginning of the period to the number at the end of the period and dividing by two.

ABSENTEEISM

Absenteeism, sickness, and leaves without permission cause many problems in the food service industry. Since most operations are relatively small, the absence of even a few employees has a serious effect on work schedules, duties of the other employees, and sales volume. Generally, operations that have the most casual attitude towards absenteeism have the highest rates of absenteeism, while those that make an effort to curb it usually meet with some success.

Causes of absenteeism vary considerably from place to place. Some authorities have tried to classify the many reasons under three broad categories: on-the-job causes, community causes, and personal causes. On-the-job causes might include poor supervision, kitchen heat, fatigue, dirty working conditions, or poor morale. Community causes could include poor transportation, inadequate police protection, or lack of child care facilities. Personal causes can include illness, alcoholism, family responsibilities, or psychological problems. The employer can do much about on-the-job causes and can sometimes help in personal causes.

Some techniques that have been found helpful in combating absenteeism are given below.

1. *Checking on the absentee.* A quick telephone call or a short visit to the absentee's home may reveal that the employee is not really sick but has gone fishing. It also indicates management's concern for the the employee and his absence.

2. *Bonuses for attendance.* These can be given to the employee for a period of perfect attendance. Unused sick time may be given as a Christmas or year-end bonus. A supervisor may also be rewarded for high attendance in his department.

3. *Preventive medicine.* Employees might be required to have regular physical examinations. These may expose some physical conditions before they become severe and cause absenteeism. The exams should be given at the time of hiring and periodically during employment and the employer might pay for them.

4. *Use of social agencies.* Many communities have agencies to which food service managers might refer employees who have problems. Alcoholics Anonymous, for example, has rehabilitated many alcoholics. Instead of summarily discharging an over imbibing employee, management could require him to utilize the services of such an agency as a condition of continuing employment. Other groups have been organized that use the collective self-help techniques of Alcoholics Anonymous for those having difficulty with drugs or gambling urges. Large industrial concerns are beginning to employ the industrial chaplain or psychologist more and more to assist their employees and cut turnover and absenteeism.

Absenteeism should be calculated at the end of each month to establish a standard pattern. This is one formula that may be used:

A (Rate of absenteeism) =

$$\frac{(\text{Number of daily absentees during period}) \times 100}{(\text{Average number of employees}) \times (\text{Number of working days})}$$

If an operation having 50 employees has 100 absences in a month with 30 working days, the calculations would be as follows:

$$A = \frac{100 \times 100}{50 \times 30} \text{ or 6.7 percent}$$

OVERTIME CONTROL

One of the best ways to encourage high labor costs is having uncontrolled overtime work. There may be instances when it is necessary to have employees work beyond their normal hours. If not controlled, however, supervisors can use overtime as a substitute for improper scheduling or planning. Employees may try to create overtime conditions for the extra money, especially if a premium overtime rate is paid. To avoid overtime, it is necessary that work loads be forecasted and the staff scheduled for the work load within the normal period. It is almost axiomatic that if overtime claims are accepted by management without question, the privilege will be abused. Two practices have been found to be very helpful in controlling overtime. One is to require a requisition in advance for overtime personnel. This requisition should include the name and the job of the employee involved, the amount of overtime the job requires, and the reason for the need. Management approves the requisition by signing it. Besides being a control device, the form requires the supervisor to correlate his personnel with the workload accurately since he must determine in advance whether he will need overtime assistance or not. There are, of course, reasons for overtime (such as breakdowns or unexpected business) that cannot be predicted in advance. In such cases, management should insist that an overtime report be prepared within 24 hours showing the amount of overtime worked and giving the reason for it. It is much easier to evaluate the need for overtime when the facts are current than at the end of the month when reasons may have been forgotten by management or invented by the employee. Figures 3 and 4 illustrate typical forms used to control overtime.

CONTROL REPORTS

One of the responsibilities of management is constant awareness of its payroll costs. For this purpose, control reports are almost indispensable. The format of the report should be developed to suit the individual operation concerned, since there is no universal form. Different operations have different labor cost problems and managers desire different informa-

Date _8/2_   Section _Sanitation_   Supervisor _Green_

Name	Position	Time	Elapsed time	Reason
John Jones	Dishwasher	8-9-45 p.m.	1¾ hours	Dishwasher breackdown caused delay

Figure 3   Overtime report.

tion regarding their own particular labor costs. To be effective, the form must be current, and it should not be so complicated that it cannot be presented to management the following day or (if it is completed weekly) by the beginning of the following week. The control reports do not, in themselves, control payroll, but they allow management to make the diagnosis as to whether or not payroll costs are within acceptable limits.

Figure 5, a daily payroll report, can be prepared either for a whole operation or for varous departments within the operation. It is a relatively simple chart and gives management its payroll operating cost. It also calls attention to overtime or extra time and the reasons for it. Amounts in the "total" column are calculated in the payroll office.

Some operations base their control on setting a standard number of

AUTHORIZATION FOR OVERTIME OR EXTRA WAGES

Number

Function_____   Date Scheduled_____

Number of Persons or Overtime Hours Required	Job Classification	Rate	Per
Remarks			

Date filed _____   Department head _____

Date approved _____   Manager _____

Figure 4

hours for different volumes of activity. Figure 6, "Staffing Table," shows the number of hours of work required for daily volumes ranging from $3000 to $3600.

Figure 7, showing a daily summary of payroll, is both an analysis and a control form. The format provides information on the number of workers used per day, the amount paid to them, the payroll cost ratio to sales, and customers served for each type of employee. It includes both today and to-date figures.

Figure 8, "Daily Cost Report," compares the actual hours worked with the standard hours for sales of $3335.60 ($3200). The example is illustrated on a daily basis but many operations prefer to calculate on a weekly or a monthly basis. The system is very helpful, since management can see at a glance differences from the predetermined standards. There are also the benefits in setting the standards that accrue from management being forced to examine the various jobs, to find ways of improving them and thereby, to increase productivity.

Figure 9 gives the staffing requirements for the food service operation of a small country club. Provision is made for the busier weekends and also for banquets.

Figure 5 Daily payroll report.

Department *Preparation*   Date *August* 2, 19—

| No. of employees | | | Hours worked | | Pay per employee | | |
Regular	Extra	Occupation	Reg.	Overtime	Daily	Overtime	Total
1		Head Cook	8		#32		$ 32.00
2		Cooks	8		24		48.00
3		Ass't Cooks ①	8	4	20	15.00	75.00
1		Pantry man	8		16		16.00
	1	Pantry man (party prep)		4		3.00	12.00
7	1	Totals					183.00

Coverage per meal

	B.	L.	D.
Head Cook		1	1
Cooks	1	2	1
Ass't Cooks	2	3	1
Pantry man		1	1
	3	7	4

Overtime

① Preparation for party tomorrow

44

Position	$3000		$3200		$3400		$3600	
	Jobs	Daily volume (hours)	Jobs	Daily volume (hours)	Jobs	Daily volume (hours)	Jobs	Daily volume (hours)
Preparation								
Chef	1	8	1	8	1	8	1	8
Cooks	3	24	3	24	4	32	4	32
Pantry girls	3	24	3	24	3	24	3	24
Total preparation	7	56	7	56	8	64	8	64
Sanitation								
Dishwashers	7	56	8	56	8	64	9	72
Potwashers and porter	2	16	2	16	2	16	2	16
Total sanitation	9	73	10	73	10	80	11	88
Service								
Hostesses	1.5	12	1.5	12	1.5	12	1.5	12
Waitresses	14	112	15	112	16	120	17	128
Busboys	4	32	4	32	4	32	5	32
Total service	19.5	156	20.5	156	21.5	164	23.5	172
Admin. and general								
Manager and assistant	2	16	2	16	2	16	2	16
Storeroom	1	8	1	8	1	8	1	8
Office clerk	1	8	1	8	1	8	1	8
Cashiers	1.5	12	1.5	12	1.5	12	1.5	12
Total admin. and general	5.5	44	5.5	44	5.5	44	5.5	44

Figure 6 Staffing table.

45

DAILY SUMMARY OF PAYROLL
FOOD AND BEVERAGE DEPARTMENT

SALES	Today	To Date
Food		
Beverage		
Total		

Day _____
Date _____

	Today		To Date				Ratio to Sales To Date			Average Covers per Employee To Date		
			This Month		Last Month							
	No	Amt	No	Amt	No	Amt	To-day	This month	Last month	To-day	This month	Last month
Preparation—regular												
Chef and cooks												
Potwashers												
Vegetable cleaners												
Pantry												
Pastry and bake shop												
Preparation—extra												
Chef and cooks												
Potwashers												
Vegetable cleaners												
Pantry												
Pastry and bake shop												
TOTAL PREPARATION												
Service—regular												
Supervision												
Captains												
Waiters and waitress												
Busboys												

Service—extra																		
Waiters and waitress																		
Busboys																		
TOTAL SERVICE																		
Steward																		
Steward and assistant																		
Warewashers—regular																		
Warewashers—extra																		
Others																		
TOTAL STEWARD																		
General																		
Storekeepers																		
Checkers and cashiers																		
TOTAL GENERAL																		
TOTAL FOOD																		
Beverages																		
Bartenders																		
Waiters																		
Others																		
TOTAL BEVERAGES																		
TOTAL FOOD AND BEVERAGES																		

Figure 7

47

DAILY COST REPORT

August 2, 19_____

Sales _$ 3,335.60_

Position or Section	Hours		Hours		
	Standard	Actual	Over	Under	Explanation
Preparation					
Chef	8	8			
Cooks	24	22		2	_Cook given afternoon off_
Pantry Girls	24	26	2		_Needed for extra salads_
Total	56	56	2	2	
Sanitation					
Dishwashers	64	70	6		_Dishwasher break-down_
Potwasher and porter	16	16			
Total	80	86	6		
Service					
Hostesses	12	12			
Waitresses	120	128	8		_One girl sick_
Busboys	32	32			
Total	164	172	8		
Administration and General					
Managers	16	16			
Storeroom	8	8			
Office	8	8			
Cashiers	12	12			
Total	44	44			

Figure 8

USE OF STAFFING GUIDE FOR A TYPICAL SUMMER WEEK
IN A SMALL COUNTRY CLUB

	Tuesday–Friday	Extra Staff Needs			
	Daily Staff for 225 Covers	Saturday	Sunday	Friday Night Banquet	Add One Extra Man per "Covers" Bracket Below
Covers					
Average	206	325	400	250	
Excess over normal		100	175		
Kitchen					
Chef and cooks	2	1	2		70
Potwasher-Vegetable cleaner	1	1	1		250
Pantry	2	1	1		160
Warewasher-porter	2	1	2		115
Dining room					
Headwaiter	1				
Waiters	6	4	7		Combined lunch and dinner covers per 4 waiters 25–28
Busboys	2	1	2		
Grill or cocktail lounge					Food and beverage covers per $175 sales 50
Waiters	2				
Bartenders	1			1	
Buffet or banquet					
Cooks				2	125
Potwasher-Vegetable cleaner				1	300
Pantry				1	250
Warewashing				2	140
Waiters				10	20–25
Busboys				2	Per 7 waiters
Total staff	19	9	15	19	

Figure 9

chapter 4

Food Purchasing

Traditionally, the major expense of a food service operator has been the food. Although labor cost has begun to rival or surpass food cost as an expense, management still needs to use the proper food purchasing techniques to make its operation profitable and the food pleasing to its patrons.

Proper food purchasing results from management's ability to coordinate and plan. Food requirements are governed fundamentally by two factors: the menu choices and the volume of business. The menu will affect not only the efficiency of purchasing and the actual cost of food items, but the labor costs, the patron service, the selection of equipment, the kitchen layout, and the storage space as well. Of course, the volume of business determines the quantities that need to be purchased.

Management must decide what quality and quantities are best suited to the establishment in order to establish standard specifications. Proper food purchasing requires answers to the following questions:

Do you want to serve only the highest quality food available, the lowest quality that your patrons will accept, or something in between?

Where is the purveyor situated and what is the extent of his resources?

Do you have a choice of dealers, or must you deal mainly with one or two?

Can deliveries be made daily, or must purchasing plans take into account less frequent shipments?

Do you have sufficient storage space?

Your menu will be largely governed by these considerations, and purchasing must be geared to the menu.

CHANGES IN FOOD PURCHASING

Accepted food purchasing procedures have been changing, and more changes are imminent. Formerly, the buyer would contact purveyors handling different types of food items, discover the best deal, and make the purchase. Thus one operation might deal separately with purveyors specializing in fresh produce, meats, frozen foods, poultry, eggs, groceries, and baked goods. The typical purveyor specialized in one type of product. Marketing innovations are forcing the one-line purveyor to change. The changing nature of the food service industry and the many new products available are also changing the purchasing procedure.

Some of the factors causing changes in the traditional buying procedures are:

Food distributors are expanding their lines. The purveyor who formerly handled only fresh produce can now add frozen foods. Some food distributors are trying to develop "Total Shopping Capability"; that is, they have begun to supply a complete range of food items, nonfood supplies, and kitchen and dining equipment.

Purveyors are providing more nonmerchandise services, like menu planning, marketing advice, computer time sharing, and data processing.

The small local individual distributor is either growing or merging into a distribution chain that can serve much larger geographical areas.

New products change purchasing procedures. It is easier to purchase a package of frozen peas than the fresh variety; it is more convenient to buy preportioned meat items than the primal cuts. Moreover, purchasing preprepared convenience items does not present the problems found in purchasing the individual components.

Multiunit operations have begun utilizing central preparation facilities or commissaries. Thus purchasing becomes centralized: the individual dining units usually order prepared food from their commissary.

Many operations, especially the fast food variety, are built around comparatively few menu items that are not routinely changed. Even if it does not actually supply much of the food, a central organization may establish standards, make specifications, and choose the dealers. This centralized authority leads to simplified food purchasing.

Similar kinds of food service operations—hospital and school cafeterias, for example—have begun to band together to form buying groups. Their volume purchases can bring economic benefits and eliminate much purchasing at the operation level.

Food marketing is changing. Some companies have started selling directly to the operation rather than to the distribution systems, the traditional "middleman." Vertical marketing integration is more popular. That is, some companies are no longer interested in only the production or the selling. Now they may handle all aspects of production and marketing.

Rising delivery costs are limiting the amount of service a purveyor can provide. Food industry distribution costs are believed to be higher than in any other industry, and this fact is leading to fewer and larger deliveries. Accordingly, more and more product lines are now being handled by fewer and fewer suppliers.

Supermarkets, which were once concerned almost exclusively with home business, are becoming more active in the institutional supply field.

Food shortages, like the beef shortage of 1973, tend to make purchasing more of a scramble than an organized process. In times like these, the assurance of a food supply will probably outweigh cost considerations. Moreover, those operators who have established sound, reliable, businesslike dealings with purveyors tend to get "taken care of" first, when normal competitive buying procedures must be suspended.

WHO SHOULD PURCHASE?

The size of the operation, the variety of its purchases, the training and interest among the staff available, and management and company policies will determine who will do the purchasing. Various people may serve as the purchaser; however, regardless of who is appointed to do the purchasing, there are some general considerations involved. The purchaser, of course, must have adequate knowledge of food grades and prices, quantity specifications, and market fluctuations. Also, he must have the time to perform his duties properly. To determine purchase quantities, the buyer must have access to records of past purchases, yield computations, formulas to determine portion breakdown, and sales forecasts. Food purchases might be divided in categories such as:

Meat
Poultry
Fish
Fruits
Vegetables
Dairy products
Bakery items
Cake
Coffee
Ice cream
Desserts
Groceries (condiments and packaged foods)

Some operations have found it desirable to divide purchasing duties. The manager might purchase only meats and leave the vegetable, produce, and grocery purchasing to his steward. (Since the meat expense is usually by far the major part of food cost, it deserves the most consideration and care.)

There is a trend to relieve the chef of purchasing and give this responsibility to an administrator. At times, the chef may be too busy to do an adequate job of checking prices and quality, and he may be tempted merely to call in his orders. An administrative assistant to the chef, known as a "purchasing steward" (or by some other title) who is not directly involved in preparation and preparation deadlines, could spend the time necessary to do the job efficiently and economically.

For control purposes, it is desirable that the purchaser should not also be responsible for receiving and preparing food. Someone who wants to defraud his employer can do so more readily if he both purchases and receives the food. Deficits in quality or in quantity are then less easily detected. Also, when the preparation function is separated from purchasing, the preparation personnel are likely to call attention to instances where the food quality does not meet specifications. Unfortunately, too many operations in our industry have been victimized by collusion.

Although it may not be feasible for management to do the purchasing directly, it should specify, or at least approve, the purveyors from whom food is secured. This practice provides an element of control and somewhat limits the possibility of undesirable purchases. Many managers periodically check their merchandise costs against those of similar operations to see that the prices they pay do not exceed those paid by others for comparable quality and service.

THE BEST COST

In purchasing, the cheapest price does not necessarily correspond to the best buy. A case of eggs can weigh from 34 to 60 pounds. A price per pound in this case can be more important than the cost per dozen (grade and quality aside). Consideration of the amount of bones and fat in a piece of meat may make the lower price for a bone-in, poorly trimmed piece of meat actually higher than that of a similar higher priced piece which is trimmed and boneless.

The optimum cost is partially determined by the yield of the product and not only by the price per pound.

PURCHASING METHODS

There are many methods by which food can be purchased. They include:

Open market buying
Sealed bid buying
Cost-plus buying
Co-op buying

Open market buying is by far the most widely used way that food service operations secure their food. After determining needs, the purchaser obtains prices from the purveyors. The order is then given to the purveyor who quotes the lowest price commensurate with the quality specified. This ordering is usually done by telephone, but orders may be given to a purveyor's salesman or taken in person to the market. It is a good control procedure to obtain price quotations from three purveyors for each food item, although a shortage of local purveyors might make this impossible. A steward's market order sheet may be helpful. If the order is large and contains a number of items, it may be split among several different purveyors, each supplying items that they offered at the most advantageous price.

Sealed Bid buying is used mainly by large organizations and governmental institutions. This method involves determining how much of an item will be needed for an extended period of time, preparing detailed specifications for the item, and asking purveyors to make sealed bids on the item. It eliminates the problems of frequent pricing and buying and permits large quantity discounts. The sealed bid method eliminates partiality or favoritism and, therefore, conforms with public institutional policies. However, the system is cumbersome and does not let a manager take advantage of price advantages as they occur in the market.

Cost Plus buying is not used too frequently, but it does offer advantages. The operator makes an agreement with a purveyor to buy all of a certain kind of food from him at a selling price fixed at a specific percentage over the dealer's cost. Usually, the operator agrees to telephone all orders in at a definite time, and a definite delivery schedule may be agreed upon as well. The advantage to the food operator is that the dealer's markup is usually only a fraction of the normal markup. Nor does the operator have to go to all the bother of getting competitive bids and keeping records on different purveyors. The advantage to the purveyor is that he gets all of a customer's business. He knows in advance what the customer wants, and so he does not have to run the risk of stocking food that may not be needed or wanted by his customers. Moreover, time spent soliciting business is kept at a minimum. A problem may arise when it comes time to verify the purveyor's costs. The manager may have to supply more motivation for the purveyor to seek the best prices, since he knows his percentage has been guaranteed no matter what price he charges the customer. Reports issued by the United States Department of Agriculture are helpful in determining current prices, and a subsidiary agreement may be made whereby the purveyor provides his customer with a copy of his invoices.

Co-op buying involves a group of similar operations such as schools, hospitals, or fraternities that band together to secure, through mass purchasing, quantity discount prices. The group may employ a manager who investigates prices and quality on behalf of all the members of the group. The members indicate to the co-op the quantities and qualities desired, and the co-op combines the orders to get the lowest prices it can. Theoretically at least, purveyors can offer lower prices since they do not have to send salesmen to call regularly on the various members. Many co-ops purchase other items beside food for their members, and many offer other services as well.

PURCHASE SIZE DETERMINATION

To purchase properly, a manager must, of course, know what to purchase and how much of it to purchase. Normally, the menu offering and sales forecast determine the types and amounts of food to be purchased.

A number of food operations work from an inventory exclusively, and the kitchen merely requisitions food from the storeroom. Purchasing groceries, bread, dairy products, ice cream and certain vegetables can become routine—even scheduled. If a par stock of each item is maintained, an order of a predetermined size is placed when the inventory declines to a predetermined point. Foods which are not regularly and routinely needed require special purchasing care and the maintenance of par stocks here may not be feasible.

The determination of quantities in purchasing is a difficult task. After a menu has been decided upon, the expected sales of each entree must be calculated on the basis of past experience and future expectations. A record of entrees sold is a very valuable help when the time comes to determine quantities to be purchased and to schedule production. In too many cases there are no records, and the quantity to be served becomes guess work. Cooked-to-order items can be held in storage and used as needed. But this is not so with prepared roasts, fowl, fish, or other special dishes. A miscalculation could mean overproduction, underproduction, waste, a higher food cost, and possibly dissatisfied guests.

STEWARD'S MARKET ORDER SHEET (Illustration 1)

The Steward's Market Quotation Sheet, or Purchase Order Sheet, is a great help in purchasing. It lists the foods that are likely to be used and has columns to indicate how much is on hand, how much is to be ordered, and what the bids are from different purveyors. The normal practice is to call purveyors and collect quotations for each item on the list. After quotations from the various purveyors have been received, the best price for each item is circled on the Market Quotation List. The purveyor is then called back and given the order for these items circled in his column.

A copy of the Steward's Quotation List should be given to the person who will receive the merchandise to let him know what to expect. Another copy may be sent to the food controller to allow him to check invoice prices and to show him that the purchaser is using competitive bidding.

STANDARD SPECIFICATIONS (Illustration 2)

STANDARD SPECIFICATIONS[a]

CUBED STEAKS[b]

1. Grade—U. S. Good.
2. Weight—6 ounces (over or under tolerance of ¼ ounce allowed).
3. State of refrigeration—chilled or frozen as per purchase order.
4. The cubed steaks may be produced from any boneless meat from the beef carcass which is reasonably free of membraneous tissue, tendons and ligaments.
5. Knitting of two or more pieces and folding the meat is permissible.
6. Cubed steaks must be reasonably uniform in an overall shape.
7. Surface fat must not exceed ¼ inch in width at any one point when measured from the edge of the lean.
8. Surface and seam fat must cover not more than 15 percent of the total area on either side of the steak.
9. The cubed steak must not break when suspended from any point ½ inch from the outer edge of the steak.

---

[a] It is expected that the general specifications for the operation will include the requirements regarding government inspection and grading.

[b] The specifications may be abbreviated by referring to specifications approved by the USDA. Cubed steaks would be Item No. 1100 in the "Institutional Meat Purchase Specifications for Portion-Cut Meat Products" effective March 1970, and available from the Superintendent of Documents, U. S. Government Printing Office, Washington, D. C. 20402.

Illustration 2

A necessity in food purchasing is the use of standard specifications. With standard specifications, purveyors can bid knowledgeably according to quality or size. Specifications provide a basis for all purveyors to bid equally on the same item. Specifications also provide a basis for standard yields and production. A seven-rib roast of beef can weigh from 7 to 34

STEWARD'S MARKET QUOTATION LIST

WM. ALLEN & CO., N.Y. STOCK FORM 6088—PRINTED IN U.S.A.

ON HAND	WANTED	QUOTATIONS	ARTICLE
			BEEF
			Corned Beef
			Corned Beef Brisket
			Corned Beef Rump
			Corned Beef Hash
			Beef Chipped
			Beef Breads
			Butts
			Chuck
			Fillets
			Hip Short
			Hip Full
			Kidneys
			Livers
			Loin, Short
			Strip
			Shell Strip
			Ribs Beef
			Shins
			Suet, Beef
			Tails, Ox
			VEAL
			Breast
			Brains
			Feet
			Fore Quarters
			Hind Quarters
			Head
			Kidneys
			Legs
			Liver
			Loins
			Racks
			Saddles
			Shoulder
			Sweet Breads
			MUTTON
			Fore Quarters
			Kidneys
			Legs
			Racks
			Saddles
			Saddles, Hind
			Shoulder
			Suet

ON HAND	WANTED	QUOTATIONS	ARTICLE
			Provisions (Cont'd)
			Pig's Knuckles Fresh
			Pig's Knuckles Corned
			Pig, Suckling
			Pork, Fresh Loin
			Pork, Larding
			Pork, Spare Ribs
			Pork, Salt Strip
			Pork Tenderloin
			Sausages, Country
			Sausages, Frankfurter
			Sausages, Meat
			Shoulders, Fresh
			Shoulders, Smoked
			Shoulders, Corned
			Tongues
			Tongues, Beef Smoked
			Tongues, Fresh
			Tongues, Lambs
			Tripe
			POULTRY
			Chickens
			Chickens, Roast
			Chickens, Broilers
			Chickens, Broilers
			Chickens, Supreme
			Cocks
			Capons
			Ducks
			Ducklings
			Fowl
			Geese
			Goslings
			Guinea Hens
			Guinea Squabs
			Pigeons
			Poussins
			Squabs
			Turkeys, Roasting
			Turkeys, Boiling
			Turkeys, Spring
			GAME
			Birds
			Partridge
			Pheasant, English
			Rabbits

ON HAND	WANTED	QUOTATIONS	ARTICLE
			FISH (Cont'd)
			Carp
			Codfish, Live
			Codfish, Salt Boneless
			Codfish, Salt Flake
			Eels
			Finnan Haddie
			Flounders
			Flounders
			Flounders, Fillet
			Fluke
			Haddock
			Haddock, Fillet
			Haddock, Smoked
			Halibut
			Halibut, Chicken
			Herring
			Herring, Smoked
			Herring, Kippered
			Kingfish
			Mackerel, Fresh
			Mackerel, Salt
			Mackerel, Spanish
			Mackerel, Smoked
			Perch
			Pickerel
			Pike
			Porgies
			Pompano
			Rednapper
			Salmon, Fresh
			Salmon, Smoked
			Salmon, Nova Scotia
			Scrod
			Shad
			Shad Roes
			Smelts
			Sole, English
			Sole, Boston
			Sole, Lemon
			Sturgeon
			Trout, Brook
			Trout, Lake
			Trout, Salmon
			Weakfish
			Whitebait
			Whitefish
			Whitefish, Smoked

ON HAND	WANTED	QUOTATIONS	ARTICLE
			Vegetables (Cont'd)
			Estragon
			Egg Plant
			Garlic
			Horseradish Roots
			Kale
			Kohlrabi
			Lettuce
			Lettuce, Ice Berg
			Lettuce, Place
			Leeks
			Mint
			Mushrooms
			Mushrooms, Fresh
			Okra
			Onions
			Onions, Yellow
			Onions, Bermuda
			Onions, Spanish
			Onions, White
			Onions, Scallions
			Oyster Plant
			Parsley
			Parsnips
			Peppermint
			Peas, Green
			Peas
			Peas
			Peppers, Green
			Peppers, Red
			Potatoes
			Potatoes, Bermuda
			Potatoes, Idaho
			Potatoes, Idaho
			Potatoes, Sweet
			Potatoes, New
			Potatoes, Yams
			Pumpkins
			Romaine
			Radishes
			Rhubarb, Fresh
			Rhubarb, Hot House
			Sage
			Shallots
			Sorrel
			Sauerkraut
			Spinach
			Squash Crooked Neck

ON HAND	WANTED	QUOTATIONS	ARTICLE
			FRUIT (Cont'd)
			Dates
			Figs
			Gooseberries
			Grapes
			Grapes
			Grapes, Concord
			Grapes, Malaga
			Grapes, Tokay
			Grapefruit
			Grapefruit
			Guavas
			Lemons
			Lemon
			Limes
			Limes, Florida
			Limes, Persian
			Muskmelons
			Oranges
			Oranges
			Oranges
			Peaches
			Peaches
			Pears
			Pears
			Pears, Alligators
			Pineapples
			Plums
			Plums
			Pomegranates
			Quinces
			Raspberries
			Strawberries
			Strawberries
			Tangerines
			Watermelons
			Watermelons
			BUTTER
			Print
			Cooking
			Sweet
			EGGS
			White
			Brown
			Mixed Colors
			Pullets

LAMB					
Breast	Quail	VEGETABLES	Squash Hubbard	CHEESE	
Fore Quarters	Venison, Saddles	Artichokes	Tarragon	American, Kraft	
Feet	SHELL FISH	Asparagus	Thyme	American, Young	
Fries	Clams, Chowder	Asparagus	Tomatoes, New	Bel Paese	
Kidneys	Clams, Cherrystone	Asparagus, Tips	Tomatoes, Hot House	Camembert	
Loins	Clams, Little Neck	Asparagus, Fancy	Turnips, White	Camembert	
Legs	Clams, Soft	Beans	Turnips, Yellow	Cheddar	
Lamb, Spring	Crabs, Hard	Beans, Lima	Turnips, New	Cottage	
Racks, Double	Crabs, Meat	Beans, String	Watercress	Cream	
Racks, Spring	Crabs, Oyster	Beans, Wax	FRUIT	Cream, Phila.	
Saddles	Crabs, Soft Shell	Beets	Apples, Cooking	Cream, Phila.	
Shoulder	Crabs, Soft Shell Prime	Beets, Tops	Apples, Baking	Edam	
PROVISIONS	Lobsters, Meat	Broccoli	Apples, Crab	Gorgonzola	
Bacon	Lobsters, Tails	Brussels Sprouts	Apples, Table	Liederkranz	
Bologna	Lobsters, Chicken	Cabbage	Apricots	Parmesan, Grated	
Bologna	Lobsters, Medium	Cabbage, Red	Bananas	Roquefort	
Crepinette	Lobsters, Large	Cabbage, New	Blackberries	Roquefort	
Salami	Oysters, Box	Carrots	Blueberries	Roquefort, Broken	
Hams, Corned	Oysters, Blue Points	Carrots	Blueberries	Stilton	
Hams, Fresh	Oysters	Cauliflower	Cantaloupes	Store	
Hams, Polish	Scallops	Celery	Cantaloupes	Swiss	
Hams, Smoked	Shrimps	Celery Knobs	Honey Balls	Swiss, Gruyere	
Hams, Virginia	Turtle	Chicory	Melons, Casaba	Swiss, Gruyere	
Hams, Westphalia	FISH	Chives	Melons, Honeydew	Miscellaneous	
Head Cheese	Bass, Black	Corn	Melons, Persian		
Lard	Bass, Sea	Corn	Melons, Spanish		
Lyon Sausage	Bass, Striped	Chervil	Cherries		
Phil. Scrapple	Blackfish	Cranberries	Cherries		
Smoked Butts	Bluefish	Cucumbers	Cherries		
Pig's Feet	Bloaters	Dandelion	Currants		
Pig's Head, Corned	Butterfish	Escarole	Chestnuts		
		Endive			

pounds. The number of servings from each of these seven-rib roasts could, therefore, vary tremendously, depending on whether the rib was light or heavy. Specifications should be used by the receiving clerk as a basis for accepting or rejecting items. Without them, he would be forced to use his own judgment, which might or might not coincide with management policy. With specifications, it is much easier for a new employee to take over the ordering. To be most effective, specifications must be available to the buyer, to the purveyor, and to the receiver.

Many sets of specifications are available; what is important is that you develop or adopt the best ones for your particular operation and use. You may want to accept the standard published ones, but be sure to experiment and first test to see that they are the most suitable for your operation. A 20-pound roast may give the highest yield, but there is no sense in buying this roast if you can sell only two-thirds of it at a time.

OVERBUYING

There is a strong temptation to overbuy when a "good deal" appears, but the temptation tends to cloud some of the hidden costs involved in a bargain. Money, both interest and principal, which could be invested or put to other profitable uses, is tied up in the large purchase. It costs money to maintain and to refrigerate or heat storage space. The greater the supply of food on hand, the easier it is to pilfer; and costs may also go up because employees exercise less care when apparently unlimited amounts are available. Outright spoilage or deterioration in quality may occur. (And there is always the chance that the price of your "good deal" will drop even further.)

Sometimes, of course, it is necessary to buy over normal amounts. Climatic conditions may be such that a shortage can be definitely assured and it may be necessary to buy to protect prices or even to insure a supply. Temporary food shortages may, therefore, justify some overbuying that in usual times would be ill-advised. Unfortunately, it is often difficult to beat the wholesalers who raise prices in anticipation of food shortages.

FORECASTING FOOD NEEDS

Knowing the number that will be served is essential to wise purchasing. Purchasing too much food often results in waste or spoilage; purchasing too little food leads to dissatisfied customers. Many operations prepare a business forecast to help alleviate both problems. The forecast may be prepared by an individual or by a committee. One effective system starts by estimating the total number of covers that will be served during a meal period, day, or other period. Factors involved in this forecast are records of, for example, the number of people served on the same day during the past year, or during the past week; the weather conditions; and other miscellaneous factors affecting local business and general business trends. Percentages of total customers ordering the various courses—the appetizers, the salads, the a la carte items and the desserts—are usually rather constant for a specific operation, and it is easy to obtain the number of servings for each course by multiplying total covers by the percentage for each course. It is somewhat more difficult to determine the sales of individual items in each course. This is especially true if the menu is constantly varied. Fried chicken might be very popular with one set of companion items, but not nearly as popular with another set. A cycle menu is very helpful in this regard and simplifies forecasting sales if records are kept of the relative popularity of items. Some of the food cost accounting systems described in Chapter 11 have forecasting features.

STANDING ORDERS

Standing orders are of help to organizations that have a steady volume. These orders are prepared in advance, often on a monthly or weekly basis, and eliminate the necessity to call in frequent orders on such regularly used foods as bakery and dairy products. The standing orders specify how much of each item should be automatically delivered each day of the week or month. It is usually convenient to have the standing order items supplied by only one vendor. Where volume fluctuates, standing orders should not be used; moreover, consideration must always be given to holidays or special occasions when fluctuations can be expected in the most steady operations. Frequent checks of supplies on hand and tabulations of current needs must also be made to prevent spoilage.

Standing orders may also be used in conjunction with par stocks. The delivery would correspond to that amount needed to raise the stock to a predetermined level.

SALESMEN'S VISITS

Calls by salesmen can be of considerable help to the food purchaser. Salesmen can provide market trend information, introduce new products and provide information about unusually good buys. Many buyers find it expedient to specify the times when salesmen should make their visits or telephone calls. This practice is helpful to both the salesman and the buyer. The buyer can then organize his day without being interrupted by unplanned visits, and the salesman can expect that the buyer will be prepared to discuss an order with him.

WRITTEN PURCHASE ORDER

Some larger organizations employ written purchase orders for food items. These purchase orders are sent to the vendor and usually specify quantity, price, and delivery time. They may also include quality specifications and payment information. The purchase order helps eliminate errors in pricing and quantities and may be useful in the receiving process. The frequency of ordering, the short time between ordering and delivery, and the clerical work involved do not make purchase orders feasible for the typical operation, except possibly in the special case of large orders of canned goods or nonperishable items where there is a great deal of money involved and complete agreement on quality and purchasing details is important.

CAN CUTTING TESTS

When one buys large quantities of a canned item, he may want to have an occasional can-cutting session. He asks different purveyors to send samples of their products that meet his specifications. The containers are emptied. The label net weight, the actual weight, and the drained weight are noted, along with a count of the items in the can or the yield by portions. Unlabeled samples are inspected by a panel of at least three people who rate such items according to quality, color, yield, syrup, absence of defects, and taste. Price may or may not be considered at this time, depending upon whether the operation's emphasis is on cost or quality. Many operations use can cutting for each new pack of food.

chapter 5

Receiving

Receiving is not just the accepting of and signing for merchandise. It includes verifying that the quality, size, and quantity meet specifications and that the price exactly reflects the items ordered and billed. Tagging and marking perishables with the date received is also part of the process. Finally, the items received must be recorded accurately on the daily receiving record. The merchandise must then be moved promptly to storage and preparation areas before it gets lost or deteriorates. Receiving is an area where alert management can prevent a great deal of grief. The more consistent and the more routine the receiving function, the less chance that attempts will be made to defraud the operation during the delivery of merchandise.

ESSENTIALS FOR GOOD RECEIVING

Competent Personnel. Receiving personnel must have the four "I's": intelligence, integrity, interest, and information about food. A conscientious employee who takes enough interest and time to detect old merchandise, excess shrinkage, short weights, and foods not up to specifications is an essential member of the management team. These people are valuable and should be paid accordingly. Accepting poor quality and paying for short measure is tantamount to losing money from the cash drawer. If the operation is too small to afford a regular receiving man, deliveries should be arranged for definite times so that a competent person can be assigned to receive them. Many operations require that all meats, poultry, and seafood be delivered at a specific time and received by the manager or a responsible employee, especially since these items reflect about 50 percent of all food purchased.

Facilities and Equipment. The first consideration for good receiving is a proper receiving area. In the normal food operation, the receiving area may also be used as an employees' entrance, a trash storage area, the salesmen's entrance, and a place for general storage. Coping with this inherent clutter and confusion requires good back-door management. Ideally, the receiving room should be located near the storeroom and refrigerators so that the movement of food takes a minimum of time and effort. The receiving department requires certain equipment. Accurate scales in good working order are a must. One survey discovered that 30 percent of scales used in receiving departments could not give correct weights, yet management thought shipments were being properly weighed. Why not test your scale periodically with a known weight to check its accuracy? Both platform and counter scales should be available, but a platform scale is more important. Large operations have begun to use scales that print the weight on the reverse side of the invoice or packing slip; other scales print a tape which is then attached to the merchandise. This system eliminates any doubt in the weighing-in process.

There should be an unloading platform of a convenient height to unload trucks and a ramp to facilitate unloading of other vehicles. The receiving man should have a desk where he can do his paper work and keep invoices and forms in order. Some receiving areas have duplicating machines to make copies of invoices that have been marked "received" and have been stamped numerically. Copies can then be sent to the bookkeeping department for payment, to the cost department, and to the storeroom, and can be retained in the receiving department as a permanent receiving record. Proper dollies and hand trucks are important to a receiving department; they help to expedite the movement of merchandise with the least amount of effort. If frozen foods are held for any length of time in the receiving area, enough freezer capacity should be provided to prevent deterioration of the food.

Specifications. The person who receives orders should know the standards that the purveyor must meet and be instructed to accept nothing below this standard. The purchaser's written specifications should also be in the hands of the purveyor. The specifications are usually given to the receiving clerk in one of two ways. A memorandum or purchase order of the food ordered showing the quantity, price, and quality or grade may be handed over to the clerk, or specifications for main food items may be posted on the wall near the scale so that weight, size, and quality can be checked.

Sanitation. The facilities should be arranged so they can be easily cleaned. A water connection that permits a hosing down of the area is almost a necessity. If insects congregate, there should be adequate screening and fly protection.

Supervision. Receiving should be checked by management at irregular intervals. It is just as important to recheck weighings, quantities, and qualities occasionally as it is to audit cash. The receiving man should be aware of management's concern for his work and the importance attached to it.

Scheduled Hours. If possible, purveyors should be directed to make deliveries at specified times. This practice makes it easier to have a qualified receiver available and helps avoid the confusion when too many deliveries come in at the same time. With the drivers all eager to be off for the next delivery, the receiving clerk may be pressured, and the goods may not be properly checked. Some operations require that perishable foods be delivered in the morning, and other groceries in the afternoon.

THE RECEIVING CLERK'S DAILY REPORT

The main record of receiving is the Receiving Clerk's Daily Report (Figure 1). This form has many uses. It provides an accurate record of all food received, the date of delivery, the vendor, and the food's quantity, weight and price. This data can be very helpful in checking and paying bills. For cost control, it is necessary to know the unit costs of all food delivered to the kitchen and storeroom. In the distribution section of the Receiving Report, there are three columns headed "Direct," "Stores," and "Sundries." These columns are required in some food cost control systems. Items in the Direct column indicate that the food has been delivered to the kitchen to be used that day, and should be included in that day's food cost. Items in the Stores column indicate that the food went to the storeroom rather than to the kitchen. (Food sent from the storeroom is charged by requisition.) The Sundries column includes nonfood items such as cleaning or paper supplies.

Checking the receiving report is a very easy way to determine how much food went directly to the kitchen on any one day from sources outside the storeroom. The receiving man who signs the report is responsible for seeing that the food has all been received by the operation and measures up to the quality specified. This record is usually prepared in duplicate. One is sent with the invoices to the cost and accounting department, and one remains in the receiving department for reference.

DATING PERISHABLES AND GROCERIES

In many well-run operations, food items are dated with a crayon or a tag. The dating can be put on the case or crate or on the individual container.

WILLIAM ALLEN & CO., N.Y. STOCK FORM 6164

RECEIVING CLERK'S DAILY REPORT

NO. _____

DATE _____

QUAN.	UNIT	DESCRIPTION	✓	UNIT PRICE	AMOUNT	TOTAL AMOUNT	PURCHASE JOURNAL DISTRIBUTION		
							FOOD DIRECT	FOOD STORES	SUNDRIES

SIGNATURE

Figure 1

67

Such a system permits the use of the older merchandise first and helps to ensure quality.

MEAT TAGGING

In food cost, meat is the largest expense in food purchasing, and many operations use a meat tag system to control this cost better. The meat tag is a card which can be attached to the individual meat item. A meat tag is shown in Figure 2. The standard card consists of two duplicate parts.

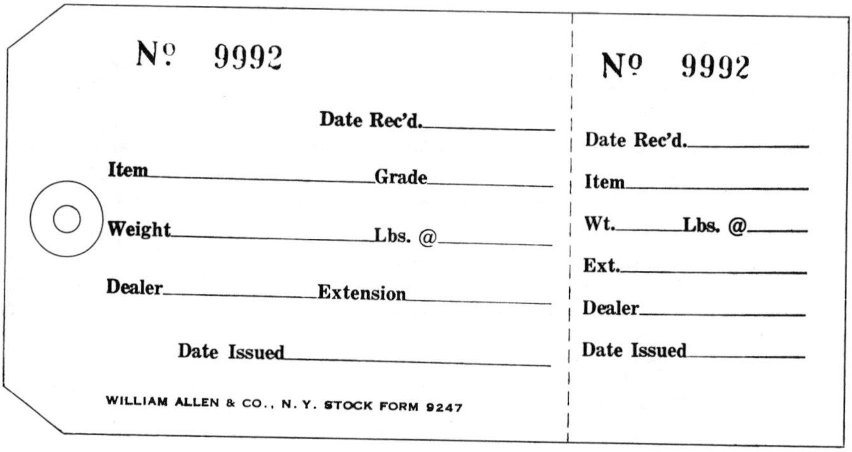
Nº 9992

Date Rec'd.______

Item______ Grade______

Weight______ Lbs. @______

Dealer______ Extension______

Date Issued______

WILLIAM ALLEN & CO., N. Y. STOCK FORM 9247

Nº 9992

Date Rec'd.______

Item______

Wt.______ Lbs. @______

Ext.______

Dealer______

Date Issued______

Figure 2

Each half has a printed number and spaces for the date, the dealer's name, the cut, the weight, the price per pound, and the total price. A procedure for using meat tags follows.

1. Both parts of the tag are filled out for each piece, box, or package of meat, fish or fowl.
2. The top half of the tag is fastened to the merchandise.
3. The duplicate bottom half is sent to the person responsible for food cost accounting.
4. The tag is removed and usually placed in a locked box when the items are used in the kitchen, and the tags are then sent to the food cost controller who adds the used tags to determine the meat cost for the day.
5. The food cost controller matches his copy of the tag with the tag that has come from the kitchen. He knows there should be mer-

chandise in storage for every unused tag; if not, the merchandise has "walked away" or has not been properly charged.

Here are some of the advantages of using a meat tag system.

1. The receiving man has to fill in a tag for each individual piece of meat, and this requires him to weigh the meat.
2. With the item already having the weight marked on the tag, a second weighing when issued is eliminated.
3. It is very easy to determine the meat cost for a day, or for any other period.
4. Shortages and disappearances of meat are brought to light when there are more duplicate tags than items in storage.
5. The tagged items make inventory very easy and, if desired, an inventory or dollar value of the items on hand can be determined just by adding the duplicate tags.
6. The name of the dealer on the tag makes it very easy to trace the item back to where it was purchased.
7. The date on the tag makes it easier to use the older items first, or to age meats.

PRICING MERCHANDISE

Some operations follow the practice of marking every can or carton with the price of the item, just the way prices are stamped on supermarket items. Proponents of the practice claim it makes pricing inventories much easier and also makes employees more cost conscious. With the price stamped on it, the item is no longer just a piece of merchandise to the employees, it becomes an article of value.

INVOICE STAMPS

To facilitate the process of handling and checking invoices, some operations stamp the delivery slip or invoice with a rubber stamp, and the person performing each function indicates it on the appropriate line.

```
Date Received _____
Quantity       _____
Price OK       _____
Extension OK _____
Entered      _____
Paid         _____
```

This practice ensures that all the steps have been performed, and it fixes the responsibility for any errors.

STANDING ORDERS

On many items, there is no daily purchase; instead, a predetermined amount may be delivered each day or at regular intervals. Bread, dairy products, eggs, ice cream, and certain nonfood items usually fall into this category. It is most imperative that delivery men do not place these items into storage and that the items be counted by the receiving clerk and stored by him.

BLIND RECEIVING

To force receiving personnel to weigh or count incoming merchandise, a number of operations employ the "blind receiving" system. The purveyor is instructed to list only the items on the shipping invoice and to omit quantities or weights. The receiving man must then count or weigh the items to fill in the invoice or the receiving report. His figures are then checked with the invoice containing counts or quantities that is mailed to the accounting office by the purveyor. An operation may supply the blind invoice forms to the purveyor.

CREDIT MEMORANDUMS

Occasionally, merchandise may be short of weight or unsatisfactory in quality, and credit should be received for it. A printed form may be used that should be prepared in triplicate. One copy should be attached to the invoice, initialed by the delivery man, and sent to the bookkeeping department. Another copy should be given to the delivery man to take to the purveyor. And one copy should be kept by the receiving department. In addition, the invoice should be properly marked, as should the driver's receipted copy showing the discrepancies. A phone call to the vendor may also be in order.

The credit memorandum should contain the name of the purveyor, the date, and number of the invoice, the discrepancy, and the amount of credit. Formal credit memorandums are used more generally where times for deliveries have been scheduled and the receiving man has an opportunity to fill them out properly. Regardless of whether a printed form is used, it is important that application for credit be made as soon as possible, while the facts are clear.

SOME RECEIVING PITFALLS

There are many ways in which an unscrupulous person can successfully defraud an operation. Here are some of the tricks.

1. Packing merchandise in excessive moisture or wrappings or ice to make weighing more difficult and add more weight.
2. Repacking produce and putting a lighter weight in the new crates while keeping the price the same as for the heavier original crates. (It is wise to spot check the weights of crates and cartons.)
3. Placing satisfactory merchandise on the top level that is visible, but inserting merchandise of poorer quality underneath.
4. Not sending the grade specified in the hope that it will not be noticed.
5. Sending incomplete shipments with the full bill, and neglecting to send the remainder.
6. Supplying short weights. (Insisting that merchandise be weighed is one of the most important parts of receiving.)
7. Charging for boneless meats while leaving the bone in, substituting larger boned cuts than specified, or leaving excessive fat on the meat. (Specifications and the insistence on their use can help eliminate this practice.)
8. Using excessive packaging to increase weights, a practice somewhat akin to the old time butcher leaving his thumb on the scale.
9. Trying to get the receiving man to make a bulk weight for all the items under the pretense of saving time so that, say, the amount of hamburger can be increased and the amount of sirloin decreased by a similar amount, with the total weight remaining the same as the total weights of the invoices.
10. Delivering merchandise directly to the kitchen without passing it through the receiving department.
11. Allowing delivery men to place merchandise directly from the truck into the storeroom or refrigerators without checking quantity and quality in the receiving area.

RECEIVING PROCEDURE

It is management's responsibility to see that proper receiving procedures are established and adhered to. (It is easy to establish procedures but difficult to adhere to them.) A good set of procedures includes the following steps.

1. All items are counted, weighed and marked.
2. All pieces of meats, fish and poultry are weighed and inspected individually, and their tags are prepared.
3. Cartons of fruits and vegetables are opened at random to inspect for quantity and quality.
4. All items are checked against purchase specifications.
5. Invoices prices are checked against the purchase order or the buyer's quotation sheet.
6. All receiving invoices, after verification, are stamped and signed by the receiving clerk.
7. All merchandise, food, and supplies are written on the receiving report.
8. The unit price is put on each item and then placed in storerooms or refrigerators.
9. Management periodically checks its receiving procedures.

chapter 6

Storage, Issuing, and Inventory

STORAGE

Vital to any food service establishment is the operation of its food storage facilities, and in any evaluation of such an establishment, the adequacy of its storage area should be one of the prime considerations. Here, the food items that represent money must be kept until needed. They must be protected from theft and kept in prime physical condition. Contents should be placed in an organized manner, and the premises should be scrupulously clean. Too often, however, food storage is synonymous with disorder. Food is piled helter-skelter, and sanitation may be largely overlooked. Management cannot tell what is on hand, and both wastage and spoilage are greatly increased.

The food storage area is usually divided in two sections: a place for the dry food items—those in cans, bags, and cartons that do not require refrigeration—and a refrigerated section where frozen foods and foods susceptible to spoiling are kept.

The Storeroom (Dry Storage). Too often when planning a food facility, the architect relegates any left over space in his floor plans to "storage" without any real thought of precise storage needs. Considerations in planning for dry stores should include:

Adequate space.
Nearness to receiving and preparation areas.
Security of contents.
Temperature, humidity and lighting.
Shelving types and arrangement of contents.
Protection from vermin and insect infestation.

Adequate Space. The space required for dry stores depends on many factors, like the type of operation, its menu, its volume of business, its purchasing policies, and the frequency of deliveries. An operation serving a varied and changing menu will have different storage requirements than one serving a fixed, limited menu. Operations that can have food delivered daily and readily do not have the problems of the operation that is isolated, and which may receive only weekly, or even more infrequent, deliveries of some items. Other operators like to purchase large quantities of foods at one time and they must make extra provision for food storage.

Although each type of operation is different, there are several general rules which they may use as guidelines. One approach is to specify necessary floor space in terms of square footage per meal. Proponents of this method often recommend one-half to one square foot of floor space per meal served. Another method is to determine storage needs in terms of the supply on hand. A two-week supply is generally suggested; after calculating the amount of dry stores that will be used in a two-week period, the manager calculates the amount of space that it will occupy.

Although many food operators believe they can use as much dry food storage space as they can get, too great a storage area presents problems. Every square foot of storage area costs money to heat and maintain, so too great an area will require a larger capital expenditure. There is a tendency to want to fill up a storeroom, so an overly large area may promote an overly large inventory. If the area is not filled with foodstuffs, other supplies may be put into it. This habit complicates security, since it encourages more goings and comings, perhaps by people not controlled by the food department. Obviously, too small a storage area also presents problems. It retards ready access to items; some may be hidden; many must be stored in open areas; and it is more difficult to keep the premises clean.

Location. Theoretically, the storage are should be located between, and adjacent to, the receiving area and the preparation area. This is sometimes impossible. Many storerooms are located below the kitchen with an elevator or a dumbwaiter providing access to it. Unfortunately, in some large institutions, the dry stores area may be located blocks away from preparation, necessitating much hauling. If space is severely limited, it may be desirable both to have limited storage facilities close at hand and to utilize bulk storage elsewhere.

Security. A prime purpose of the storage area is to protect the contents which, after all, represent money in the form of merchandise. For tightest security, access to the storeroom should be strictly limited. Ideally, only the storeroom personnel and management are ever permitted in the room.

Merchandise should be delivered by the delivery men to porters at the storeroom entrance, or to storeroom personnel solely responsible for deliveries. A Dutch door that has a top half and a bottom half with a counter or ledge over the bottom half may be very helpful. This adjustment permits merchandise to be handed out and also keeps people from entering. Operations that allow personnel to enter the storeroom indiscriminately invite trouble. Not only are they apt to experience more pilferage, but they will find it practically impossible to pinpoint the guilty individuals as well. The open storeroom may also be used as a lounging place, away from the eyes of supervision.

Security is also promoted by installing only a limited number of entrances. Only one is desirable. Some operations with doors opening to the outside have found pilferage greatly reduced by locking the outside door and throwing away the keys (assuming, of course, that there is an inside means of entrance).

Temperature, Humidity, and Lighting. Some operators feel that although care must be given to raw or perishable items, there is little need to worry over canned or boxed items. This simply is wrong; with few exceptions, almost every food begins chemical deterioration immediately after processing. Infestation by roaches, flies, weevils, and rodents is also possible, and there is a definite natural deterioration in the quality of canned foods stored over long periods. This deterioration is accelerated by high temperatures and sudden fluctuations in temperatures, which can cause condensation in the products. The dry foods storeroom should be kept relatively cool; a 60-to-70 degree temperature is satisfactory, but maintaining a 50 degree temperature will help to maintain better quality in most foods. One study showed that foods in general keep three times as long at 70° F as they do at 100° F. Other studies have revealed that nutritional losses in foods increase as storage temperatures rise. Unfortunately, many storerooms have heating and water pipes running through them. The heating pipes may cause excessive heat, especially if there is little ventilation. The water pipes may cause condensation in the summer. This condensation creates dripping and humidity problems. It is desirable that relative humidity be around 50 to 60 percent, and lower for cereals. Operations with excessive humidity may want to install a mechanical or chemical dehumidifier. On the other hand, if the relative humidity is too low and the air is too dry, a humidifier or basins of water distributed around the storage area may be helpful.

The storeroom should be ventilated, and four air changes per hour are desirable. Ventilation haphazardly installed may also cause security, insect, and dust problems.

A problem in many dry food storerooms occurs when refrigeration compressors and condensers for refrigeration units are installed in the dry storeroom. These not only give off heat but also require periodic servicing, which creates still another security problem. Moreover, in some closed storerooms the compressors raise the temperature high enough in the closed area to cause mechanical problems.

Some products, like beer and beets, are affected by direct sunlight, so storeroom windows should be frosted. Clear glass can also transmit radiant heat to sealed containers and raise the temperature inside them higher than the surrounding room temperatures. Of course, the storeroom should have adequate illumination. One good rule of thumb dictates two or three watts of light for every square foot of floor area, but it should be noted that low ceilings and high shelves can hinder proper light distribution.

Shelving and Arrangement of Contents. Shelving is required whenever less-than-case lots must be stored or where management does not want to leave canned goods in full cases. Shelving should be adjustable and can be either metal or wood. Metal shelving takes up less space than wood, is easier to clean, can be more easily adjusted, and eliminates danger of splinters. Wood shelving, on the other hand, is somewhat softer than metal—better suited to storing glass jars. But it requires more care. Shelving space usually depends on the size of a No. 10 can, which is 7 inches high and 6¼ inches in diameter. Shelves 19 inches wide and 16 inches high will permit three rows of No. 10 cans to be stacked two tiers high, or four rows of No. 2½ cans stacked three tiers high. Unless special equipment (a rolling ladder, for example) is available, items should not be stored above 7½ feet or, in any case, beyond normal reach. Bulk supplies, such as cartons of breakfast food, case lots of canned goods, and bags of flour, may be stored on pallets that are raised eight to ten inches above the floor. Any merchandise stored directly on the floor or against outside walls may absorb moisture, create cleaning problems, and cut down ventilation. For this reason, merchandise on shelves should be kept two inches away from outside walls. If bags or crates of goods are kept on pallets on the floor, those bags and crates should be piled in a crisscross arrangement. This allows for better ventilation and, in some cases, easier stacking. It is also suggested that they not be stacked more than six tiers high.

Arranging foods in the storeroom involves several considerations. First, there should be a definite place for each item. Second, the fast-moving items should be stored close to the entrance. One effective system breaks the foods down into groups and then arranges them in that group alphabetically on the shelves. If fruit juice comprises one of the groups, the cans would be placed on the shelves, apple juice first, then cranberry, grape, and grapefruit, for example. The various groups do not necessarily have to be placed alphabetically; for example, frequently used items should be stored so that they may be easily reached.

The American Hospital Association, in one of their publications, suggests the following classification of groups:

a. Beverages, milk products, and mineral waters.
b. Candies.
c. Cereals, prepared.
d. Cereals and flour.
e. Chocolate and cocoa.
f. Cookies, cakes, and crackers.
g. Colorings.
h. Condiments and spices.
i. Extracts.
j. Fats and oils.
k. Fish, shell fish, and sea foods.
l. Fountain and ice cream supplies.
m. Fruits, canned.
n. Fruits, dried and glace.
o. Fruit juices and cocktails.
p. Fruit preserves and jellies.
q. Fruits, spiced and pickled.
r. Gelatin and gelatin desserts.
s. Leavening agents.
t. Nut meats and nut products.
u. Pickles and olives.
v. Sauces and relishes.
w. Sugar and related substances.
x. Vegetables, canned.
y. Vegetables, dried.
z. Specialties.

Having a definite space for each type of food item requires somewhat more space than if foods were placed haphazardly in an empty area, since foods may not require all the space allotted to them at one time. However, a great deal of time is saved by not having to hunt for items, which would most likely be necessary if they were stored randomly. In addition, the operator can readily determine exactly what he has on hand, if his foods are stored systematically. If inventory sheets are made up to correspond with the allotted spaces on the shelves, a great deal of time can be saved in taking the inventory.

Too often, new merchandise gets used while the old merchandise gets older and staler. FIFO (first in, first out) is the process of rearranging the merchandise so that the older containers are in front and issued first. It takes extra work to effect FIFO, but it pays off by eliminating the problem of stale merchandise. Some operations use a dating stamp on containers or cases to help show which merchandise is the oldest.

Protection from Vermin and Insect Infestation. Food must be protected from infestation by flies, roaches, weevils, and rodents. The grains and cereals are especially vulnerable to such vermin. Protection from pests requires the elimination of all holes or openings in the walls, ceilings, and floors of the storeroom. (Some mice can enter a half-inch hole.) Windows should be tightly screened. Provision should be made for regular cleaning and spraying so that insects may be controlled. Trash—especially garbage—should never be placed in the storeroom. If pipes must penetrate the walls of the storeroom, the walls should be tightly sealed around the pipes.

Bulk supplies of cereals, dried fruits, and vegetables should be kept in metal or heavy plastic containers with tight fitting lids. The cans should be labeled and perhaps mounted on rollers.

Summary. Here are some basic guidelines for dry storage.

1. A thermometer to indicate excessively high temperatures should be kept in the storeroom.

2. People allowed in the storeroom should be strictly limited and controlled.

3. Goods should be marked with the date of delivery and the FIFO system should be employed.

4. Merchandise should be stored six to ten inches above the floor and two inches from walls.

5. There should be a definite space for each food classification.

6. Employees' personal belongings should not be kept in the storeroom.

7. The storeroom should be locked when authorized personnel are not manning it. An emergency key in a sealed envelope may be kept in the manager's office.

8. The storeroom should be cleaned and sprayed regularly, with particular attention given to dark corners and to the areas under the shelves.

9. Foods packed in glass should not be exposed to direct sunlight or to any strong light.
10. "G.I." cans or large plastic containers that are used for bulk storage should have tight lids and it may be desirable to mount them on rollers for easy maneuverability.

REFRIGERATED STORAGE

Refrigeration is absolutely necessary for perishable items and extends the quality and life of some semi-perishable foods. Besides maintaining quality, refrigeration is necessary to curtail the growth of bacteria and control the food poisoning that results. Storage is generally classified as "refrigerated" when temperatures above freezing are maintained; frozen food storage exists when a temperature of 32 degrees or lower is maintained. Equipment is usually classified as "reach-in" when food is removed from outside, and "walk-in" when it is necessary actually to enter the unit. Specialty refrigeration units, such as beer coolers, salad refrigerators, and milk dispensers, are also in common use.

Amount of Refrigeration. There are no established rules to determine how much refrigeration is required in an operation. The number of entrees, the amount of convenience foods in use, the frequency of deliveries, the policy on leftovers, and fluctuations in business will all affect the amount of refrigeration required. To determine the size of the unit, one must determine the quantity of food that will be stored and its volume. Refrigeration space is sometimes dvided (somewhat arbitrarily) into a third for meats, a third for fresh produce and vegetables, a sixth for dairy products, and a sixth for frozen foods, but again this allocation depends on menu deliveries and the amount of frozen convenience foods used, among other things.

It is difficult to be exact in these calculations unless one expects to serve a very standard menu to a constant number of customers. Refrigeration storage space is rated in cubic feet, and some designers recommend one to two cubic feet per meal served.

Obviously, an excessive amount of refrigeration increases capital costs and operating expenses but perhaps even more important, it encourages a tendency to allow leftovers to accumulate and to spoil. Some operations have found that by strictly limiting the amount of refrigeration, they curtail overproduction and overordering.

Reach-in-refrigeration is very efficient since space does not have to be provided for personnel to move around in; however, walk-in units are necessary for storing large quantities of food. Many operations provide relatively small reach-in refrigeration handy for cooks in the preparation area while maintaining larger, walk-in refrigeration some distance away. Issues for the day, or for the meal, can be delivered at one time to the smaller units, and subsequent trips are largely eliminated. Efficiency in storage can be increased by installing adjustable shelves and racks that can be arranged according to the size of the articles stored. These adjustable shelves also help to eliminate unused storage space.

Physical Construction. It is poor economy to try to save money on cheaply constructed refrigeration units. Proper insulation is vital since outside heat can enter the unit by direct transmission. Vapor barriers are necessary to prevent water vapor from condensing in the insulation and making it less effective. All openings should be tightly fitted with some sort of stripping or gasket. Doors on walk-in units should be able to be opened from the inside, and a light, or some other signal, should be provided so that a person trapped in the unit can indicate his presence there. (Glass and plastic refrigerator doors are becoming more popular.) The inside construction of walk-ins should include walls that allow easy cleaning. Durable floors are especially important. The floor of the unit should be flush with the outside hall so that carts can readily be wheeled in. Portable shelving is very desirable. Stainless steel casing outside is very attractive and very durable but it is also very expensive; cheaper finishes can be just as efficient, though possibly less attractive. (Some of the new vinyl finishes provide a great flexibility in aesthetic design.) The handles, latches, releases, and other hardware used in the units should be the best available, and thought should be given to the availability of spare parts.

Temperatures and Humidities. Some large operations maintain over a dozen different temperatures in at least as many units. Optimum temperatures have been established for different foods, but most operations with a limited number of units have to make compromises. A prime function of refrigeration is to prevent the growth of bacteria which usually multiply most readily in the 50 to 120° F temperature range; therefore, all refrigerated foods should be kept colder than 50° F. Humidity also affects refrigerated foods. An excessively high relative humidity allows food to become slimy, encourages bacteria growth, and lets spoilage take place faster. Too low a relative humidity causes food to dry out. Too low a relative humidity can often be overcome by covering items with a wet cloth or dampening them directly. However, open containers of water should not be kept in the units to increase humidity because of the sanitation problems they create.

Separate refrigeration is often provided for three types of products: meats, fruits and produce, and dairy products.

Meats require temperatures of 32 degrees to 36 degrees and a relative humidity of 75 to 85 percent. If there is no provision for separate meat storage, meat should be kept on the lower shelves where it is coldest. Too low a temperature will cause meat to darken. Hanging meats should not touch each other and, of course, should be stored off the floors and several inches from the walls to allow for ventilation and air movements. Ground meats, fresh fish, and fresh poultry should be used as soon as possible and, in any case, should not be kept more than a few days.

Fruits and vegetables can be kept at temperatures between 35 and 45° F, and a higher relative humidity, from 85 to 95 percent, is desirable. Remove any decaying pieces so they can not spoil others in the containers. (Such vegetables as potatoes, squash, and eggplant can be kept at temperatures up to 60° F.)

Dairy products should be kept at temperatures in the 38 to 46 degree range and at a relative humidity of between 75 and 85 percent. If eggs are stored in crates, the crates should be cross-stacked. Butter should be wrapped tightly, since exposure to light and air causes rancidness.

A reach-in refrigerator in general use should be maintained in the 34 to 40 degree range. Fresh fish always presents a storage problem; it should be kept at around 30 degrees and only for short periods. Packing it in ice is usually the best way to preserve it. Leftovers should be stored in low flat pans rather than in deep ones. It takes a long time for heat to dissipate from the center of the deeper pans, so bacteria may grow, even while the food is under refrigeration. Loading refrigeration units with a great deal of hot food may raise the temperature, and time will be required to lower it again. Again, bacteria growth may result. Foods can be precooled by placing them in pans which are set in a sink of cold water. However, they should remain at room temperature only for a limited time.

TABLE 1
TEMPERATURE AND RELATIVE HUMIDITY GUIDE

	Temperature (°F)	Relative Humidity (%)
Meats	32–36	75–85
Fruits and Vegetables	35–45	85–95
Dairy	38–46	75–85
General purpose (reach-in)	34–40	75–85

Other Refrigerated Storage Considerations. Cleanliness of the refrigeration unit is vital for good management, housekeeping, and sanitation.

The contents of the unit should be put in order daily, and any spilled foods should be wiped up immediately. Warm, soapy water can be used to wash inside walls, but they should be quickly rinsed. Walk-in floors should be mopped daily.

If food items become "slimy," the temperature may be too hot or air movement may be inadequate. These problems may be caused by a blocked evaporator or frosted coils. Normally, a unit should be defrosted when there is an accumulation of a quarter-inch of ice. Besides maintaining efficiency, defrosting reduces electrical power costs. Self-defrosting units further reduce labor cost.

If the food appears to be dried out, the temperature may be too low or there may be too much air movement. If there is no fan control, blocking part of the evaporator (the coils inside the unit) may help.

A germicidal or ultraviolet ray lamp can help. Some operations recommend them because they reduce the mold that accumulates on aging meat. However, others feel this advantage is outweighed by their tendency to speed fat breakdown.

Some operations have an alarm light or a buzzer that is activated when temperatures rise above a certain level. This system helps prevent food loss by alerting personnel. If the trouble takes time to repair, temperatures may be kept down by placing ice or dry ice in the highest part of the unit. One common refrigeration trouble is the loss of the refrigerant. Since replacing the refrigerant is relatively expensive, it is wise to locate and correct leaks as soon as any difficulty is detected. Every unit should have a thermometer installed, and it should be checked regularly. Sometimes the thermometer gauge is installed outside of the unit for easier visibility.

FROZEN FOOD STORAGE

The use of frozen foods is steadily increasing with the increased use of convenience items and more and more consideration will be given to frozen food storage. The most important factor in frozen food storage is, of course, the temperature, which normally should be from zero to minus ten degrees. Even though foods stored at 32 degrees may be technically frozen, chemical changes and microorganism growth can occur in this temperature range. It is sometimes said that every temperature rise of ten degrees in frozen food storage cuts the storage life in half. Vegetables like peas and lima beans will become discolored and lose flavor in two months at ten degrees, but can be held up to a year at zero degrees. Frozen peas deteriorate 60 times faster at 30 degrees than at zero degrees.

Frozen food should be wrapped in moisture- or vapor-proof material; this will prevent the food from losing moisture and suffering freezer burn.

Freezer burn occurs when fat under the surface becomes rancid, causing a brown discoloration. A high humidity should be maintained in the freezer area, since the cold dry air will seek moisture from the foods stored in it.

Foods that have been allowed to thaw should not be refrozen. Rejuvenated microorganisms can cause spoilage, and changes in the food cell structure can cause a loss of quality. Most frozen foods can be cooked or reconstituted directly from the frozen state. Large pieces of meat, however, must be thawed, or partially thawed, before further processing. To prevent rapid growth of bacteria, these items should be thawed under normal refrigeration temperatures, rather than at room temperature. There may be less shrinkage when unthawed meats are cooked, but cooking times may be longer and fuel costs higher.

As in the regular refrigeration process, a thermometer gauge to check the temperature of the freezer units should be visible, and it is very desirable to have an alarm system that activates if the freezer temperature rises above a certain safety level. Air circulation should be provided inside the units; circulation is facilitated when items are not placed directly against the walls and ceiling, or on the floor. To ensure FIFO (first in, first out) it is helpful to have items stamped with the date of storage.

ISSUING

Issuing is the process used to supply food to the preparation units after it has been received by the operation. It also entails a control on food sent to preparation, a means of providing information for food cost accounting, and in some cases, providing information for a perpetual inventory system. Issuing can be done directly from the receiving dock or from the storerooms. If the issues are sent from the receiving area without going through a storeroom they are called direct purchases or direct issues. Direct issues are, presumably, used on the day they are purchased, since the kitchen is not a storeroom. The dollar value of direct issues is found from the direct column of the Daily Receiving Report (Figure 1, Chapter 5), and from this report management can determine the various items that are sent directly into the preparation unit.

All food items that are received but are not used the day they are purchased are considered storeroom purchases. They are storeroom issues when delivered from the storeroom. Thus, if a food item is received, sent to the storeroom, and issued from the storeroom and used the same day, it would be considered a storeroom issue. The control for storeroom issues is the requisition, and no food should be issued from the storeroom unless it has been recorded and ordered on a requisition form. By adding the total direct purchases and the total value of the requisitions, it is relatively easy to determine the food cost for the day or for the period under examination. *Direct purchases plus storeroom issues for the day equal daily food cost.*

Direct Purchases. To have accurate food cost information and better control, it is necessary that direct purchases (or issues) be limited to food that actually will be used on the day of delivery. If the food is not used the same day, the recorded food cost for the day of delivery would be unrealistically high, and the recorded food cost on the day it actually gets used would be unrealistically low. Some incoming purchases may have a portion of their value charged as direct purchases and sent directly to the preparation units, while a portion may be charged to the storeroom and sent there.

Storeroom Issues. All food provided by the storeroom should be recorded on a requisition like the one in Figure 1. If the requisitions are prenumbered, duplicates and missing requisitions can be more easily traced. Although most operations do not need numbered requisitions, the numbering may have some psychological value in that workers tend to be more careful with them. The name of the ordering department—the kitchen, pantry, and bake shop, for instance—should be filled in along with the date. The requisition should provide columns for the quantity of each item, the size of the unit desired, and the name of the item. There should also be spaces for the unit price and the total cost or "extension" (which is determined by multiplying the number of units and the cost of each unit). A line should be included for the person authorized to request the articles to sign or initial. The storeroom should not give out any merchandise without this authorizing signature. There should also be space for the person issuing the food or filling the requisition to sign. In addition, it may be desirable to provide a space for the person entering the requisition on the bookkeeping records, or extending the costs, to sign or initial. If there is trouble regarding deliveries, the person delivering the food from the storeroom may also have to sign.

Some operations use only one original requisition, while others feel that control is facilitated by the use of duplicate copies. Duplicate copies may be used to provide a copy of the requisition for the ordering department, to supply a duplicate to the food cost controller, to provide a copy for perpetual inventory, and to allow a copy to be returned with the order. The duplicates may be made out with the original requisition, or they may be made out by the issuing storeroom. Since the duplicates are largely informational, they would not necessarily have to be signed by the person making out the original.

Difficulties sometimes arise when food is requisitioned for preparation prior to the actual serving day. These difficulties are best handled by mak-

REQUISITION   ORDER

No. _____   Date _____ 19

To _____

Please deliver to _____

Remarks

Signature

WHITNEY DUPLICATING CHECK CO., NEW YORK 1, N. Y. – FORM 5006

Figure 1   Requisition.

ing two requisitions: one with the date that the food is issued, and the
other with the date that the items will be used. The food is released on
the basis of the first requisition, but only the second requisition is recorded on the date of use for cost control purposes. Care must be taken
at the end of an inventory period that items issued but not charged be
given credit on the inventory.

If the storeroom cannot supply an item on the requisition, it should be
marked "out." In some cases, it is desirable to call the person requesting
the item immediately so he can make substitutions or purchase arrange-

ments. The storeroom should not make changes on requisitions or accept requisitions over the telephone.

Pricing the requisitions and calculating extensions may be done in the storeroom or elsewhere. With constantly changing prices, finding the exact cost of the item may be a problem. A very effective and easy way to determine this cost is to stamp or mark the containers with the unit cost when they are received. When filling out a requisition, it is very simple to record the cost. This also simplifies pricing inventories. It eliminates the necessity of checking back through the receiving report, the invoices, or the perpetual inventory cards to find the purchase cost. Some operations cost out the requisition at the last purchase cost, but this practice can lead to some difficulties in resolving inventory valuations.

If a meat tag system is employed, the meat tag can be used for costing purposes. It saves reweighing the item and also eliminates inventory shrinkage calculation, since the item is issued at the weight on the tag, which is the weight received.

Figure 2 correlates the requisition with the standard recipe card. The

REQUISITION

Date_____   Item_____

Ingredients	Quantity	50 Servings	100 Servings	150 Servings
Eggs	_____	9 eggs	1½ dozen	2¼ dozen
Shortening	_____	¾ pound	1½ pounds	2¼ pounds
Vanilla	_____	⅛ cup	¼ cup	⅜ cup
Salt	_____	¾ teaspoons	1½ teaspoons	2¼ teaspoons
Sugar	_____	2 pounds	4 pounds	6 pounds
Flour	_____	2 pounds	4 pounds	6 pounds
Baking powder	_____	1¾ ounces	3½ ounces	5¼ ounces
Dry milk	_____	3 ounces	6 ounces	9 ounces

Figure 2

items required are already listed and only the quantities have to be entered. This system, of course, requires that a standard recipe sheet be used every time the item is prepared.

INVENTORIES

Food inventories may be divided into two general types: the *Physical Inventory*, in which the merchandise is actually counted, and the *Perpetual Inventory*, in which purchases and requisitions are recorded, providing a continuous balance on hand. The balance of the perpetual inventory can be checked with the actual count of the physical inventory. Inventories are necessary to calculate the food cost (the cost of goods sold) accurately. They also reveal shortages and help guide purchasing.

Physical Inventory. Without proper physical inventory, it is possible for one to maintain a misleadingly low food cost by not recording requisitions and not replacing food taken from storage. This practice will eventually come to light when the storeroom grows bare and requires extensive restocking. The restocking will return costs to normal levels all of a sudden, and the understating of the food costs will be revealed. In calculating food cost, one needs an opening inventory value figure (the closing inventory of the previous financial period) and a closing inventory value figure. These figures can be accurately determined only by counting the merchandise in storage and determining its value. The formula for determining food cost is given below.

The value of the opening inventory
plus food purchases
equals the total inventory available
less the closing inventory
equals the cost of the food consumed
      during the period.

The cost of food consumed is known as the "gross" cost. If employees' meals are deducted from this amount, the resulting figure is referred to as cost of goods sold. Although food cost can be ascertained on a daily basis by adding direct purchases and storeroom requisitions, inventory fluctuations must be taken into account for a truly accurate figure.

Normally, inventories are taken once a month, usually at the end of the month or whenever the financial period may end. An inventory at the end of December would be the closing figure for the year (and the opening inventory for the next year) if the financial year runs from January 1 to December 31. However, physical inventories are taken whenever management needs an accurate food cost figure.

Two people can take inventory easily if one counts while the other records the figures. To ensure control, at least one of the inventory takers should be free of connections with the storeroom or the kitchen and should not be influenced by their personnel. Someone from the manager or food controller's office usually does the work. The inventory is sometimes taken on looseleaf inventory sheets, which list the items in the same order as they are placed on the shelves. Space should be left on the inventory sheets for new items that might be added during the year. To facilitate pricing, unit prices, if marked on the merchandise, should be called when the merchandise is counted. No more than one food group should be listed on each inventory page, and each page should be subtotaled. These subtotals are combined for a grand total, on a recap sheet, and the personnel taking the inventory should sign it to fix responsibility.

A popular method of taking inventory is to use a twelve-month inventory bound book. This book allows the inventory takers to write the items only once, and by folding half pages they can match the items each month for their monthly counts. The system makes inventory taking easy; it makes comparing the amounts held in stock easy; and it makes it easy to spot slow-moving items.

Storeroom inventories should be taken after the close of business on the last day of the financial period, but this is not always possible. In any case, they should not be taken until the day's purchases are in the storeroom and issues have been made.

Some operations that have a very stable inventory have found that their count of items in the storeroom varies little from month to month. In some cases, it has proven economical not to count most items but to assume that they remain constant. Only expensive and fast-moving items are counted. This method sacrifices some accuracy and control but does eliminate much of the tedious job of inventory taking. It should be employed only where experience has shown that there is little variance from month to month, and of course, a full inventory should be taken periodically.

Kitchen or production inventories represent goods that have been charged to preparation departments but have not yet been consumed. These inventories are usually taken by the person in charge of the unit or department, but spot checks should be made by personnel responsible for food cost control. Meat is usually the item of largest cost in production inventories, so the food cost control personnel may want to take part in this inventory especially. Kitchen inventories are added to storeroom inventories for a total inventory value figure.

Storeroom Reconciliation. Figure 3 shows a format for storeroom reconciliation. Besides opening inventory, purchases, issues and closing inventory, other credits are subtracted and debit transfers are added. It may be desirable to reconcile commodity groups, especially if there is a large discrepancy, and it is important to discover where this discrepancy occurred.

Slow inventory turnover may indicate an excessive amount of goods on hand—stale or unusable, goods that are still carried as assets. Many operations figure that their inventory should turn over three to five times a month. Thus, an inventory value of $5000 should be reflected in a monthly cost of food-consumed figure of $15,000 to $25,000. Inventory turnover is calculated by dividing the value of the inventory into the cost of food consumed during the period. If the cost of food consumed is $25,000 and the value of the inventory is $5000, the inventory turnover is

---

STOREROOM RECONCILIATION

Beginning inventory value	$ 2,000.00
Food stores purchased	8,000.00
Total	$10,000.00
Issues per requisition	8,050.00
Balance	$ 1,950.00
Ending inventory value	1,925.00
Over or (short)	$ (25.00)

Figure 3

five times. This figure will vary according to the operation; a limited menu fast-service operation, for example, will have a considerably higher turnover. There will usually be some difference between the value of the physical inventory and the figure that could be calculated if purchases were added and issues subtracted from an original figure. Normally, an overage or shortage of one-fourth of one percent of the cost of goods sold is considered acceptable.

Perpetual Inventory. A perpetual inventory keeps purchases and issues constantly recorded for each item in storage so that the balance on hand is always available. Perpetual inventories require considerable labor to maintain and usually are utilized only by very large operations which make purchases for several months' consumption. With the use of data processing increasing, perpetual inventories for purchase determinations and cost analysis may become more routine. In a noncomputerized operation, advantages that may accrue from the use of a perpetual inventory include the following:

a. It guides buying. The perpetual inventory indicates when it is necessary to reorder.
b. It controls overbuying and underbuying. It is easier to see how much food has been used and how much will be needed.
c. It provides a constant inventory figure. Although the perpetual inventory should be checked periodically against a physical inventory, it is possible to take a quick inventory from the cards at any time.
d. It shows item variations. The perpetual inventory indicates how much of each item should be on the shelves, and it helps to pinpoint items that show unusual variances.
e. It helps move old items. By glancing at the cards, it is possible to see

which items are not being used so that they can be incorporated into menus.

As mentioned before, a perpetual inventory entails a great deal of work and, to be effective, must be constantly kept up to date. Some operations keep a perpetual inventory on fast moving items, like butter or coffee. Such ratios as pounds used per $100 of sales, or pounds used per 100 customers, will indicate whether food usage is within bounds.

The perpetual inventory can be kept on cards (Figure 4). These cards may be kept in any convenient manner, like flip rings or file drawers, which allows ready access to and entries on the cards. Buying and cost information may be kept on one side of the card, the perpetual inventory on the other side.

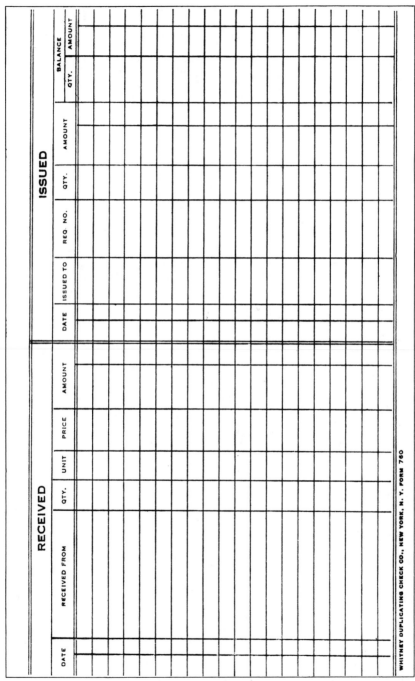

Figure 4   Perpetual inventory card.

91

chapter 7

Preparation and Portion Control

KITCHEN CONTROL

The term "kitchen control" implies both the most efficient utilization and scheduling of personnel and equipment and the production of a predetermined amount of food so as to have it ready at a designated time. There should be as little overproduction and waste as possible, and the food should be the highest quality suitable for the operation.

Control, in general, is a basic function of management, and kitchen control is, most particularly, a management and supervisory concern. For control to be effective, management must constantly inspect, check, instruct, and evaluate. No operation that "runs by itself" has effective control.

Forecasting. Estimating how much to produce is vital to kitchen control. In institutions with a definite patron census, these estimations are relatively easy to make; however, in operations serving varying volumes of different items, it becomes a problem to forecast total sales volume and the volume of individual selections. (Forecasting procedures discussed in Chapter 4 are, of course, applicable to the problems of forecasting demand and scheduling production.) Production estimates must be performed in advance so that proper planning and purchasing can be more exact, and forecasting the number of each item that will be sold requires past performance records such as a Sales History Card (Figure 1).

FOOD PRODUCTION SHEET

The Food Production Sheet (Figure 2) augments the Sales History Card. Figure 2 illustrates one type of Food Production Sheet, although there

SALES HISTORY CARD

Date	Day	Price	Lunch (Number Sold)	Percent	Dinner (Number Sold)	Percent	Comments
6/1	Mon.	$2.00			40	20	5 over
6/3	Wed.	2.00			40	18	Ran out 7:15
6/5	Fri.	1.75	25	12	15	5	Special for dinner out 6:30
6/18	Thur.	2.00			50	22	6 Over
6/22	Mon.	2.00			45	20	15 Over heavy rain, 150 entrees

Figure 1. Fried chicken

are many variations of this performance record. The Food Production Sheet shows forecasted orders, the quantity actually prepared, the number of orders sold, the number of leftovers, the discrepancy—the difference between the number sold and leftovers, compared to the number prepared —and a space for comments. The information for the Sales History Cards may be taken from this form.

FOOD PRODUCTION SHEET

Date and Day: Monday, June 1

Weather: Fair

Total Meals Served: 200

Meal Supper

Item	Forecasted	Prepared	Number Sold	Percent	Leftover	Discrepancy	Comments
Fried Chicken	45	45	40	20	5		Employee meals
Filet of Sole	30	25	22	11	3		
Baked Ham	70	70	61	31	2	7	Poor Portioning
Pot Roast	80	75	67	33	8		
Lamb Chop	5	10	10	5			Employee meals
	230	225	200	100	18	7	

Figure 2

Work Assignment Sheet. Figure 3 shows a Work Assignment Sheet, which

---

WORK ASSIGNMENT SHEET

Station: _____
Employee(s): _____

Date:_____

_____
_____
_____

Item	Recipe No.	Quantity	Preparation Time	Needed	Comments

Figure 3

may be used for those individuals or stations in the kitchen who are responsible for advance food preparation. (If designed for a station, the Work Assignment Sheet should indicate the personnel assigned to the station.) With a Work Assignment Sheet, a supervisor need not personally instruct employees what to produce. Since the orders are written, there is less chance of error and confusion regarding quantities. In making out the work assignment sheet, the supervisor must give thought to the equalization of work loads. In the example shown, there is a column for listing items that the individual or sections must prepare, the recipe number (if a numbering system is used) and the quantity desired. Listing the preparation time helps the supervisor determine work loads and also gives an employee an indication of the time required to produce the item. The "Needed" column shows when the product should be ready. When small batch cooking is desired, the time schedule is shown for the required amounts needed. The "Comments" column allows space for special instructions, other jobs to be performed, equipment to be used, or any additional information the supervisor might want to transmit.

Quality Control. Quality control, besides being difficult to achieve, is also illusive to define. At one time, it was informally thought to be descriptive of only highly skilled personnel using the finest ingredients to produce a consistently superior product. Now it is recognized that the ingredients do not have to be the finest available, but that they should be the best for the level of quality desired. Skilled help is not always readily available, so other ways must be found to substitute for the missing skills and artistry. Moreover, "consistency" has become as important as "quality." So now "quality control" implies that every product measures up to a predetermined standard and sells at an appropriate price, rather than necessarily being outstanding. Quality control today is just as important for a hot dog stand as it is for a gourmet restaurant. At one time, the industry stressed the periodic and final inspections to discover defects and maintain quality; today it recognizes that quality control comes, in large measure, with the proper planning of facilities and production processes and the careful instruction of those employees carrying out these processes.

Quality control requires the proper equipment and its correct use. Some tools of quality control in food service include measuring scales, written specifications, standard recipes, accurate thermostats, and modern, light, cool, spacious working conditions.

Besides planning and providing the physical equipment, it is the job of management to motivate employees to be conscious of product standards. Concern for and insistence upon quality is mandatory. With the relative abundance of good jobs in other industries and the low esteem in which many food service jobs are held, it is difficult to create in an employee a sense of pride in his work. Therefore, some operators try to motivate their employees by exposing them to other operations. They encourage a cook to visit, at company expense, another restaurant with his wife to get ideas and to evaluate the quality of the competition. Hostesses and other key employees should also be sent to view competitive operations.

Quality control may be somewhat easier in the future, with the increase of mechanization and convenience foods. The more automatic the equipment, the easier it is to maintain quality. Convenience foods that are produced in large production runs in a central plant can develop a high level of quality control and product standardization.

Standard Recipes. At one time, standardized recipes were the anathema of chefs and fine cooks. Their reputation, after all, rested on their ability to prepare a wide variety of food products relying solely on their own ability and experience. Since they were proud of their training, it would have been an insult to place a recipe in front of them. Formerly, the cook had to be able to make allowances for variations in raw food quality, and these "allowances" could not be incorporated into a recipe. However, the quality of today's processed raw food products is very uniform and rarely presents problems in recipes. The master cook who could work strictly from his own knowledge is vanishing; where he remains, he must often admit that even he can produce even better dishes with the help of standard recipes.

Standard recipes are very useful to a food service operation for these reasons.

a. They facilitate uniform quality and taste. The patron who orders a product and smacks his lips in fond remembrance of past enjoyment will again enjoy the same taste, not another cook's different interpretation. Your patrons have a right to expect the same item each time they order it.

b. They give predictable yields. It is known exactly how much the recipe will produce. This knowledge will also effect portion control, since the number of servings from a particular recipe can be determined in advance. Portion control, in turn, is necessary for accurate costing.

c. They require less supervision. The standard recipe gives instructions which a supervisor might otherwise have to give orally and supervise in person.

d. They require less trained help. Standard recipes not only substitute, in part, for the lack of staff expertise, but they also serve as a media of staff instruction. Employees can learn from clear-cut instructions as they do the work.

e. They establish food cost control. With standard recipes it is possible to secure accurate food costs, since quantities and kinds of ingredients are established in advance. Standard recipes make possible the calculation of labor time and costs, since the preparation procedure may also be specified.

f. They create independence. With standardized recipes, other people can produce items which may be the speciality of one employee, and the operation is not dependent solely upon that employee. (To be candid though, one must admit that even with standardized recipes, some employees do a better job than others on particular items.)

Many operations have sets of standard recipes displayed impressively on the supervisor's desk, where their only real purpose seems to be to attract attention and dust. Having standard recipes is important but their application is far more important. It is good business to require that each time an employee prepares an item (apart from such routine items as eggs, hamburgers, and french fries) he uses a standard recipe, which contains the procedures and quantities that have been determined by management. The recipe can be mimeographed and discarded after the item is prepared or it can be enclosed in plastic and returned to the file after completion. Photo reproduction processes, such as Xerox and Thermofax, can also be used to provide work copies. Work areas and equipment should be provided with racks, clips, or other means to hold recipes in such a way that they are readily visible during the preparation process and the worker does not actually have to handle them. If permanent cards are used, there should be one complete set in the appropriate preparation units, a set in a master file in the office, and a set in the food cost control section. In many operations, the standard recipe includes a picture of how the food should appear when served.

There are many sources of standard recipes, most of which are very good, but each recipe should be tested and then adapted to your particular operation. In testing, it is necessary to judge the quality of the product

RECIPE FOR: Swiss steak				NUMBER: A 106
TOTAL WEIGHT YIELD	NUMBER OF PORTIONS 100–4 oz. servings			SIZE OF PORTION 1 steak each
INGREDIENTS	WEIGHT lbs.	oz.	VOLUME OR MEASURE	PROCEDURE
Beef, cut in 4 oz. servings	25	—		1. Season flour with salt and pepper. Dredge steaks in seasoned flour. Cook steaks in fat until browned on both sides. Place in serving pans.
Flour, hard	2	—		
Salt	—	—	¾ cup	
Pepper	—	—	1¾ tsp.	
Fat	2	—		
Bay leaves	—	—	2 each	2. Boil together bay leaves, cloves and garlic in 2 qts. stock for about 20 min. Strain.
Cloves, whole	—	—	½ tsp.	
Garlic, crushed	—	—	3 cloves	
Beef stock	—	—	2½ gal.	
Tomato puree	—	—	2¼ cups	3. Mix together beef stock, tomato puree, soy sauce and flour. Stock should not be too hot or the flour will not blend. Simmer about 10 min., stirring constantly.
Soy sauce	—	—	1½ cups	
Flour, soft	—	—	5 cups	
Onions, chopped	2	—		4. Add onions and simmer 10 more minutes. To the stock in which the spices were boiled blend celery, salt, thyme and savory; add to sauce and mix well. Pour sauce over steaks to cover.
Celery salt	—	—	1 tsp.	
Salt	—	3		
Thyme, ground	—	—	1 tsp.	
Savory, ground	—	—	½ tsp.	
RECIPE FOR: Swiss steak	PREPARATION TIME 1 hr. 30 min.		TEMPERATURE 350°F	COOKING TIME 2 hours

Figure 4

according to the customs of your operation: decide on seasoning or flavoring changes that would make it more appealing to your patrons; convert the amount of ingredients used to produce your desired yields (the conversion process may also cause some changes in the ingredient proportions); cost out the recipe; and determine the necessary selling price appropriate for you.

Figures 4 and 5 are illustrations of standard recipes used in a veterans' hospital. Quantities of ingredients are given. Columns are provided for ounces or other measurements. The preparation procedure is listed in sequence with appropriate temperatures and times included. The total yield in weight or portions, the yield per pan, the type of pan, and the size of the portions should be included. Cooking temperatures and times should be specified, and so should special equipment, such as a particular kind of oven that might be required. Preparation times are very helpful for planning work loads; it may be desirable to have a numbering system of recipes for easier reference; and many standard recipes include the ingredient and portion costs to facilitate pricing and cost controls. Finally, it is important that the date of the last testing or revision be shown to indicate if the version is the latest one.

RECIPE FOR: Fricandeau of veal				NUMBER: B 098	
TOTAL WEIGHT YIELD 37 lb. 7 oz.		NUMBER OF PORTIONS 100		SIZE OF PORTIONS 6 oz.	
TYPE SERVING PAN Roast pan		AMOUNT PER PAN 18–12 oz.		PORTIONS PER PAN 50	
	WEIGHT		VOLUME OR		
INGREDIENTS	lbs.	oz.	MEASURE	PROCEDURE	
Veal, cubed, E. P.	20	—		a. Melt fat.	
Shortening	—	11		b. Add veal and brown.	
Onions, diced	4	—		c. Add onions, carrots, celery,	
Carrots, sliced	4	—		salt, pepper and parsley. Bake	
Celery, diced	1	10		in moderate oven 350°F for	
Salt	—	—		30 min.	
Pepper	—	—	2 tsp.	d. Add tomatoes and cook until	
Parsley, chopped	—	3		tender, about 30 min., basting	
Tomatoes, canned	6	10		frequently.	
Flour	—	4½		e. Remove meat and vegetables.	
				f. Thicken liquor with flour mixed to a smooth paste with cold water, cooking and stirring until thick.	
RECIPE FOR: Fricandeau of veal	PREPARATION TIME 30 min.		TEMPERATURE 350°F	COOKING TIME 1½ hours	

Figure 5

Meat Cookery. The most expensive cooking ingredient is usually meat. Some cost aspects to consider in meat cookery follow.

a. *High temperature* accelerates shrinkage. One study showed a shrinkage loss of 15.8 percent at 325° F and 30.4 percent at 500° F. Using the lower temperature prevented 2.4 ounces of shrinkage per pound or approximately 15 percent of the meat cost. A temperature around 300° F is recommended for roasting, and lower temperatures also produce a product that is juicier and more evenly browned. The length of the cooking period also influences the amount of shrinkage. Rare meat shows less shrinkage than medium or well done meats. The newer, liquid-filled roasting skewers are even more effective than plain metal ones.

b. *Meat thermometers* provide the most scientific way to determine if the meat is ready for serving. In beef, a 140° F reading indicates rare, a 160° F reading indicates medium, and a 170° F reading indicates well done.

c. *Different grades* of meat have different yields. Generally the lower grades have less shrinkage, due to the coarse texture of the meat and the absence of fat.

d. *Convection ovens* have decreased cooking time and shrinkage.

Vegetable Cookery. For a long time vegetable cookery in this country was largely ignored, in contrast to some European and Asian areas where the preparation of vegetables is a fine art. Here, vegetables are too often prepared in large quantities and allowed to overcook and become soggy and bland. Today, the most satisfactory way to obtain large quantities of firm, tasty cooked vegetables cheaply is through frequent small batch cookery. Often a counter top steamer is used, although other cooking apparatus can also give satisfactory results. Unless all your patrons are served at one time, small batch cooking can provide a continuous supply of freshly cooked vegetables with most of their palatability, color, and nutritional qualities preserved. Preprocessed frozen vegetables are being used extensively in quantity cooking. Their quality can be good and they require less labor than the preparation of fresh vegetables.

PORTION CONTROL

Portion control is vital in the operation of a food service facility. It requires two definite steps: determining a definite size to be served, and making certain that this designated portion is always served.

A facility may have excellent control in all other phases of its operation, but if it serves a five-ounce portion of an entree instead of the planned four ounces, its profit has been considerably reduced. Serving meager portions or uneven portions will cause customer resentment and dissatisfaction. The serving personnel in cafeterias may occasionally show partiality for favorite patrons to the dismay of the others. Unfortunately, portion sizes are too often left to the discretion of the serving or preparing personnel, with little thought given to what might be the ideal portion size.

Determining the Proper Portion Size. The proper portion is one which has been determined by a consideration of the type of operation, customer satisfaction, the cost of food and service, and merchandising problems. Published standard portion charts can be used as a guide, but specific standard portion charts should be developed for the individual operation.

The cost approach involves determining what your clientele will pay for an item and determining how much of the item you can provide for that price. If roast beef will sell for $6.00 a la carte, and a 40 percent food cost is your goal, the portion of roast beef should cost around $2.40.

The quantity approach requires a determination of the amount of food your average patron prefers.

Unfortunately, average portions may be too much for some and not enough for others. Cost, quantity, quality, and sales prices all affect the determination of portion sizes. Unusually large portions may be served for merchandising purposes—that is, to attract attention—like a nine-inch-high piece of cake. Some operators serve large portions in order to secure more sales which they hope will compensate for their higher costs. With rising costs, some operators cut their portions until they encounter visible or audible customer resentment. This is a dangerous practice as one can never tell how much resentment and lost patronage has occurred before resentment becomes evident. One of the least effective ways to set your portions is to copy blindly those of your competition. Your competitors may be in error, and there is no reason for you to suffer for their mistakes. In any case, portion sizes must satisfy the customer. Since sales volume will signal this approval, it is important to analyze the sales and the cost of your bestsellers. If your profit is acceptable and if the item is selling briskly, your portion sizes are probably correct. Also, it is well to observe the food that is returned to the dishwashers. Such informal observations sometimes give clues as to whether or not the quality of the food is acceptable and the portion sizes are too small, too large, or just right.

Serving the Proper Portion Size. After the proper portion size is determined, you must arrange for it to be served as specified. Personnel must be made aware of this proper size, and written instructions containing this information should be readily available to all personnel who portion-out food. Large institutional operations serving a single menu may ask a supervisor to demonstrate the proper portions before the serving period and to make up sample platters for the benefit of serving personnel.

Portion control scales are invaluable. They can be used to measure portions of such meat items as steaks and chops and patties before they are cooked. Often preparation personnel feel that they can judge sizes and weights without the aid of a scale, but even the most experienced cook will do a better job if he weighs what he is cutting or forming. It may not be necessary to weigh every steak or patty, but it would be wise to weigh every third or fourth. Scales can also be used to weigh prepared entrees. There are scales on the market that can be adjusted to account for the weight of the platter, thus showing the weight of the portion directly on the dial.

The dish or glass size often controls portions. A four-ounce glass will serve about three and one-half ounces of liquid. Vegetable dishes can determine the amount of vegetables served. Desserts may be controlled by the size of their containers. The serving plate is most important. A smaller serving plate should be used for small portions that would look incongruous on a large plate.

Paper service is becoming more popular for portion control. Paper souffle cups are very handy for such side garnishes as, apple sauce and mint jelly. Paper creamers and condiment and jelly containers are also useful in controlling portions, figuring costs, and reducing labor. Not only do they help determine portion size, but they also prevent garnishes from mixing into the other foods.

A specific size ladle, scoop, or serving spoon can standardize the portion. Thus, a number-eight scoop will serve a half-cup or four ounces. (Scoop size is determined by the number of scoops per quart.)

Cooking utensils can be used in portion control. An eight-inch pie tin yields six slices. Uniform sizes can be obtained by using a marker or scoring the pie tin. If a standard recipe is used for hard puddings, jello, or sheet cakes, a marked pan can delineate standard quantities and sizes. Portion sizes are often determined by cut lines along each side of the pan. Casserole dishes automatically control portion sizes.

Portion control is closely tied to purchase specifications. A half-crate of fresh grapefruit weighing 36 pounds can contain anywhere from 18 to 48 grapefruits, depending upon their size. It is necessary, therefore, to determine what size grapefruit is desired and to specify this size in purchasing. A half grapefruit from the 48 count is far smaller than one from the 18 count and it would presumably command a lower menu price. Frankfurters and bacon strips come in various sizes, and the number per-pound should be specified. Baked potatoes and many other vegetables depend on precise specifications for portion control.

Effective portion control requires five steps.

1. Determining the desired size per portion.

2. Making sure these portion sizes are known and available to all personnel.

3. Requiring use of specifications in all purchases for properly sized food items.

4. Providing the means for measuring portions.

5. Checking and constantly rechecking to see that your personnel are serving the specified portions—and this can be the hardest part of the whole process.

CONVENIENCE FOODS

One of the most significant changes in food service operations in recent years has been the greatly increased use of convenience food items. These are also referred to as "efficiency foods," "ready foods," or "preprepared foods." The introduction of convenience food items may affect the various subsystems of menu planning, procurement, production, serving and sanitation, and their introduction is helped by a systems approach.

Convenience foods are not new. Since earliest times, techniques such as drying, pickling, and salting have been used to preserve food and postpone spoilage. Utilizing these techniques has required a certain amount of pre-preparation and has reduced the effort required to serve the food at the time of consumption. A major development in convenience for food items was canning, developed in the early 1800s with support from Napoleon who desired to make his army independent of local food supplies and seasonal shortages.

Although food service operations have been using convenience items, such as canned goods, commercially baked bread, and packaged cereals for many years, technological advances have only recently permitted the widespread use of refrigerated or frozen convenience items. At the same time this technology was being developed, the industry was finding itself under severe pressures. Labor costs were rising at a rapid rate; skilled workers were in short supply; customers were demanding more sophisticated foods; competition was increasing; and profits were declining. It was natural to try to solve or alleviate some or all of these problems with the large number of newly available convenience items. It was also natural to try to obtain the full benefits of convenience foods by integrating them into the whole operation with a systems approach, rather than merely substituting convenience items for conventionally prepared foods.

Advantages of Convenience Foods

a. Labor savings. A great deal of labor time can be saved by having convenience food items produced under assembly line conditions. However, if the food operator maintains the same staff, who formerly prepared conventional foods, to reconstitute these convenience foods, he will sacrifice his labor savings. Some operators have reduced preparation manpower requirements by as much as 60 percent using largely convenience items. However, labor preparation costs are only a small portion of the costs of serving a meal, and even major savings in this area can cause only a moderate reduction in total costs.

b. Variety and sophisticated foods. In the usual operation the production crew has time to prepare only a limited number of items. If some of these are already prepared and need only to be taken from storage and reconstituted, it is possible to offer considerably more items on a particular day with the same staff. An operation may also want to offer a food item that is beyond the capability of its staff to prepare. Or, perhaps the staff can prepare the item but the small demand for it does not justify special preparation. If the item is available in convenience form, it could be taken from inventory and served when requested.

c. Less skilled personnel. Since the skilled preparation is performed outside of the kitchen, it is not necessary to have personnel in the kitchen competent to produce all items.

d. Less food loss. In the usual kitchen it may be hard to utilize unsold quantities of prepared items. Little lead time is required with convenience items, and they can be reconstituted as needed with little leftover. The volume production run of an item under factory conditions causes far less waste than frequent short production runs of the same item in the kitchen. If the convenience item is frozen or suitable for dry storage, the problem of spoilage found in fresh items will be largely eliminated.

e. Lower food costs. Lowering food costs has been a topic of considerable discussion. Some operators feel that if built-in labor, space requirements, equipment costs, working capital, and overhead costs are considered, convenience foods have a definite advantage. Others feel that even considering these costs, they can produce food at a lower cost using conventional methods. The answer for a particular operation depends on the needs and capabilities of the operation and how the convenience items fit in with its total system.

f. Less equipment investment. If the major portion of the food preparation is performed elsewhere, less equipment may be needed in the serving kitchen. This assumes, however, that there will be no conventional preparation requiring the equipment. Even though there may be less total equipment, more equipment may be required for specific purposes. If frozen convenience items are used, there may be more need for freezer space, and microwave ovens would be required if they were essential in reconstituting the items.

g. Nutrition and quality. The nutritional value of vegetables processed quickly at the peak of their season may surpass the quality of the vegetables if there is a delay between harvesting and use. For example, frozen vegetables cooked quickly from their frozen state may retain nutrients better than fresh vegetables that have been stored. A factor that may decrease the quality of frozen items is a temperature that fluctuates between initial freezing and time of preparation. During transportation and storage periods, the products may defrost. Although the items may be quickly refrozen, defrost-refreeze cycles can have marked adverse effects on quality.

Disadvantages of Convenience Foods. Convenience foods have some disadvantages that sometimes limit their feasibility. These disadvantages are discussed below.

a. Poor quality. Many convenience items are of excellent quality, but unfortunately not all. Some operators who would like to use convenience items cannot find items that meet their standards for all their menu needs. Their efforts to install a convenience system will be limited accordingly. In addition, the quality may not be uniform in a shipment. For example, an operator may find only enough sauce in a package to cover four of the six items packed. The quality of convenience items has increased considerably in the last few years, but a company may produce a product that would be acceptable in a school lunch program but unacceptable in a fine restaurant.

b. Unavailability. Some areas have difficulty securing convenience items. Local purveyors may not carry desired items or full lines of items. Deliveries may be complicated by the need for refrigerated trucks. With the increasing use of convenience items, however, availability and delivery problems are decreasing.

c. Adverse employee reaction. In some instances there has been adverse reaction by some employees to the large-scale introduction of convenience foods. This reaction has been traced to a natural reluctance to change, a fear of job loss, or the feeling that convenience foods are an insult to the culinary ability of the employee. Whether or not these reactions are expected, there should be some orientation and explanation when convenience foods are introduced. Besides preparing employees psychologically for the changeover, the program can acquaint them with the new system and how to be more proficient in their jobs.

Adoption of Convenience Foods or Convenience Food Service Systems. Changing to convenience foods, or programming a new operation for convenience foods, does not consist simply of substituting the convenience items for conventionally prepared ones. The convenience system should provide food and service at least as good as the food and service supplied with the resources available from a conventional system, and they should also produce economies in operation. It is not necessary to convert completely to convenience foods as these items can supplement conventional items, and the two can be integrated. For best results, this integration must be planned carefully rather than effected haphazardly.

In considering the large-scale introduction of convenience items, the operator must keep the goals of his organization constantly in mind. For a commercial operation, this goal would probably be the maximizing of profits while providing food and service acceptable to patrons. A non-profit institution might have the goal of providing the best food and service that its resources permit. The first step in implementing these goals is a market analysis. The operator must carefully analyze his prospective patrons. How old are they? What is their economic status? Does he expect to cater to men, to women, or to families? What ethnic groups are prevalent in his area? How much time do they have available for dining out? Through these and other analyses, he can define target markets that determine the groups to whom he is trying to appeal. It is also necessary for him to determine what his customers want and what "market mix" of services and facilities he should provide. The "market mix" includes not only the food and its service but also many other factors such as location, decor, hours, pricing, and parking. The factors will vary according to the type of operation.

When the target markets, menu, and service aspects of the "market mix" have been determined, the specific choices of food items and methods of service must be settled. Consideration must be given to facilities available and subsystems necessary to support the type of operation desired. Subsystems for the preparation of food include procurement, receiving, storage, pre-preparation, preparation, serving, clean-up, and sanitation. How can these be accomplished best for the type of operation planned? For a fast food operation with minimum investment, space, and employees, a total convenience system utilizing disposables or vending machines may be best. Most of the subsystems are simplified or eliminated by their use, and a product can be produced that is acceptable to the operation's patrons. An analyis would also have to be made to assure the operator that his costs are appropriate. A gourmet restaurant may find it can use few convenience items and cannot do away with its well-integrated group of subsystems. An operation that serves largely conventionally prepared food may find convenience items desirable when business rises above normal levels, and its regular organization cannot handle the volume. An operation that wants to add more variety to its menu, without increasing personnel, may find convenience items ideal.

Make-or-Buy Decisions. It is not necessary that all convenience items be procured from outside the operation. More and more operations are preparing items on an assembly line basis in their own kitchens. These items are prepared in quantities suitable for an extended period rather than for the immediate meal. The food is portioned into appropriate units and stored until needed. Then it is pulled from storage, reconstituted, and served. The production of food on a mass basis and its storage present some technical problems in the preservation of quality but most of these can be easily overcome.

One of the reasons for labor inefficiency and high manpower requirements in food service has been the peaks and valleys in kitchen activity. A staff that can cope with the busy periods must be available, yet, during parts of the day, there may not be enough work to keep everyone busy. This inefficiency can be substantially decreased by preparing food in large quantities on a continuous assembly line basis regardless of meal period times. Another saving comes from elimination of much of the time lost due to frequent get readys, teardowns, and cleanups inherent in small-batch cookery. Scheduling working hours has traditionally been a problem in food service. Personnel have to be on duty early in the day to start production and late in the day to clean up. Since food is served over weekends and holidays, production personnel must be on hand. The assembly-line concept, with the pre-prepared food being put into storage (or inventory) until needed, allows more preparation personnel to work regular hours and normal work days.

Even with his own assembly line, an operator may need to purchase some items from outside purveyors to supplement his production.

It may not be feasible for him to prepare food for inventory, but assembly line or more efficient methods may be utilized nevertheless Some school systems have found economy and high quality in utilizing a central commissary where most preparation takes place on an assembly line basis. It is then shipped to the satellite schools where it is served. The satellite schools require little in cooking facilities or capability, and the advantages of centralized control can be achieved. Even though it may not be possible to schedule normal hours in a kitchen, it may be possible to reduce the number of hours in the kitchen by using an Ingredient Room that can be scheduled during normal hours.

Scale for Convenience Food Use. A Raw to Ready Scale* can be used to illustrate the degree to which an operation can utilize convenience foods. At the lowest end of the scale, no pre-processed food is used. At the highest end of the scale, the restaurant takes advantage of all the appropriate pre-processed food available to it.

Raw										Ready
0	1	2	3	4	5	6	7	8	9	10

The lower end will require maximum personnel, skills, equipment, and organization. The upper end has the largest amount of labor "built into" the foods and will require a minimum of personnel, time, and equipment. A luxury restaurant would rank low on the scale while a simple operation serving all convenience foods would rank high. A traditional cafeteria might rank in the 2-to-4 range while one programmed for convenience items could fall in the 6-to-8 area.

An operator planning further use of convenience foods could determine his present status on the scale and then determine the level to which he should rise, considering his customer markets, facilities, sources of supply, and economic resources. He might also consider how many of his non-convenience items could be exchanged for or replaced by the "convenient" type, such as dairy products or fresh fruit desserts, where no fabrication is required. At least one major producer of convenience foods has ranked products according to the scale, and as more producers rank their products, it will become increasingly easy to see what products are available at the various levels.

If a new preparation facility is being planned, the location on the scale will help indicate which of the basic kitchens are required.

Full production. The kitchen is fully equipped, and the operator expects to make most of his items from scratch.

Production—semiconvenience. There will be a mix of made-to-order and convenience items, and the kitchen will require a variety of equipment.

Full convenience. The operation will concentrate mainly upon reconstituting items that have been pre-prepared; the personnel and equipment requirements are low.

Short order and convenience. The kitchen will produce made-to-order

* Developed by Richard K. Rodgers, Kelley Rodgers and Company, Chicago.

items usually requiring a minimum of skills and equipment; all prepared items will be of the convenience type.

Short order only. Often, in a fast food operation the kitchen's menu is
very limited and items are produced at the time of the customer's order.
There may be some pre-preparation, such as preformed hamburgers or
blanched french fried potatoes.

INGREDIENT ROOMS (Food Production Control Centers)

Some operations, especially large hospitals, have found that Ingredient
Rooms, or "Food Production Control Centers" as they are sometimes
called, increase efficiency and effectively implement a food delivery system. The Ingredient Room is an area where pre-preparation is performed
on food items before they are issued to the cooking personnel. Pre-
preparation can include weighing, measuring, cleaning, chopping, slicing,
and peeling. After pre-preparation, the items are delivered in the quantities needed for the recipes at the time preparation begins.

Conventional materials handling differs from an Ingredient Room.
Under the former, food is requisitioned according to the various recipes.
The food is then issued in standard amounts, rather than the exact ones
called for in the recipes. After issuance, it must be stored in the preparation unit until work on it begins. Exact weighing to conform to recipes
must be done in the kitchen. Excess amounts from issues must be returned
or be kept in the kitchen until they are used in other items. This complicates requisitioning for new items, since consideration must be given to
the goods already in the kitchen. Because pre-preparation and preparation are mixed, cooks must often perform the work that less skilled workers could perform. With conventional materials handling there is also
considerably more handling and moving of items, which can result in
higher costs and a need for more labor.

The first step in the operation of the Ingredient Room involves food
quantity planning. The operator determines his production quantities
from his market forecasts. Then, determining the quantities of specific
items he needs from the standard recipes for the various menu entries, he
requisitions his ingredients from the storeroom, making sure to consolidate
the ingredients duplicated in different recipes on one requisition.

In the Ingredient Room, the amounts of the various ingredients for
each recipe are exactly weighed or measured, and pre-preparation such
as cleaning or trimming is performed. Both the ingredients and a copy of
the recipe are then delivered to the proper work center or area in the
kitchen at the time preparation is scheduled to begin. All the pre-preparation has been finished, and final preparation can start immediately.

A daily production schedule is prepared which conforms to both the

Ingredient Room and kitchen operations. Consideration is given in the production schedule to meal times, personnel utilization and availability, equipment utilization and availability, and advance preparation necessary.

The advantages in using the Ingredient Room concept are:

a. Better utilization of personnel. In many operations skilled cooks spend less than half their time actually cooking. They often spend valuable hours weighing, cleaning, trimming, and performing other pre-preparation work. With an Ingredient Room, unskilled personnel do more of the less skilled work, so fewer skilled personnel may be required.

b. Less materials handling. Exact quantities are sent from the Ingredient Room to the proper kitchen area. Differences between recipe amounts and issue quantities do not often occur, therefore the need for storage space in the preparation unit is also reduced.

c. Better quality. With more exact weighing and ingredient control, the quality of the meal can be enhanced. A cook is no longer liable to misjudge his proportions, and he becomes less liable to proceed carelessly. Since the cooks are primarily cooking and do not have to bother with pre-preparation duties, they can concentrate on the preparation. Food items are delivered only when preparation is to start, and cooks cannot prepare the food ahead of time and have it deteriorate in quality while waiting to be used.

d. Lower food costs. Food issues in excess of the required quantity are eliminated. Exact amounts sent to the kitchen cut down opportunities for pilferage. The Ingredient Room can often be located closer to storage areas than the kitchen, which can significantly reduce transporting distances.

e. Better control. By separating weighing, counting, and other pre-preparation steps from the final preparation, an operator can achieve better control in both phases, and he can give more attention to the weighing of ingredients.

f. Easier costing. With exact amounts rather than approximate requisitions determined in the Ingredient Room, it is much easier to cost production. Instead of many requisitions (and trips) between the kitchen and the storeroom, relatively few consolidated requisitions from the Ingredient Room are all that are necessary.

An Ingredient Room may require extra clerical help to combine quantities needed for the same items used in different recipes. However, this requirement is more than offset by the handling and processing of fewer requisitions. Moreover, an Ingredient Room lends itself to automatic data processing. Computers may be efficiently used to determine item and total food costs, provide nutritional analyses, keep inventory counts, and determine purchasing needs when the operation uses exact quantities of ingredients. Finally, since the delivery time from the Ingredient Room to the kitchen must be specified, supervisors can give more thought to the most efficient scheduling of personnel and tasks both in the Ingredient Room and in the kitchen.

chapter 8

Menu Control

In the past, most operations designed and built their facilities and then simply wrote up a menu. However, today the menu determines the type of facilities used, the number and type of personnel required, and the merchandise ordered. In short, the menu-type should be one of the first decisions made in a proposed food operation; it is a prime sales tool, and it is essential to both sales promotion and production planning.

A menu can affect an operator's cost in many ways. Purchasing, storage, preparation, payroll, food cost, service, and scheduling are all heavily dependent on it. The trend toward short-order speciality operations with standard menus is, in part, attributable to the desire to simplify problems caused by elaborate menus and the high costs associated with them.

MENU PLANNING

Menu selection has a very definite effect on sales, ease of production, and costs. While it is easy to draw up an attractive list of foods without considering the physical and personnel resources in the kitchen or the cost of the food compared to what the patrons are willing to pay for it, it is both foolish and costly to do so. A menu must be planned.

For example, a menu should:

a. Depict an appetizing and appealing array of foods that the diner will desire to buy and consume.

b. Achieve the best utilization of personnel and equipment. (Too often, a menu may overburden one section of the kitchen while another area remains relatively idle.)

c. Incorporate the best seasonal buys. (Generally when foods are at their peak of quality, they are also cheapest.)

d. Offer the foods that will either keep the operation within cost limits or produce the desired profit. (In planning a menu, care must be taken to see that the food items do not go over the budget or are not too expensive in relation to what customers are willing to pay.)

Writing the Menu. The primary goal of any food operation is to plan, prepare, and serve attractive, appropriate meals at a reasonable cost for the type of operation. In many institutional operations, the manager must also consider the nutritional needs of his patrons. Menu writing is related to cost control, consumer preference, market availability, sales promotion, kitchen layout, personnel capabilities, and food budgets or food selling prices. Although menu preparation is often done hurriedly in the midst of the kitchen activity, it is much better to prepare a menu in a quiet place with files of past records, ideas from trade publications, item sales history cards, and sales forecasts readily accessible. Many operations that offer a new menu daily maintain standard items and a la carte selections; they actually change only a portion of their menu each day. Other operations feature specific items on different days of the week as a merchandising plan. Thus, Tuesday may be steak day and Wednesday fish day, with different customers attracted to these specific items on the designated day.

Two of the main pitfalls in menu writing are the temptation to include items on the basis of their appeal to the writer and the habit of listing the same old selections over and over again. Meat ball stew may be your favorite food, but your patrons probably do not share the preference and should not be subjected to it too often. With attractive new menu items appearing constantly in publications and being advertised by food distributors, there is no reason for not trying some of them on your menu. These can be a rewarding adventure in eating for your patrons and a lively challenge to your personnel. But some operators offer the same bill of fare for years, feeling that it must be satisfactory if no complaints arise. Perhaps there would be more patrons, and happier ones too, if the menu changed occasionally. The menu should also be modified seasonally: seasonal food should be included when it is best and cheapest, and customary. (For example, patrons normally want somewhat lighter foods on the menu in warm weather.)

Other operators make up their new menu by crossing out and adding items on an old menu. Others may use a blank menu form, such as Figure 1. Usually the meat, or entree items, are chosen first. They represent the item of greatest cost and, to a large degree, set the cost and pricing pattern. They are also the principal source of appeal for your patrons. Once the entrees are decided upon, vegetable choices are made to complement and supplement them. For example, sweet potatoes go naturally with baked ham, french fried potatoes with deep fried fish items, and stewed tomatoes with baked macaroni. Salads, in many cases, may complement the entree choices. A Waldorf salad goes well with roast pork, and cole slaw complements most fish items. Appetizers, desserts, and breads are chosen last. In addition to the obvious cost criterion, menu items should

DATE_____

DINNER

APPETIZERS

_____

_____

SOUPS

_____SOUP   _____CONSOMME

CHEF'S SUGGESTION

_____

ENTREES

_____

_____

_____

_____

_____

_____

_____

_____

VEGETABLES
(CHOICE OF TWO)

_____   _____   _____

_____   _____   _____

_____   _____   _____

DESSERTS

_____   _____   _____

_____   _____   _____

Figure 1

be checked for arrangement of form, flavor, texture, and color combinations. A single platter should not, for example, include such red items as baked ham, red beets and tomatoes. Nor should it feature a texture combination of frizzled beef on toast, applesauce and creamed onions; all have an insubstantial texture. A monotonous form combination would certainly be fish sticks, french fries and asparagus spears—all long items. There should be a variety of flavors. The Pennsylvania Dutch serve seven sweets and seven sours and, like these famous food lovers, a manager should employ the principle of opposing flavors while planning his menus.

Number of Items. In the past, fine restaurant menus offered an elaborate number of courses and several choices for each course. This was possible when food and labor costs were lower. Today, there is a definite trend toward limiting the number of prepared items on the menu, for both cost savings and quality control. If a large selection of items must be kept and prepared for a relatively small turnover, the quality and freshness of many of these items frequently suffer. The larger the selection, the more labor required, since more items will need separate, time consuming, preparation. Some operations are using convenience foods and pre-prepared items to expand their menu selection, and these operations can sometimes offer a greater variety with limited personnel and facilities. In planning the menu, a manager should take into careful account the time needed to prepare the items and the difficulty of this preparation.

Leftover Control. Overproduction always affects the profit of an operation adversely. Good managers know in advance how they can utilize their overproduction, but, in almost every case the reutilization leaves much to be desired. Using the food in other dishes (leftover roast beef in beef pot pie, for example) takes care of the leftover roast beef but makes for expensive pot pie because of the lower selling price and the double labor involved in preparation. Serving leftovers to the staff can also be expensive. Often leftover food is placed in containers under refrigeration —which at least removes it from sight. If it is not utilized rapidly, however, it must be dispensed with: a complete loss and a high food cost. Overproduced items may also be run as specials at a later period. Not only does this practice often result in substandard food, it also increases the possibility of other first-run leftovers on the day the leftovers are added to the menu.

The ideal answer to overproduction is not to have any. Some operations achieve this ideal by planning to run out of their prepared items, hopefully towards the end of the meal. Other items, usually of a short-order nature which can be kept on hand, are then substituted easily. Advocates of this system feel that it serves the needs of both their operation and their customers. Without the cost of leftovers, more food and fresher food can be given to the customer. Other operators feel, however, that as part of their total service to their customers they should be able to serve substantially the same menu items one minute before closing that they offered one minute after opening. To these operators, a menu with a number of items not available—even near closing time—is bad public relations. They believe that leftovers are part of the cost of doing business, and they include this cost in their menu prices.

Much can be done to reduce overproduction. Accurate forecasting can help. In addition, continuous small batch cookery, besides giving better quality, allows production to match demand. Freezing prepared items provides more flexibility and greater production control. Some operations prepare many food items in advance, freeze them, and then reconstitute them according to demand.

The more prepared-in-advance items on a menu, the greater the left-over problem. So limited menu selections help control leftovers. Limiting the amount of advance preparation, and stocking more short order or prepared-to-order items, reduces overproduction. Management should have an inventory of leftovers each day to decide on their utilization. Some operations have a specific area in the refrigeration unit for leftovers so the manager can readily see them. In these operations, dates are placed on the trays so the ages of the items are apparent.

Menu Costing and Menu Pricing. Charges for various menu items can be determined in various fair and logical ways, even though selling prices pulled out of the air often seem to be the rule. A competitor's prices may be used as a guide, but there is no assurance that these are realistic. Without competition, prices may be determined by what the traffic will bear.

In the past, pricing was often based on a certain mark-up of raw food costs. Some operators still multiply their raw food cost by two, two and one-half, or three to determine the menu selling price. This, in effect, gives a percentage food cost of 50 percent, 40 percent, or 33 percent, but this system may present problems. For example, some items, like gelatin desserts, would have selling prices considerably below what customers will pay; or prices on many standard items, like eggs, fluctuate consider-ably throughout the year, yet should not be sold to customers at fluctuat-ing prices. High priced items, like expensive steaks, can have a high per-centage food cost, yet still return a higher dollar profit per unit sale than lower priced items with lower percentage food costs. Basing menu prices solely on food cost does not take labor into consideration. However, the labor cost is greater than the food cost in many operations, and the amount of labor required for menu items can vary considerably. The in-creasing use of convenience foods, where a great deal of labor expense is included in the cost of the food, can affect the use of markup costing.

Besides being a cost function, menu pricing is also a merchandising function. A decision has to be made regarding pricing policy—should selling prices be low to produce larger sales volumes that might increase net profit? Or can net profit be best increased by higher selling prices, even though these higher prices may discourage some potential business? What type of service will be offered to the customer—will he use linen or paper napkins? And how will the type of service affect prices?

Today, although meal pricing is probably based primarily on the cost of food, some operations include the calculated labor cost in determining menu prices for individual items. With the increased use of electronic data processing, it may soon be easier to include labor costs—and other costs—in the calculation of specific selling prices.

Figure 2 shows the calculation of food costs for a pot roast dinner in an operation that bases its menu pricing on the maintenance of a food cost percentage. At a 40 percent food cost, the selling price should be $3.05 (prices are usually rounded off to the nearest nickel). Rather than calculate the cost of the non-entree items, many operations add a standard amount to the entree cost for total item food cost. If other food costs from Figure 2 were generally standard, 67 cents would be added to any entree cost, plus ten percent of this total to determine total food cost. In calculating food costs, ten percent may be added by unproductive items as it usually is not practical to determine costs of seasonings and general kitchen supplies. The total food cost would then be divided by the desired food cost percentage to obtain the selling price.

COSTING A POT ROAST DINNER

Platter items	
Five ounce serving of meat	$0.44
Gravy	0.03
Potato	0.045
Other vegetable	0.07
Beverage	0.08
Salad	0.14
Appetizer	0.09
Bread item	0.065
Dessert	0.15
Total raw food cost	1.11
Unproductive costs—10%	0.11
Total Cost	$1.22
Selling Price, 40% food cost $\frac{1.22}{.40}$	$3.05

Figure 2

Labor Costing. Labor costs are as important as food costs, and it would be very desirable to have menu prices directly reflect the amount of labor involved in producing the item. In general manufacturing, it is usually feasible to calculate the labor necessary to produce a product, especially when employees work at a steady rate. If one worker's part of the production sequence takes fifteen minutes, he should complete his work on four objects in an hour. In the kitchen there are uneven periods of activity; a cook may produce many objects during meal preparation periods but do relatively little in between. Moreover, the variety of items produced makes it difficult to allocate production time to each one.

Nevertheless, some operations analyze the labor time necessary to produce the different menu items, and the resulting figures may be used as a factor in pricing and also in scheduling. Figure 3 shows the calculation for pot roast. To calculate accurately, a manager should break the time required to produce a menu item into skilled, semiskilled, and unskilled labor. By multiplying the average wage of each class by the amount of time required, a manager can arrive at an approximate labor cost. Notice, however, that this cost assumes that workers will be working at full speed all day—a faulty assumption since food preparation has peaks and valleys of activity.

At present, cost of raw food is probably the main determinant in setting menu prices, but a high or low labor cost for a particular item should cause some adjustment in its menu price, especially if the item requires considerable skilled labor. It would be very helpful if direct labor costs could be unerringly included but, as we have seen, this is not always practical. It is possible though to find the *average* labor cost per meal and use both this figure and the food cost to determine a menu price. The

---

CALCULATION LABOR COST PER SERVING OF POT ROAST
30 SERVINGS PER ROAST

Time Required[a]	Labor Classification	Cost per Hour	Cost per Roast	Cost per Portion
20 minutes	Skilled	$3.50	$1.17	$0.040
40 minutes	Semi-skilled	3.00	2.00	0.067
20 minutes	Unskilled	2.40	0.80	0.027
Total			$3.97	$0.134 or 13¢ per portion

[a] To prepare, cook, and slice roast.

Figure 3

labor cost per meal is found by dividing the total number of meals served in a specified period (usually the previous month) into the total labor cost (including fringe benefits and payroll taxes) for the period. If labor costs for a given period are $70,000, and 100,000 meals are served during that period, the average labor cost per meal would be 70 cents. Assume that a 65 percent prime cost (food and labor) is desired, and the raw food cost is 60 cents. The prime cost would then be $1.30 and the menu price would be $2, or $1.30 divided by 65 percent. The use of both the labor cost factor and the food cost factor theoretically provides a better basis for menu pricing than food cost alone. But to ensure the absolute accuracy of this calculation, a manager would have to serve uniform meals, all requiring about the same amount of labor. Of course, the amount of labor scheduled varies with patronage volume. During a busy month, the labor cost-per-meal may be lower because employees work beyond normal rates; conversely slow periods produce higher labor costs since not everyone scheduled can work at full capacity. The average cost of labor per meal would, in each case, be distorted, and the menu price would, in turn, be distorted as well.

Another way to use labor cost in menu pricing is to balance all costs against a projected profit. For example, an operation maintains a 33 percent labor cost (of sales) and its operating expenses are 19 percent. It wants an 18 percent profit. Presently, the profit and the non-food expenses total 70 percent of sales, leaving 30 percent for food cost. The food cost percentage (in this case 30 percent) for each item is divided into its raw food cost to find the menu selling price. If the raw food cost is 60 cents, the menu selling price would be $2. This method has the advantage of building a profit into the menu price, but the profit markup of different food items varies and must be changed accordingly. One profit markup schedule is included here:

High priced entrees	10–20%
Fast moving entrees	15–18
Slow moving entrees	20–22
Appetizers	20–50
Desserts	34–36

Menu Profit Comparisons. How can a food service operator learn how profitable in terms of food cost a particular menu is? This information may be calculated on the basis of actual gross profitability per cover. A manager often wants to compare one menu against another to determine the relative profitability of his menu mix. (He knows, of course, that the "actual profitability" will vary according to the volume of business during the period.) One system of menu profit comparison employs three basic steps, and it may be used on the basis of forecasted sales to evaluate a potential menu before actual use, or it may be used with actual sales to determine the profitability of the particular item mix. In using the three-step system, one must cost all menu items and keep records of the number of each item sold—but this is only good food management. In practice, only the entree items need be counted. A manager can add a predetermined amount to the entree cost to estimate the total cost of the meal, since the amount added is usually the same for all entrees.

The three steps involved follow:

1. Multiply the number of each entree sold by its gross profit. (The gross profit is the difference between the selling price and standard cost of the entree.)

2. Add the gross profits of all entrees to obtain a total gross entree profit.

3. Divide the gross entree profit by the total number of entree covers served that day to calculate the average gross profit per cover. The higher the profit per cover, the more profitable the entree combination on the menu for that day.*

In Figure 4, the average gross profit per cover for menu A is $3.12. For menu B it is $3.04. Menu A, then, is the more profitable arrangement of menu entrees. Further examination reveals this difference is probably due to customers switching from the more profitable roast beef to filet mignon that has a lower gross profit. Since the profit figure is an *average* per cover, it is not affected by total volume of business. A busy day's menu may be compared with the menu on a low volume day.

It is possible, of course, to increase the average gross profit per cover by increasing menu prices, but if these become excessively high, the actual profit may suffer when patrons stay away. Therefore, close watch should also be kept on the volume of business and percentages of a la carte sales. In most operations the entrees on the menu are the items management wants customers to buy. If a high percentage of customers choose ala carte items instead, it may indicate that the menu does not have sales appeal. Comparing the number of entree sales to the total covers sold will give an indication of the desirability of the entree items compared to a la carte items. However, some a la carte sales may be desirable if the a la carte items are more profitable than regular menu entrees.

---

* We have drawn upon, but considerably modified, a procedure of Menu Scoring originally suggested by Michael Hurst. See David W. Stewart, "Score Your Menu for Pinpoint Profit Control," *Food Service Marketing* (then *Food Service Magazine*), August, 1960, p. 35ff.

AVERAGE GROSS PROFITABILITY PER COVER

MENU A

	Selling Price	Cost	Gross Profit (per Item)	Number Sold	Gross Profit
Roast beef	$5.50	$2.10	$3.40	120	$ 408.00
Baked ham	4.25	1.55	2.70	65	175.50
Roast turkey	4.50	1.50	3.00	110	330.00
Lobster tail	6.00	2.70	3.30	45	148.50
Total				340	$1,062.00

$$\text{Average gross profit per cover} \quad \frac{\$1,062}{340} = \$3.12$$

Total customers served   365

entree items   93%

MENU B

	Selling Price	Cost	Gross Profit (per Item)	Number Sold	Gross Profit
Roast beef	$5.50	$2.10	$3.40	85	$ 289.00
Rainbow trout	4.15	1.50	2.65	58	153.70
Filet mignon	6.00	3.00	3.00	85	255.00
Roast turkey	4.50	1.50	3.00	100	300.00
Total				328	$ 997.70

$$\text{Average gross profit per cover} \quad \frac{\$998}{328} = \$3.04$$

Percentage of customers eating
entree items   95%

Figure 4

An operation may establish a certain gross profit-per-cover figure as its goal. If a particular menu is below the goal, it may mean that pricing is too low or the menu mix does not include enough profitable items.

CYCLICAL MENUS

Menus are vital to the success of a food operation, and preparing appealing menu variations normally requires a great deal of a manager's effort and expertise. This need for variation has led to the development of the "cyclical menu": the menu used in regular rotation, but on different and continually changing days of the week. A cyclical menu helps add control since costs of the same menus are calculated on various days allowing better cost comparisons.

Cyclical menus have many advantages:

1. They eliminate much of the time necessary to prepare several menus, so more time is available to analyze and plan better menus to be used in the cycle.
2. They simplify purchasing, since the menu pattern is definite for the cycle period. There is more lead time for purchasing than when the menu is made up a day or so before the food is prepared. Quantity purchasing is also facilitated.
3. They ease employee scheduling problems. Menus and workloads are known in advance and employees needed for the production of certain items can be scheduled.
4. They improve forecasting, since continuous experience over an extended period gains knowledge of the amounts of the various choices consumed.
5. They allow training or instructional periods to be arranged in advance.
6. They provide for the systematic utilization of leftovers.
7. They improve labor efficiency since workers become more familiar with the menu items.

Normally, a food service operation tends to repeat the items on its menus. Cyclical menus provide a better means of checking that an item does not appear too often.

chapter 9

Sales and Cash Controls and Security

CASH CONTROL

In the average food service operation, cash control from sales centers on the cashier. The cashier usually performs four duties in handling the operation's money:

a. She prepared the change fund for business.
b. She accepts money.
c. She makes change.
d. She accounts for and records receipts and sometimes prepares the bank deposit.

Most cashiers operate with a change fund, a definite amount of money used for making change. The fund remains constant, and any surpluses or shortages are reflected in the day's cash receipts. Many operations find it most feasible for each cashier to have a separate fund which, except for management checks and audits, only she has accesss to. The fund may be stored in a locked container in the safe when the cashier is off duty. In preparing the change fund, there must be a predetermined amount of coins and bills available to make change. Normally, the cashier arranges this before going off duty. Some operations give the cashier a new fund each day. The cashier should immediately count the money.

When a customer presents his guest check for payment, the money should be placed first on the register shelf or on top of the cash drawer. Then the cashier should recite the amount of the check and the amount of money presented aloud: "Eight-forty out of twenty," for example. This procedure helps the cashier keep the transaction clearly in mind, gives the figures to the patron who may not have been concentrating, and allows any disputes over payment to be resolved before the money becomes merged with the cash fund and other receipts. Only after the customer accepts his change, signifying approval of the transaction, should the cashier place the money in the cash drawer. Bills of over a twenty dollar denomination should be kept separate, perhaps under the change tray. If these procedures are not followed, a customer may claim that he proffered a larger bill than that for which he received change. (If this, in fact, does happen, the cash drawer, if possible, should be counted at that moment or at least at the end of the shift. If there is commensurate surplus, the money can be returned to the customer.)

There are three steps in making change. The first is to count up from the amount of the check to the amount of money tendered audibly. Begin, "eight-forty out of twenty." Tender a dime calling out "eight-fifty"; then a half dollar, calling out "nine"; a dollar, calling out "ten"; and a ten, calling out "twenty." The second step is to give change in the largest denominations. It is better to give one dime than two nickels, one quarter than two dimes and one nickel, or one five-dollar bill than five ones. The more coins or bills involved, the easier it is to make errors. (Sometimes the second principle is modified in supplying change for tips.) The third principle in making change is to place the change directly into the patron's hand. It should not be left on the counter for the customer to pick up.

There are several methods by which sales and receipts can be accounted for and recorded with or without the use of a cash register. For example, guest checks can be accounted for by recording each one at the time of payment. The form is then totalled and the total compared with receipts. Another method is to record all sales through a cash register. A third method is to collect sales receipts without keeping any record at the time of collection but later to total the guest checks on an adding machine. The total on the tape should equal the receipts.

The Restaurant Cashier's Report is a form used by cashiers to report receipts. This form may record each check individually, as in Figure 1, or it may deal only in cash register totals, as in Figure 2. The amount of money the cashier has collected, over and above her initial bank amount, is the amount of cash she turns in to the office. This cash figure should be reconciled with such other figures as the register readings, the total of the guest checks, or the food checking system totals. Any difference between reported sales and actual cash turn-in should be reported as a surplus or as a shortage.

In some operations, the cashiers are responsible for all shortages. But under these conditions, a cashier may be tempted to make up for a loss by overcharging or shortchanging. Is this a good policy? Is the loss from an honest change error different from the loss of china carelessly broken or food inadvertently ruined? Many operators feel that cash shortages

Figure 1

RESTAURANT CASHIER'S RECORD

MEAL _____ DAY _____ DATE _____ 19 ___ CASHIER _____ LOCATION _____

CHECK No.	No. PERS.	CASH	CHARGE	FOOD	BEVERAGES	TAX	TIPS PAID OUT	TIPS CHARGED	NAME	ROOM No.

DESIGNED BY HORWATH AND HORWATH
CARRIED IN STOCK BY THE ALLIS PRESS
KANSAS CITY, MO.

DAILY REPORT

FORM NRA 4

DAY ____________________ DATE ____________________ 19 ______

	SUMMARY OF SALES				
	FOOD			BEVERAGE	
	REGISTER READING	FOOD SALES	CUSTOMERS SERVED	REGISTER READING	BEVERAGE SALES
YESTERDAY'S READING					
BREAKFAST					
LUNCH					
DINNER					
BANQUETS AND PARTIES					
TOTAL SALES					

CASH SUMMARY	AMOUNTS
FOOD SALES	
BEVERAGE SALES	
CIGAR STAND	
SALES TAXES	
TIPS CHARGED	
COLLECTED ACCOUNTS	

ACCOUNTS RECEIVABLE	AMOUNTS	
BALANCE YESTERDAY		
TODAY'S CHARGES		
TOTAL		
TODAY'S COLLECTIONS		
ALLOWANCES		
BALANCE TODAY		

Figure 2

OTHER RECEIPTS

TOTAL RECEIPTS

DEDUCT

TIPS PAID OUT

CASH PAID OUTS

ACCOUNTS CHARGED

TOTAL DEDUCTIONS

NET CASH RECEIPTS

CASH IN DRAWER

DEDUCT CHANGE FUND

CASH DEPOSIT

CASH - OVER OR (SHORT)

BANK BALANCE

BALANCE YESTERDAY

TODAY'S DEPOSIT

TOTAL

CHECKS DRAWN

BALANCE TODAY

PETTY CASH PAID OUTS TODAY

NAME	ITEM	AMOUNT

TOTAL CASH PAID OUTS

Figure 2 (continued)

DESIGNED BY HORWATH AND HORWATH
CARRIED IN STOCK BY THE ALLIS PRESS
KANSAS CITY, MO.

FORM N R A 4

DAILY REPORT

DAY_____

DATE_____ 19___

CUSTOMER'S ACCOUNTS CHARGED

CHECK NUMBER	N A M E	TOTAL AMOUNT CHARGED	TIPS CHARGED

TOTAL ACCOUNTS CHARGED

CUSTOMER'S ACCOUNTS COLLECTED

N A M E	AMOUNT PAID	COLLECTION FEE	TOTAL ACCOUNT

Figure 2 (continued)

TOTAL ACCOUNTS COLLECTED

ALLOWANCES

NAME	REASON FOR ALLOWANCE	AMOUNT

TOTAL ALLOWANCES

Figure 2 (continued)

should be reported, and be considered as a normal operating expense. Repeated shortages, of course, may cast suspicion on a cashier. Obviously all surpluses should also be reported.

Charge sales have the same value as cash sales and should command the same rigid control. Because of the rapid expansion of credit cards, charge sales have become substantial, even predominant, in many food operations. It is most important that the charge chit be properly prepared and signed and that the correct address be recorded. Figure 1 provides for charge sales as well as cash sales.

The cashier is also generally responsible for recording the sales tax, where applicable, and for the proper handling of gratuities. She may also be responsible for such non-cash duties as the controlling of guest checks and the recording of the various entree sales on an analysis sheet.

THE CASH REGISTER

In some operations the cash register now does nearly all of the income bookkeeping and most of the food cost record keeping. Despite refinements and innovations, however, cash registers retain such common elements of cash control as these:

1. *Attention.* A bell or buzzer signals each time the register is opened or used.
2. *Publicity.* The amount of the sale is readily visible as the transac- action is handled. Usually, amounts are shown on both the front and back of the machine.
3. *Recording.* A detailed printed tape is provided for all transactions, often with additional information being provided by code numbers. Some machines provide input for electronic data processing equipment.
4. *Control.* Accumulated totals for various classifications provide control and audit checks.

There are hundreds of different models of cash registers with features suitable for a wide variety of operations. (Company sales representatives are uniformly eager to make recommendations for any individual business.)

Some control features helpful to the food service field include:

1. Automatic change computers which help eliminate errors and speed customer turnover.
2. A check printer with a paper tape receipt which adds control, pro-

vides a record for the customer, and in some cases can be used as a bar or food requisition.

3. A write-in space on a paper record tape which provides room for notations.

4. Flexible keyboard combinations that can be customized for a particular operation.

5. An automatic breakdown of sales into food, liquor, beer and miscellaneous or other desired classifications. (The new cash registers are able to provide income classifications for as many items as needed.).

6. An adding machine feature which does not interfere with the register totals.

7. Special provision for credit sales.

8. Individual sales records for control of employees and determination of sales achievements.

9. Automatic sales tax calculations.

10. A lock control which allows totals to be reset with a special key only.

11. Individual cash drawers for individual employees.

12. Printed control figures for bookkeeping and tax purposes.

13. Visible totals that can be read any time.

14. An automatic spacer which eliminates the need to space the check manually in the register.

15. Preset prices on certain income items. (A key with an item caption is depressed rather than amount key.)

16. Inventory control of entree items.

17. An employee time clock that functions together with an employee work schedule analysis.

Cash register totals are an important part of cash and cost control. There are certain procedures that should be followed regarding these readings.

1. Readings should be continuous and the machine should never be reset to zero.

2. Readings should always be taken and cash reconciled after each change of cashiers.

3. An occasional spot check of readings should be made by the manager or owner.

4. Each transaction should be recorded individually. Never allow several transactions to be recorded under one figure.

When the operation is closed, the cash drawer ought to be left open. This practice dissuades thieves from breaking open the machine and inflicting costly damages upon it.

In order for the cash register to function properly as a control device, all transactions, sales, cash received, charges, taxes, and tips should be properly recorded. Any incorrect cash register "ring-up" makes it difficult to reconcile the control totals. Management must insist on accurate cash register operation and provide sufficient instruction for cashiers. A separate written record should be maintained for incorrect recordings or errors. This facilitates reconciliation with cash register readings.

SECURITY

Security includes the protection of all cash, merchandise, equipment, and supplies. Theft in any form represents a loss of profit and is part of the area of management control and concern. Since most theft losses are due to management complacency and carelessness, management's effort can go far in reducing these losses.

Theft is a major problem not only for the food service industry but for industry generally. Theft losses, which run into the billions of dollars for industry in general, have been estimated for the hospitality industry to be around one or two percent of sales—and the percentage is rising.

In the food service industry the three areas of most frequent dishonesty are money thefts, food pilferage, and collusion between employees and purveyors. Money is most easily concealed and disposed of and thus represents the most attractive target. Money is accessible to cashiers, serving personnel, and bartenders.

Food is vulnerable to the many employees who have access to the kitchen and storage area. Obviously it is consumable in any household.

The food industry is very susceptible to collusion between purchasing personnel and receiving people, on the one side, and purveyors and their delivery personnel, on the other. The collusion usually takes the form of falsely inflated prices with the difference split and one-half "kicked back." Or the delivery might not be made at all with the value of the merchandise not received shared by the colluding parties.

Perhaps there is a bit of larceny in all of us, for petty thievery abounds. It is not likely that it will be reduced by better morals or stricter consciences in the near future, since moral remedies have not seemed to work. However, grand larceny cannot be tolerated.

Most authorities place the blame for rising business theft on management ineptitude, complacency, bad executive example, and the failure of management to adopt preventive security programs. Much money and property lost could be saved through tighter control, and the key to theft control is management interest, concern, and vigilance.

Why do people steal? Here are some widely hypothesized answers.

a. Desire for material possessions. Very few of us have the where-withal to satisfy all our material wants. Our economy constantly exhorts us to purchase this and consume that. Theft becomes a means to obtain new and different things. For some low paid employees or for those who squander their income, theft may be almost essential to satisfy the desire for new things.

b. Temptation. There is an old adage that a small part of the population is completely honest, a small part is incorrigibly dishonest, and the remainder is as honest as circumstances permit. If it is difficult to steal, people will be less inclined to steal. If it appears easy, they will try. It is management's job to keep these temptations, and the prospect of success, at a minimum. Providing attractive temptations makes management partially responsible for stealing.

c. Fond memories. Some stealing is simply the acquisition of souvenirs or momentos taken by people who do not need the item or could readily pay for it.

d. Social distance. People who would not steal from an individual have fewer scruples about stealing from larger anonymous impersonal organizations. In their eyes, taking from a large restaurant chain is less of a crime than taking from a small restaurant owner.

e. Anger and resentment. An employee is unhappy or a patron has received an unsatisfactory meal. He may feel that the operation owes him something, or he may want to strike back and satisfy these feelings by stealing.

f. Kleptomania. Some unfortunate people have an abnormal and persistent impulse to steal.

g. Thrill. Stealing may present a challenge to some. It is an accomplishment to them to remove items, and the risk of apprehension adds zest to the adventure.

h. Social problems. Personal need may become so acute that normally honest people resort to thievery. Such overpowering expenses as the maintenance of a drug habit or the bills following a long illness are examples.

EMPLOYEE THEFT

Employee thievery is the cause of seven percent of all bankruptcies, and it is estimated that property lost through inside jobs is more than twice that lost through burglaries, holdups, and car thefts. One authority claims that 85 percent of all employees have stolen at least something from an employer. Many employees would never become involved in theft if they were not once tempted and emboldened by management laxness and poor security policies.

A good internal security program usually begins in the employment office. Good food service employees are at a premium, and the industry tends to resort to spot hiring without investigation. However, one should always contact the applicant's past employers to inquire about his work habits and to determine if he had any honesty problems. Too often employees are fired from one job for stealing, walk around the corner, and get another job the same day. Local police will often check their files for names submitted to them by employers. In some areas, local law requires that all employees be checked. For employees who have responsible positions and have the opportunity to cause considerable loss, a complete investigation should be conducted. (One of the advantages in having employees bonded is the investigation made by the bonding company.)

Checks should be made occasionally and unexpectedly on all parcels carried out by employees. Each employee should know that any package he takes out may be inspected. Some employers require all packages to be checked and held by the timekeeper.

Checks should also be made of trash and garbage containers, since they have been used as a means of moving merchandise outside the building for a later pick up. (Management may even find it wise to rake over its refuse occasionally.)

Do not maintain unobserved employee entrances and exits. One operation with heavy theft losses solved its problem by keeping the receiving door locked at all times except when supervised deliveries were made. It is best to have an employee entrance that is observed at all times; a closed circuit TV system may even be used.

The attitudes and activities of other personnel, especially supervisors, will have a great influence. If an employee sees another take merchandise, he may be inclined to try. If he knows the chef has under-the-table dealings with purveyors, he may be inclined to reward himself at the operation's expense. Thievery is contagious.

Anger and resentment towards an employer can prompt an employee to steal. It makes for wise personnel policy and good human relations to bring an employee close to the operation and to alleviate causes of friction. It also discourages dishonesty.

Food service wages are often low. When someone's family is hungry or desperately in need, he is tempted to steal. If his wages are adequate, the need to steal will be reduced.

To control employee thievery in the food service field, some employers use a polygraph or lie detector. This device, some say, sees five times as much use in business as it does in law enforcement. The polygraph is used mainly as a deterrent. Normally, an employee won't pilfer if he knows that he may be questioned and that his honesty will be evaluated electronically. When a polygraph service is installed in a food service operation, all employees are told that the system is being used to detect those who may discredit the establishment and to protect honest employees. Management stresses that it is not interested in the past, but will question employees about their activities only from the time of their notification of its use. The system often promotes employee relations because employees are discouraged from bad procedures. It also rehabilitates former larcenous employees who suspect that they are being observed. Savings in food costs (as high as two percent), as well as lower bonding premiums can be achieved by the installation of the polygraph.

Some operations hire outside protective agencies to conduct periodic checks and to review security practices regarding employees while on duty. Just the knowledge of the presence of the service is a deterrent to many would-be thieves.

Bookkeeping is an area where fraud may be perpetrated, and the examples of trusted employees defrauding their employers over many years are legion. This type of stealing can be countered by frequent management checks and by having audits performed by reputable private concerns.

THEFT BY PATRONS

Thefts by patrons are hard to control, and management must always be wary of possible lawsuits. Souvenir collecting is one cause of stealing. A name, logotype, or monogram is really the thief's target in these cases, and the simple elimination of the monogram frequently reduces the stealing. Also, offering the items most often stolen for sale at the cashier's desk or in a giftshop allows the patron who wants them to buy them— and at a profit to the establishment.

A little psychological ingenuity may reduce patron thievery. A card on a room service table, stating that the waiter is responsible for the service items, shifts the loss from an impersonal organization to a visible individual. Many will take advantage of the former but not the latter. Signs indicating that a protective service agency supervises the operation may discourage a thief. A very obvious closed circuit television camera in fire corridors, gift shops, or news stands may also prevent theft since the patron never knows whether or not he is being monitored.

Some operations burden their serving personnel with the responsibility for expensive and desirable items that can be easily removed. A waitress financially responsible for these items has an increased incentive to see that patrons do not remove them.

Patrons who pay their check themselves at the cashier's desk have been known to alter the addition on the check for their own benefit. It requires an especially alert cashier to detect these changes. The cashier should be situated so that a patron will not be tempted to walk out without paying.

One final, common source of loss: Customers often use expensive napkins to wrap extra food for their pets (or children) at home. Some restaurants provide "doggie bags" for this purpose and save small fortunes in table linen in the bargain.

RESTAURANT GUEST CHECK CONTROL

The handling and controlling of guest checks presents some special problems. Most transactions involve rather small amounts, and normally there is no tangible merchandise that can be seen and checked (as there is in most retail establishments) when the customer settles his bill. A single entry and exit and the fact that a number of customers are often covered by one check may tempt some customers to stroll out without settling their bills. A counter service operation may employ one person to write out the order, pick it up, serve it, present the bill, collect payment, and then put the money in the cash register. Better control is obtained by separating functions and employing a cashier, but there is still ample room for confusion, theft, and negligence. The more items recorded on a check, the greater the chance for error. And a waiter or waitress who may be adept at giving good table service may write sloppily, add incorrectly, or remember prices poorly.

There are many ways that both serving personnel and customers can defraud an operation that has poor guest check control. For example, an unscrupulous waiter could collect a check, then keep both the check and the money. He might use his own checks to collect payment and, again, pocket the money if no other record of the sale exists. A waiter might total the check higher than the figures call for, collect the higher amount, correct the total before turning in the check, and keep the difference.

Customers and serving personnel may work in collusion. Items may be purposely left off the check in exchange for a higher tip from the knowing customer. Expensive items may be served, but inexpensive ones listed on the check the patron pays. Customers may connive to get two different checks during their service and pay only one.

In order to keep personnel and customers from defrauding, an operator must have control over guest checks. Elements of this control include:

a. The use of guest checks. (If money is collected and sales rung up without any substantiating checks, it is impossible to determine if all sales have been accounted for.)

b. Distinctive identification for all checks. (It is very easy to purchase pads of the common green checks from variety stores. The use of these checks permits easy substitution for fraudulent purposes. The check should be distinctive enough that its substitution will alert other personnel and customers.

c. Checks printed on erasure proof paper. (This type of paper shows when changes have been made—for whatever reasons. Mistakes should be crossed out, not erased.)

d. Use of pens or indelible pencils. (This precaution, like the previous one, helps prevent figure finagling.)

e. Prenumbering of all checks. (Accountability is basic to guest check control. Checks should be numbered in such a way that it can be determined precisely who is responsible for specific checks. The common green unnumbered checks make it difficult to determine whether all the checks have been turned in.)

f. Requiring all waiters to sign for their checks (and their duplicates) when they are issued to them. (With numbering, accountability can be obtained. If questions of propriety arise, it is possible to determine the food server involved. Figure 3 shows a Waiter's Signature Book that might be used. Some operations require food servers to turn in unused checks at the end of the day and to secure new ones at the beginning of each day.)

g. Including the number of people in the party and their table number on the check. (With this information, it is easier to check the number of items served against the number of customers. Also, meaning-

Waiter Signature Book

Date .... 19 ....

WAITER NO	GUEST CHECK			DUPLICATES			WAITERS SIGNATURE
	From	To	Closing No.	From	To	Closing No.	

Figure 3   Courtesy of Whitney Duplicating Check Co.

ful cover and average check statistics can be developed from these two figures.)

h. Auditing checks periodically for pricing and addition errors. (It may not be practical to audit every check, but every food server should know that his checks will be audited occasionally. Besides revealing mistakes, this practice provides the psychological motivation to eliminate errors since there is a greater chance for their discovery. Some operations which do routine auditing impose a fine or penalty for each mistake discovered.)

i. Accounting for all used checks. (When a check is paid, it is taken out of circulation and the possibility of its being used again is thereby eliminated. If used checks remain unaccounted for, it may be a sign that they are being reused to divert the payment. Figure 4 depicts a form that can be employed to keep track of used checks.

CONSECUTIVE NUMBER RECORD

HUNDRED_____   SERIES_____

WM. ALLEN & CO. STOCK FORM 7029

00	50	00	50	00	50	00	'50	00	50
I	51	I	51	I	51	I	51	I	51
2	52	2	52	2	52	2	52	2	52
3	53	3	53	3	53	3	53	3	53
4	54	4	54	4	54	4	54	4	54
5	55	5	55	5	55	5	55	5	55
6	56	6	56	6	56	6	56	6	56
7	57	7	57	7	57	7	57	7	57
8	58	8	58	8	58	8	58	8	58
9	59	9	59	9	59	9	59	9	59
10	60	10	60	10	60	10	60	10	60
11	61	11	61	11	61	11	61	11	61
12	62	12	62	12	62	12	62	12	62
13	63	13	63	13	63	13	63	13	63
14	64	14	64	14	64	14	64	14	64
15	65	15	65	15	65	15	65	15	65
16	66	16	66	16	66	16	66	16	66
17	67	17	67	17	67	17	67	17	67
18	68	18	68	18	68	18	68	18	68
19	69	19	69	19	69	19	69	19	69
20	70	20	70	20	70	20	70	20	70
21	71	21	71	21	71	21	71	21	71
22	72	22	72	22	72	22	72	22	72
23	73	23	73	23	73	23	73	23	73
24	74	24	74	24	74	24	74	24	74
25	75	25	75	25	75	25	75	25	75
26	76	26	76	26	76	26	76	26	76
27	77	27	77	27	77	27	77	27	77
28	78	28	78	28	78	28	78	28	78
29	79	29	79	29	79	29	79	29	79
30	80	30	80	30	80	30	80	30	80
31	81	31	81	31	81	31	81	31	81
32	82	32	82	32	82	32	82	32	82
33	83	33	83	33	83	33	83	33	83
34	84	34	84	34	84	34	84	34	84
35	85	35	85	35	85	35	85	35	85
36	86	36	86	36	86	36	86	36	86
37	87	37	87	37	87	37	87	37	87
38	88	38	88	38	88	38	88	38	88
39	89	39	89	39	89	39	89	39	89
40	90	40	90	40	90	40	90	40	90
41	91	41	91	41	91	41	91	41	91
42	92	42	92	42	92	42	92	42	92
43	93	43	93	43	93	43	93	43	93
44	94	44	94	44	94	44	94	44	94
45	95	45	95	45	95	45	95	45	95
46	96	46	96	46	96	46	96	46	96
47	97	47	97	47	97	47	97	47	97
48	98	48	98	48	98	48	98	48	98
49	99	49	99	49	99	49	99	49	99

Figure 4

When a check has not been accounted for, the food server to whom it was issued may be identified by the Waiter's Signature Book. A check stub receipt, retained by the waiter and endorsed by the cashier, can show that the cashier has accepted responsibility for the check.)

Figure 5 shows a typical guest check. Notice that it has three parts. The top part, or heading, usually contains the name of the operation. In addition, it contains blanks for the date, the waiter's number or initials, the table number, and the number in the party. It should also contain the check numbers, serially. The middle, or body, of the check is the place where the orders are written and the prices entered. The last line of the body may specify the total figure to be paid.

If a waiter's receipt system is employed, the last part of the check, the bottom, is known as the stub. It is separated from the body of the check by perforations and contains a second printing of the check number which appears in the heading. It may also have spaces for the waiter number, for the cashier symbol and for the total cost of the meal. When a waiter turns in the check and its payment, the cashier stamps it "paid." Part of this "paid" stamp appears on the stub, together with some method of identifying the cashier. It is then torn off and retained by the waiter for a specified period, usually three days. If any questions arise, the waiter can present the numbered stub which, because the portion of the cashier stamp shows, indicates that it was turned into the cashier. If the check were missing, she would then be responsible for it.

An operation should have different, distinctive checks for its various dining areas and beverages. Often this distinctive difference can be achieved with different colored paper stock. Beverage sales may be recorded on the reverse side of food checks, possibly in a space provided specifically for that purpose.

Guest sales should be audited. All used checks should be accounted for. The dollar total of a day's checks (or the checks for a certain meal period) should be compared with the Restaurant Cashier's Sheet, the register tape totals, or the cash receipts. If a food checking system is used, the total sales should be checked against the totals produced by the checking system. Any discrepancies must be investigated. The checks should be at least spot-audited for pricing and arithmetic errors.

There are different systems for pricing meals, totaling these prices, and receiving payment for them. The waiter may mark the price at the table, or item prices may be printed on the check by a checking machine or a food checking device. In some operations, the waiter does not price the check; the food checker does. The waiter or cashier may total the check. (Having the cashier do this job increases the element of control but may

DATE	SERVER	TABLE NO.	PERSONS	CHECK NO. 4467
1				
2				
3				
4				
5				
6				
7				
8				
9				
10				
11				

PAY ONLY THIS TOTAL 👉

FORM CK–3   WHITNEY DUPLICATING CHECK CO., N.Y.

SERVER'S RECEIPT   DO NOT PAY THIS STUB

DATE	SERVER	TABLE NO.	PERSONS	CHECK NO. 4467

Figure 5

delay service at the cashier's desk.) The waiter may collect payment for the check, take it to the cashier, and return with the change. Or the patron may pay when he leaves the dining area. The waiter who collects payment is usually able to see that no one leaves without paying. (He can also present the change in such a way as to encourage the patron to tip generously.) Some feel that having the waiter handle the details of payment is a subtle nicety of table service. However, having the waiter take the check to the cashier adds still another chore to the waiter's work. Another approach is to allow waiters to carry money and to make their own change. Their responsibility is to turn in the total amount shown on their guest checks and any bank funds that might have been issued to them. Of course, control diminishes when one person takes the order, picks it up, makes up the check, and collects the money. Control increases when other people are involved in the procedure.

FOOD CHECKING SYSTEMS

A good food checking system provides an independent record of the sales value of food that is taken from the kitchen. The value of this food should equal the total amount shown on the guest checks received by the cashier. There are many ways for an operation to be defrauded on the payment of its food served, and the comparison of these figures provides a strong element of control. In fact, food checking systems combined with guest check control can go far to alleviate defrauding.

Most food checking systems originally employed separate food checkers: the familiar lady just inside the kitchen door recording the value of the food leaving the kitchen and also checking portion amounts, neatness, and the appropriateness of utensils. The present trend is toward the elimination of the separate food checker, and the rationale is economic. Although systems without checkers can control food leaving the kitchen, they cannot inspect the trays for violations of serving procedures.

The first modern food checking system was said to have been installed in the Parker House in Boston around the turn of the century. Since that time there have been a number of different systems. Modern cash registers and specialized checking equipment have added new dimensions to food checking, and considerable improvement in this area is expected. Most food checking systems used today are one of two types: the duplicate check system or the checking machine system. Both systems can be used with or without separate food checkers.

Duplicate Check System. The Standard Waiter Duplicating System and the Whitney Duplicating Check System are two examples of a system which provides a duplicate copy each time information is written on the guest check. The machines use a Waiters' Book, Figure 6, containing a supply of regular checks, carbon paper, and a supply of duplicate checks. By means of a hinge on the book, it is possible to place any duplicate check under any regular check. The information written on the original check is transferred to the duplicate by the carbon paper. If a food checker is employed, the waiter presents the duplicate to the checker who retains it when the food is taken from the kitchen. It is easy for the checker to see whether the items on the tray appear on the duplicate checks, and the duplicates thus provide a record of food taken from the kitchen. The duplicates are numbered, so each food server's duplicates may be compared with the original checks.

It is possible to use a number of duplicates with one regular check. For example, a waiter can take the order for one course, write it on the original and duplicate, and turn in the duplicate when he leaves the kitchen. When he takes another course order, he can use the regular check but another duplicate. In some operations the checker also prices the guest check. If a checker is not used, the duplicate becomes both the order and the requisition for the preparation departments. Food is not released unless a duplicate is presented to the cook, the pantry, or the dessert department. The duplicate is retained—often placed in a locked box with a slot in the top. At the end of the period, these duplicates are separated according to food served and then compared with the original checks that have been turned in. If more food has been issued than the server has accounted for, further investigation is required.

The duplicate check can be helpful in some operations by serving as an order memo. The order does not have to be called out under this system. Duplicates are placed sequentially on a rack, the preparation personnel take each one in turn, and no one has to remember the orders. Since the duplicates contain the same information as the check itself, duplicate systems reveal the items listed on a missing check as well as the value of that missing check. Use of a duplicate checking system without a checker requires that management insist on allowing no food to leave the kitchen without duplicates.

Checking Machines. Originally, machine checking systems always employed a checker. In this system, the server brings the tray to the checking station. The checker notes that the items on the tray are listed on the check, inserts the check in the machine, and prints the prices on the check with the machine. In printing the prices, the machine also keeps a record of the total sales. Separate figures may be kept for different servers or for different classifications of sales, such as food and beverages. At the end of

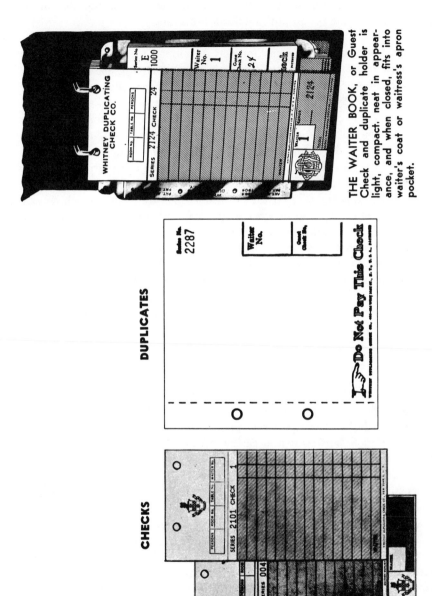

THE WAITER BOOK, or Guest Check and duplicate holder is light, compact, neat in appearance, and when closed, fits into waiter's coat or waitress's apron pocket.

DUPLICATES

CHECKS

Figure 6

145

the period, the total figure from the machine should equal the total of all guest checks or the restaurant's total sales receipts.

Prechecking Systems. Prechecking was developed to permit control over food sent from the kitchen to the dining room without having to use a separate checker. One prechecking system utilizes precheck cash registers. After the order is written on the guest check, the server takes the check, inserts it in the printing table, and records the prices of the items. The prices appear on the guest checks and on a separate "printout requisition chit." The "printout requisition" is the authority needed by the preparation unit to release the food to the server. The server must write the items, or their symbols, on the requisitions where the prices have already been printed. He may then initial the "printout." The requisition (which can be used instead of vocal orders) is given to the preparation unit. After being filled, the requisition is spindled or put in a locked box to prevent reuse. This system contains several control features: totals are locked in the register; food is issued by requisitions which may later be checked; separate totals may be accumulated for different food and beverage categories and for each server; and the number of checks used is recorded. The register can also total the checks and allow the server to act as cashier. The requisition system can be applied to selected expensive food items, the entree, a complete dinner, or (theoretically, at least) each cup of coffee.

Food Checking Systems for Self-Service and Takeout Operations. Special checking machines have been developed for cafeterias and other establishments where there are large amounts of activity and the customer brings his merchandise to the cashier to be priced. In these situations, there is no prior guest check. Instead of using amount keys, the cashier pushes item keys which correspond to items on the tray. These preset registers automatically print the item's selling price, add prices of subsequent items to those of previous ones to give a total, calculate and print the sales tax, keep a running count of the number of each item sold, and provide an itemized slip for the customer. This automatic, or preset, pricing has several definite advantages. It facilitates the use of odd-cent pricing, eliminates mistakes in addition, permits a fast traffic flow, and eliminates pricing guesses or mistakes. Since the machine can also add sales taxes, it can keep a total of taxes collected. A separate keyboard can be used to handle sales that might not be included among the item keys. Finally, the portion counters are very helpful for ordering, forecasting, inventorying, determining profit percentages, and analyzing sales and cost control according to items sold.

chapter 10

Utilities Control

Many food service operators shrug off any suggestion that they might reduce their utility costs. They feel that since the rates are set, often by regulatory agencies, and since there is no competitive bidding and usually only one supplier, they can do little about their utility bill. However, utility costs average about two percent of sales, and many operations have been able to develop worthwhile savings by shaving this percentage.

WATER

Water, an essential commodity for life, is indispensable in food service operations. But these operations have traditionally been careless with water so that half of the water used in connection with food service is probably wasted. With water shortages beginning to occur, it may become necessary to eliminate this wastage not only to control costs but also merely to maintain the supply.

Common causes of wasted water are leaking faucets and running toilets. Both problems can lead to costly damage beyond the cost of the wasted water, but fortunately both problems are easy to remedy. Usually, all that is needed for a leaking faucet is a new rubber washer. For the running toilet, it is usually necessary to replace only the flush tank ball. Parts are available at any hardware store, and the work does not require a plumber. Figure 1 outlines the cost of various sized leaking faucets—and at a very low water rate.

Cleaning with "hard" water, which contains excessive calcium and magnesium salts, also increases the use of water. Hardness of water is measured by the number of grains of these mineral salts in a gallon. "Three grains hardness" means that there are three grains of mineral salt per gallon, or 50 parts per million. Water softening systems usually pay for themselves with soap savings, longer wear for fabrics, and easier cleaning. The softening also prevents the build-up of hard water "scale" in pipes which both curtails the flow of water and decreases the efficiency

Amount of water lost and cost per month through various size openings. Forty pounds pressure and a rate of $0.20 per thousand gallons.

	Gallons Lost	Cost
½ in.	1,230,800	$246.16
⅜ in.	692,400	138.48
¼ in.	307,700	61.54
⅛ in.	76,900	15.38
¹⁄₁₆ in.	19,200	3.84
¹⁄₃₂ in.	4,800	0.96

Figure 1

of heating systems. In many areas about the country it is not necessary to purchase a water softening system, since the water softening ion exchange tanks and their necessary replacements can be secured on a service basis. If it is not feasible to supply conditioned water to the whole operation, it may be desirable to supply the softened water, at least, to the dishwasher and laundry. Not only will there be water savings, but there will be cleaner dishes, brighter linens, and a smaller detergent expense. (Most detergents contain a large amount of water softening compound, so presoftened water requires less of it.)

Some operations waste a great deal of water in their air conditioning systems. By using cooling towers, an operator can cycle his cooled water over and over again.

CONTROLLING KITCHEN FUEL COSTS

Fuel is needed in the kitchen to supply heat for the cooking processes. But it has been estimated that in some cases less than 50 percent of the heat is actually used to cook foods. The rest heats the kitchen and roasts the cooks. Besides being very uncomfortable, excess heat and humidity is costly to remove.

Insulation can control much of this heat loss. All steam and hot water pipes should be insulated not only for economy in operation but also for safety. Ovens are usually insulated, but many other types of common cooking equipment are not. Insulating a fryer can preserve over one-third of the heat input. Insulation can also be used on steam-jacketed kettles, toasters, water heaters, and dish machines. The result is not only lower fuel costs but a more comfortable kitchen.

Old fashioned cooking equipment took such a long time to reach the proper temperature that cooks would turn on the burners in the morning and keep them going all day so the cooking temperature would always be hot enough. Although modern equipment, with its rapid recovery capacity eliminates the need for all day heating, some cooks out of habit, still like to keep all their equipment hot. (Even with the older equipment, one doubts that all the equipment had to be turned on all the time.)

There are two kinds of heat: "sensible heat," which is measured by a thermometer, and "latent heat," which is water vapor in the air. A boiling pot gives off heat which raises the temperature (sensible heat) but it also adds hot vapor to the air (latent heat) causing an increase in humidity. Since temperature and humidity are definitely related, both types of heat can be uncomfortable. In kitchens, the open bain marie is a prime offender. Cooking pots, steam tables, and steam kettles should be kept covered. It takes only a small portion of the fuel needed to boil the contents of an uncovered pot to boil the contents of a covered one. And, again, the kitchen will be considerably more comfortable.

Kitchen equipment has not reached the automated sophistication of much factory equipment, and there is a great need in kitchens for automatic timers and automatic thermostats, for example. Good food is often left too long in cooking equipment because the cook is too busy elsewhere to remove it; he may not even be aware it is finished. Automatic devices that signal with a buzzer or a light when items should be removed are readily available. Some devices, like the automatic fryer baskets, even remove the items automatically; others turn off the heat when a certain temperature is reached or a certain time has elapsed. If mechanical devices are not readily available for a certain piece of equipment, it is frequently possible to devise your own. Not only will savings in fuel result, but there may also be savings in the amount of labor required and the quality of the product may be enhanced.

When thermostats and timers need adjustment and a thorough cleaning, higher food costs result. It pays to have these checked periodically and, in some localities, utility companies will do this checking for you. Variations in atmospheric pressure, moisture, dirt, and foreign substances can affect the adjustments.

COMPARING KITCHEN FUEL COSTS

The two fuels most used for kitchen production are electricity and gas. Both industries mount aggressive sales promotions and each can present statistical data that flatters its fuel. Both fuels claim greatest speed and flexibility, the best cooking results, and the widest acceptance. The issue is further complicated by the fact that rates for each fuel vary drastically from one locality to another. An economic saving in one area may not be duplicated in another having a different set of rates. Among the welter of claims and counter-claims, however, there are certain factors which may be relied upon for economic comparison.

The unit of measurement for heat is the British thermal unit (Btu). (A Btu is the amount of heat required to raise 1 pound of water 1° F or roughly the heat given off by a wooden match.) Natural gas is usually sold by the thousand cubic feet (MCF) or by the hundred thousand Btu or therm. The heat value of natural gas is approximately 1000 Btu's per cubic foot, or 1,000,000 Btu's per thousand cubic feet (MCF), or 100,000 Btu's per therm. Electricity is usually sold by the Kilowatt hour (Kwh) and each Kwh provides 3412 Btu's of heat. On the basis of cost per input Btu, natural gas is usually cheaper than electricity. However, gas cooking equipment requires more Btu's to produce the same amount of heat as the comparable electric cooking equipment. The gas industry can produce figures showing that it takes 1.6 Btu's of gas in gas equipment to equal one Btu of heat from electricity in electrical equipment. The electrical industry can produce figures showing that it takes closer to three Btu's of gas in gas equipment to equal one Btu of electricity in electrical equipment. The industries would agree that different equipment has different ratios. The smaller the energy ratio—the number of Btu's of gas to match equivalent results in electricity, which requires fewer Btu's—the more attractive gas looks.

In summary, gas fuel for the kitchen is cheaper in terms of input Btu's per dollar, but gas equipment requires more input Btu's than comparable electric equipment. In theory, gas and electricity can be compared by determining the number of Btu's required by gas equipment and dividing this by the cost-per-thousand cubic feet or therm. This would give the cost for gas. The total number of Btu's required by electricity, once determined, could be multiplied by the rate per Kwh (including demand charges). The result would be the cost of electricity as fuel. The rate per Kwh is sometimes hard to determine, since the increased use of electricity could affect the rate. It could also change the maximum demand which could affect the rate as well.

Electrical Rates. Electrical rates are usually based on one or two factors: the amount of electricity actually used; and the "demand charge," the price the utility charges for being able to supply the maximum amount of electricity an operation might require during its peak demand periods. Although the peak demand periods may occur infrequently, the electric utility, nevertheless, must have the capacity available to meet them whenever they do occur. Since large quantities of electricity cannot be stored, the demand charge helps defray the expense of maintaining a generating capacity that, much of the time, is not needed. Therefore, it may help a food service operation to plan its use of electricity so as to avoid peak loads. For example, it could use electric water heaters only during off-peak periods and store the hot water; or it could arrange to operate large electric appliances only during off-peak periods.

Figures 2 and 3 are offered as format guides for comparing fuel costs. However, because of the many variable factors—lower prices and availability of the service, for instance—it is difficult to determine absolutely reliable figures.

In addition to being used to compare the two fuels, these calculations may be used to determine how the actual fuel cost compares with the calculated cost. A wide discrepancy should initiate further examination and probably a search for areas of fuel wastage.

Besides the cost of fuel itself, it is necessary to consider the cost of

	Gas		*Electricity*	
Btu's required per meal	_____		_____	
Meals served per day	_____		_____	
Energy required per day	_____	Therms	_____	Kwh
Day per month	_____		_____	
Energy required per month	_____	Therms	_____	Kwh
Energy rate	_____	per Therm	_____	per Kwh
Energy cost per month	$_____		$_____	
Energy cost per year	$_____		$_____	

Figure 2. Comparison of Cooking Cost (based on number of meals).

Total Btu input	_____	Total Kw input	_____	
× % in put at one time	_____	× % in put at one time	_____	
= Btu used per hour	_____	= Kw in use per hour	_____	
÷ by 1000 for number of cubic feet or				
÷ by 100,000 for number of therms	_____			
× Cost per cubic foot or therm	_____	× Cost per Kwh	_____	
= Cost per hour	_____	= Cost per hour	_____	
× Hours used per day	_____	× Hours used per day	_____	
= Cost per day	_____	= Cost per day	_____	
× Days per month	_____	× Days per month	_____	
= Cost per month	_____	= Cost per month	_____	

Figure 3. Comparative operating costs (based on connected load).

original equipment, installation costs, maintenance or service costs, and amortization costs as well. Cost of physical changes required to install one of the fuels may be a governing factor. Only cost factors regarding the choice of fuel have been explored here. Each fuel claims certain advantages—centering on such vague notions as speed, reliability, longevity of equipment, cleanliness—beyond the direct costs of operation, and many operators feel that these are more important.

Figure 2 shows one method of comparing fuel costs. The operator should receive from each utility an estimate of the number of Btu's that would be required per-meal. This figure is used to calculate the number of therms (100,000 Btu's) and Kwh's that are needed for each fuel. By multiplying these by the utilities' rates, a cost comparison may be made.

Figure 3 shows a method of calculating fuel operating costs that bases the usage on a percentage of the connected load. For gas, the total Btu input of all appliances is calculated, and the total Kw input for electric appliances is calculated. It is assumed that this equipment will be used a certain percentage of the time. (Sixty percent is a common figure.)

SPACE HEATING

Besides its use for food preparation, fuel will also be needed to heat the premises. Savings in fuel consumption may be obtained by proper insulation, which often pays for itself. Another source of loss is incomplete combustion. Besides wasting fuel, incomplete combustion will build up soot on the heating surfaces of any furnace, which sharply reduces its efficiency. A one-thirty second of an inch layer of soot can cause a 2.5 percent increase in fuel consumption while a one-eighth inch layer can cause an increase of 8.5 percent. A three-step preventive maintenance program to achieve proper combustion includes:

1. Maintaining the proper fuel-air ratio as specified by the burner manufacturers.
2. Keeping the burners and orifices clean, properly aligned, and in good mechanical condition.
3. Maintaining the fuel oil temperature and pressure at recommended levels.

The furnace and burner should be periodically checked, adjusted, and cleaned for efficient trouble-free operation. Besides promoting economy, efficient combustion will help minimize air pollution.

Cost Comparison. It is easy to determine the approximate relative costs of various fuels by determining the number of Btu's received per one cent expended. There are, of course, such other considerations as energy conversion efficiency, availability and continuity of energy supply, space for fuel storage, operating expenses, labor, comfort standards, and physical plant investment, which cannot be so readily compared. Figure 4 depicts raw energy and Btu cost comparisons for oil, natural gas, coal, and electricity.

Oil

Btu per gallon	142,000		
Cost per gallon	$0.15	$\dfrac{142,000 \times 0.75}{15}$	= 7,100 Btu's
Burner efficiency	75%		per one cent

Natural Gas

Btu per cubic foot	1,000		
Cost per 1000 cubic feet	$0.75	$\dfrac{1000 \times 1000 \times 0.75}{75}$	= 10,000 Btu's
Burner efficiency	75%		per one cent

Coal

Btu per pound	13,000		
Cost per ton	$12.00	$\dfrac{13,000 \times 2000 \times 0.70}{1200}$	= 15,170 Btu's
Furnace efficiency	70%		per one cent

Electricity

Btu for Kwh	3,412		
Cost per Kwh	$0.01	$\dfrac{3,412 \times 1.00}{1}$	= 3,412 Btu's
Efficiency	100%		per one cent

Figure 4. Calculations showing Btu's received for expenditure of one cent for various fuels.

chapter 11

Food Cost Accounting

GENERAL INTRODUCTION TO FOOD COST ACCOUNTING

The primary objective of any food cost accounting system is to produce useful information about the results of the food operation. It must provide sufficient information so that corrective measures may be instigated immediately should food costs become too high.

Although older accounting techniques dealt with past data in analysis, newer systems concentrate on forecasting sales and calculating costs for these sales. Automatic data processing will undoubtedly provide new dimensions to food cost accounting.

Food cost accounting, once merely an analysis of past data on cost and sales, is now concerned with potential profits involving both sales and costs. The food cost accountant can provide data for the manager pricing a menu for the greatest sales and profit. He can determine whether it is better to sell lower food-cost items or items with a high cost that may produce a higher gross profit. The food cost accountant can keep track of customer preferences and the relative popularity of menu items. He should determine how much cost should be added for special touches and specialty items such as chafing dish service, exotic foods, and off-season foods. In sales analysis, he must forecast sales volumes, demands, and menu selections.

A kitchen is a type of factory, but there are significant differences between food cost accounting and general factory cost accounting. In factory cost accounting, the finished product may be broken down into its various cost components and appropriate allocations made for different materials, labor, overhead, and burden.

A factory usually has long production runs of comparatively few items and produces for inventory instead of for immediate sales. A kitchen, on the other hand, cooks many items to order or has only short production runs for limited periods. Food is perishable and normally must be disposed of rapidly, rather than put into stock or inventory. An excess amount of production and inventory cannot readily be moved by clearance sales or price reductions. Some foods must be purchased, prepared, and consumed within a period of a few hours, which does not allow time for elaborate cost records.

Pricing of menu food items is usually chaotic compared to most other products. A dessert costing five cents may be sold for thirty cents, but milk costing seven cents may be sold for only fifteen cents. Food operations find it impossible to perform cost analyses on the finished product but, instead, have developed methods of cost accounting based on the total cost of the raw food.

Food Cost Accounting History. Food cost accounting is comparatively recent. Prior to prohibition, many food operations were subsidiaries of a beverage operation; food was actually given away in the "free lunch" bars. Food was an attraction to draw people as underpriced food and entertainment are used to draw people to casinos today, where more profit lies in gambling. With beverages outlawed, some operations, by necessity, had to survive on the food business, and every assistance was needed. Food cost accounting provided such assistance, and its importance has grown steadily through the years.

Up to the beginning of this century, many food operations had one price for as much as could be eaten. Many commercial hotels operated on the American Plan and included meals in the room rate. The dining room was a merchandising tool to attract people to the hotel. Many hotel owners were far more concerned about their reputations for fine table fare than about the cost of their food: Food and labor were cheap; profit was in the sale of guest rooms; so why bother with food costs as long as restaurant operations broke even? Other operations had a "meal ticket" system where the meal ticket allowed as much as could be consumed at a sitting.

Though the control of costs was in his hands, the chef was a despot in the kitchen, often more concerned with his creations than with their cost. Perhaps by using sauces to cover up cheaper foods and by astute buying, he might be able to show, if so inclined, a profit—or at least minimize the loss. The total amount available for food expenditures was the only control. Menu pricing was often erratic and was based on what the customer would pay or what competition might be charging, rather than on any relation to the cost of the food.

The one-price meal plan gave way to selective prices, a la carte items, and different prices for different meal course arrangements, such as a lower price for just a platter and dessert than for a full course meal. The American Plan in commercial hotels was replaced by the European Plan in which meals were not included in the room rate. This required more cost accounting, control, and information. The chef's intuition was no longer sufficient to control the involved pricing. Management found it necessary to send the food cost accountants into the domain of the autocrat of the kitchen to learn where costs were excessive, perhaps to learn where better purchasing techniques could be employed, or to learn how waste, overproduction, and too generous portioning could be controlled. Also, menu selection and pricing policies often needed changing.

Not surprisingly, there is no one universal system of food cost accounting; different operations have different requirements and have reached different levels of sophistication in their systems. The first food cost accounting system simply considered the gross amount of food purchases. A manager might simply decide that $10,000 in food purchases should provide $30,000 in sales, or for every $100 of beef sales, beef purchases should be $35. Then it became logical to relate food cost to food sales as a percentage $\left(\dfrac{\text{raw food cost}}{\text{food sales}}\right)$. As long as the food cost percentage was satisfactory, the food cost was considered under control. Many commercial food operators are still at this stage of food cost accounting.

The overall percentage could be refined, however, by breaking down the total cost into various food groups. This level of food cost accounting was (and still is) very helpful, but it did not consider sales analysis and related only what had happened instead of what should have happened.

The next logical step to be taken was to analyze food sales according to the dollars received in the different food categories and producing departments. These sales analyses were then compared to the costs. This was still mere historic information, but with the trends before him, the chief was able to make adjustments in future food preparation.

As these techniques developed, some operations began to forecast future sales and their costs. The costs of different food items were determined in advance from standard recipes (the result is called "standard costs"), and the actual costs were compared with the forecasted costs and sales. Analysis could then be made to determine whether the difference resulted from overproduction, poor preparation methods, or other factors.

Automatic data processing will become more useful in food cost accounting as new systems are designed. Computers, with their vast memories and rapid calculation abilities, will be able to correlate purchasing inventory, issuing, standard recipes, sales, forecasting, and food cost accounting. Their speed will permit almost instantaneous reports. Not only will food costs be considered but labor and other costs will also be analyzed.

The Cost of the Food. Normally a food operation will not use all the food delivered to it on a specific day, nor will it use only the food delivered to it on a specific day. Some of it probably will be used that day, some of it will be put in storage for future use, and some food used will be taken from storage. To determine the food cost on a particular day accurately, it is necesary to know the value of the food that was delivered and consumed on the day and the value of the food that was taken from storage. The foods that were delivered and sent directly to the kitchen for use the same day are called "direct purchases." The value of these foods is usually obtained from the receiving report which breaks down all food received into direct purchases or stores. "Stores" refers to food items that are received but put into storage rather than sent directly to the kitchen. The value of foods that are obtained from storage is usually obtained by costing requisition slips. Total food cost for a day (or for any other period) is the sum of direct purchases and storeroom issues.

Cost of Food for Employee Meals. An important factor in food cost accounting is to give proper credit to the food department for meals eaten by employees. This allowance can amount to a decrease of two to four percentage points in the food cost for any period.

Most operators prefer to deduct the value of employees' meals from the total cost of food consumed and to use only the value of food sold to patrons for a food cost percentage. These operators argue that food consumed by employees is a personnel cost rather than normal food cost and that it distorts a food cost percentage.

Determining the value of the food consumed by employees can be accomplished in several ways. Some operators try to calculate the value of the food consumed per average employee meal. Multiplying this figure by the number of employee meals should give at least an approximate value of food consumed by employees. Different average values can be used for breakfast, lunch, or supper. Very large operations may have separate kitchens and facilities for employees which makes determining the cost much easier; but these operations are the exception.

If guest checks for employees are utilized, several other methods may be employed. One is to determine the sales value of food consumed by employees. Multiplying the sales value by the normal food cost percentage will give a value for employees' food consumption. However, if employees are restricted from consuming the more expensive items, consideration must be given to the employees' meals having a different cost percentage than customers' meals. A very accurate method is to tally the number of each item served to employees. By multiplying the number of each item by the food cost of the item, and adding the total of all items together, an operator can obtain his employees' food cost accurately.

The government provides standard figures for employees' meals for use in Social Security tax calculations. These figures are not very realistic and are far lower than the actual cost; however, they are a common method of determining the cost of an employees' meal credit. Some managements insist that this amount be doubled; others will even triple it. In any event, most of the employees' meal credit deducted from the food cost by this method is a poor estimate of the true cost.

The Food Cost Percentage. One very important part of most food cost accounting systems—perhaps even the goal of the system—is the determination of the food cost percentage figure, the ratio of the cost of the food sold over the dollars received from selling the food. Dividing the cost of food sold by sales provides the food cost ratio, which is expressed as a percentage. If food costs are $1000 and sales are $3000, the percentage would be $1000 over $3000 or 33.3 percent.

It is also possible to calculate the "mark up" figure by dividing food cost into sales. Many food operators use a "mark up" method that increases or multiplies the cost of the food item by two and a half or three times as a guide in determining the selling price of some items. This technique will automatically yield a food cost of 40 percent or 33.3 percent respectively for the item. In the retail industry, this method is commonly used to control the cost of goods sold.

For an accurate food cost it is necessary to consider the fluctuations in food inventory. For a limited period it is possible, without an inventory, to show a lower food cost percentage by using more food from inventory than is replaced. Conversely, if the food inventory value is increased, the food cost percentage will increase unless the increase in inventory is considered. Here is the normal formula for calculating food cost and for incorporating inventory into food cost.

	Value of Opening Inventory
Plus	Food Purchases
Equals	Total Available
Less	Closing Inventory
Equals	Value of Food Consumed During Period
Less	Value of Employees' Meals
Equals	Cost of Food Sold During Period

If a requisition system is used, where food items from storage are costed, it is not necessary to know the opening and closing inventories since the value of the food from storage can be determined from the requisitions. However, periodically the food cost must be determined with the inventory values in order to adjust for requisition errors and to reveal any inventory losses.

Types of Food Cost Accounting Systems. The objective of a food cost accounting system is to show whether or not the cost of food used is within predetermined limits. There is no one universal system, but there are some good general systems, and each has its appropriate application. A small owner-manager operation may want to know only if the food cost is reasonable for the amount of sales; a larger operation needs a system that reveals the specific items on which the food cost is excessive and that provides production and forecasting controls. Although a food cost accounting system may indicate that the food cost is excessive and perhaps indicate what food category is responsible, it generally will not tell why it is excessive. It is up to management to find out if the fault is in purchasing, receiving, pricing, too large portion sizes, waste in preparation, pilfering, forecasting, or any of the many other facets of food operation.

Percentage systems are based on the premise that food cost should be within a definite percentage range of food sales. If food costs move out of the desired percentage limits, corrective action should be taken. The percentage by itself means little until compared with some goal such as a desired food cost percentage, industry averages, or past food cost percentages. Usually a cumulative or to-date food cost percentage is also calculated, which provides a more general trend than the "today" figures. Past food cost percentages, which may be used for comparison figures, can include the same day or period during the previous month, or the same day or period during the previous year. Since the percentages are compared rather than the actual amounts, past percentages are valid despite changes in prices and costs.

Standard Cost Systems are based on the industrial technique of determining in advance what the cost of materials should be and then comparing the precalculated cost with the actual cost. If the actual cost is higher than the predetermined calculated cost, the difference or variance is an area of potential savings. In food service operations, the system involves costing items in advance (standard costs), multiplying the number sold of an item with its calculated or standard cost, and totaling the figure for all the different items involved. The total dollar figure based on precost calculations or standard costs is compared with the actual cost of food used. Industry also considers unit labor costs, but these are difficult to calculate in the usual commercial kitchen.

Sales analysis is a major factor in containing food cost, and it can be used in standard cost and cost analysis systems. Records are kept of past sales for specific items and then used for more accurate forecasting of future sales and production. The estimated number of sales of an item is then compared with the actual number of sales in order to gauge the accuracy of and provide a basis for future forecasting.

Cost and sales analysis systems compare sales and costs of the various food items sold. These systems are very effective, but unless general food groups are used, a great deal of clerical work is required.

Some food cost accounting systems currently used to control food operations are described in further detail on the following pages. The systems are not necessarily completely separate since features of one system may be found in other systems.

PERCENTAGE CONTROL SYSTEMS

Simple Percentage Control Systems. Most food cost accounting systems involve calculation of the percentage of food cost (the cost of the food sold divided by sales). The food cost percentage is very helpful in revealing a high food cost, but unlike some other systems, it does not reveal where the food cost may be excessive or indicate what the food cost should be for specific items on the menu.

Figure 1 gives a format for a simple food cost percentage control system. It has columns to record food sales and food cost on a daily and to-date basis. This particular example uses the cost of the food delivered for a day as that day's food cost. It does not consider the fact that some of the food may be taken from storage or that food delivered on one day may not be used on that day. If an operation receives the bulk of its food on certain days, the food cost would be overstated for those days and understated on days when there are fewer deliveries and food is used that has been delivered previously. An accurate food cost for the month or period is found when inventory is taken. Whether or not more food has been taken from the inventory than added to it can be determined by comparing opening and closing inventory figures. The inventory change can then be incorporated in the food cost for the period. Because there is no consideration of daily inventory fluctuations, the today cost percentage is only a guide, and the to-date figure, especially after the tenth day, more accurately reflects the true cost. During the latter part of the period, the days with more deliveries are balanced out against days with fewer deliveries.

The system in Figure 1 would be suitable for a small operation that is closely supervised by an owner or manager who does not purchase large quantities for long-term future operations. It gives an approximation of the food cost percentage which is helpful, if not entirely accurate. The system is simple, requiring only the value of daily deliveries, the daily sales, the to-date additions, and two simple ratio calculations.

In Figure 1, the daily food cost varies between 21.5 percent and 53.4 percent in the first six days. The reason for the wide fluctuation is that food is charged as cost on the day delivered. If not all the food delivered is used that day, a high food cost results. If the food used comes partially from previous deliveries, there is a lower food cost. The "To-Date" column

SIMPLE FOOD COST CONTROL (WHOLE DOLLAR CALCULATIONS)

System

Month of *January*

	Sales		Food Purchases		Food Cost Ratio	
Date	Today	To-Date	Today	To-Date	Today	To-Date
1	683	——	365	——	53.4	——
2	969	1652	275	640	28.4	38.7
3	1112	2764	446	1086	40.1	39.3
4	480	3244	165	1251	34.4	38.6
5	557	3801	120	1371	21.5	36.1
6	633	4434	164	1535	25.90	34.6
29	702	19,413		6833	51,6	35.2
30	954	20,367	255	7088	26,7	34.8
31	1318	21,685	507	7595	38,5	35.0

Total purchases	7595
Add beginning inventory	2563
Total	10,158
Less ending inventory	2752
Net cost of food for the month	7406
Food cost ratio for the month	34.2

Figure 1

is considerably more accurate, and the last To-Date figure of 35.0 percent is very close to the actual food cost ratio for the month of 34.2 percent, which considers inventory fluctuations. In this example, the value of the inventory increased from $2563 to $2752.

Summary of Food Cost and Sales. Figure 2 gives an accurate daily food cost percentage; it takes into account daily inventory fluctuations. To use the format of Figure 2, it is necessary to have some record, usually the Receiving Clerk's Daily Report, which shows which food items received during the day are sent directly to the kitchen and should be included in

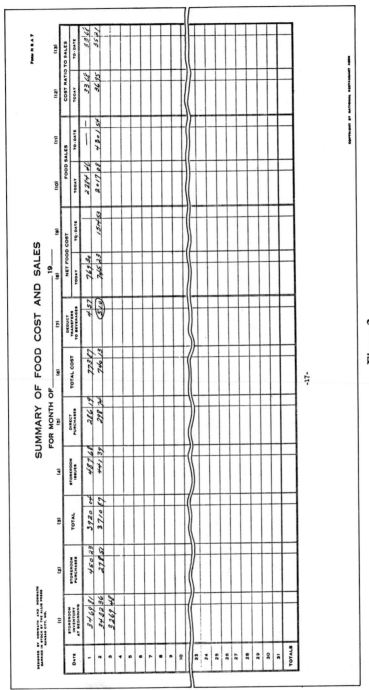

Figure 2

the day's food cost. It is also necessary to have a costed requisition system for foods sent from the storeroom so that a daily value can be determined. The daily food cost would be the value of the foods sent from receiving directly to the kitchen for use that day and the value of food used from the storeroom. Column 1 shows the dollar value of the goods in storage at the beginning of the day. Column 2 indicates purchases, which are placed in storage rather than used immediately in the kitchen. This total can be obtained from the "Stores" column of the daily receiving report. Column 3 shows the total of the opening inventory plus "Stores" purchases or additions to the inventory. Column 4 shows the value of the issues taken from the storeroom. This value is obtained by pricing and totaling the storeroom requisitions. Adding purchases to the beginning inventory, then subtracting requisitions, will give a new storeroom inventory value that should be shown as the Beginning Storeroom figure for the second or subsequent day listed vertically in Column 1. Column 5 shows the value of foods that are purchased and sent directly to the kitchen to be used the same day. The amount can be obtained from the "Direct" column of the receiving report. Column 6 shows the value of the food consumed— both the food from the storeroom and the food sent directly to the kitchen. Column 7 allows for transfers of food to other departments outside the kitchen, for example, the oranges and lemons the kitchen furnished to the bar. These transfers should be included in the bar cost and not in the kitchen food cost. A circled item indicates a bar item sent to the kitchen. Such an item should be included in the food cost. Column 8 shows the net food cost today after considering transfers. Column 9 shows the total food cost for the period to date. The figures in Column 10, which shows the day's food sales, are obtained from a source such as the sales record, the cash register reading, or the total of the guest checks. Column 11 refers to the cumulative food sales in the period. Column 12 shows the ratio of the day's food cost to the sales for the day. Column 13 indicates the ratio of the cumulative food cost to the cumulative food sales.

Figure 2 has definite advantages over Figure 1. It provides a more accurate daily food cost, and an inventory valuation figure that is helpful in controlling the inventory. It is possible to judge whether or not the inventory is higher or lower than the desired inventory, and this information can influence the volume of purchasing. It also brings an excessive inventory to the attention of management on a daily basis.

STANDARD COST SYSTEMS

A standard cost is the cost of the item determined by using the quantities given in the recipe and the current purchase prices of the ingredients. It does not take into account waste, spoilage, or other losses, so the actual cost is normally higher than the standard cost. A standard cost system compares the actual cost of all food consumed with the total of the number of each food item served multiplied by its standard cost. The closer the actual figures are to the standard costs, the more efficient the food cost control. A Standard Cost System can be used for a meal, a day, a week, a month, or any other period. It can also be used when management wants to pinpoint discrepancies indicated by other controls.

Generally, the primary objective of a Standard Cost System is to determine cost variations on a daily basis and to enable management to take corrective measures immediately. For the system to function, the standard costs must be calculated as accurately as possible. This requires the adherence to standard portion sizes, standard purchase specifications, and standard recipes. It also requires that market price adjustments be made promptly. The system is only as accurate as the accuracy of the standard costs applied. Besides the need for revising recipe costs to reflect price changes, other problems in determining standard costs include giving credit for food consumed by employees, and the cost of nonproductive items such as condiments and cooking fat. A percentage figure for other food costs is often used to include these nonproductive items.

An example of calculating standard costs is found in the standard cost for a serving of yellow cake. Ingredients, quantities, and ingredient costs for 100 servings are listed in Table 1.

The standard cost for a serving of yellow cake using these recipes, quantities, and costs would be 2.39 cents, or $.0239.

Standard Cost Systems are commonly of two general types. One system compares potential and actual costs on the basis of selected commodity groups. The other does not break foods down into commodities but calculates, on the basis of standard costs, the total potential cost of all the food served which is then compared with actual costs.

Total Estimated Costs Compared With Total Actual Costs. With this system, it is necessary for a manager to know how many portions of each item have been served. Since each item has been costed in advance, multiplying the number of portions served by the calculated (standard) cost will give the estimated food cost for each item listed on the menu, and the sum of the items for the period will give a total standard cost.

If the dinner includes an appetizer, vegetables, salad, dessert, and a drink, only the entree has to be counted. A standard cost sheet can price the side dishes as part of the cost procedure, or a flat amount can be added for these "make up" items.

Each installation usually devises its own method of costing side dishes. For example, if coffee is a separate charge in a certain restaurant, the

TABLE 1

Ingredients	Quantity	Purchase Cost
Eggs	1½ dozen	50¢ a pound
Shortening	1½ pounds	30¢ a pound
Vanilla	¼ cup	$2.80 a gallon
Salt	1½ teaspoons	4¢ a pound
Sugar	4 pounds	14¢ a pound
Flour	4 pounds	8¢ a pound
Baking powder	3½ ounces	33¢ a pound
Dry milk	6 ounces	52¢ a pound

Costing the recipe for a standard cost per serving:

	¢
Eggs—50¢ per dozen or 4.17¢ a piece	75.00
$\qquad$ 18 × 4.17¢	
Shortening—1.5 lbs. × 30¢	45.00
Vanilla— $\dfrac{\$2.80 \text{ (cost per gal.)}}{16 \text{ (cups in a gal.)}} = 17.5\text{¢ per cup}$	
$\dfrac{17.5\text{¢}}{4} = 4.4\text{¢ per ¼ cup}$	4.40
Salt—kitchen item	—
Sugar—4 pounds × 14¢ per pound	56.00
Flour—4 pounds × 8¢ per pound	32.00
Baking powder— $\dfrac{33\text{¢ (cost per lb.)}}{16 \text{ (ounces in lb.)}} = 2.06 \text{ per oz.}$	
3.5 oz. × 2.06	7.21
Dry milk— $\dfrac{52\text{¢ (cost per lb.)}}{16 \text{ (oz. in lb.)}} = 3.25\text{¢ per oz.}$	
6 oz. × 3.25	19.50
	239.11 cents

$\qquad$ or $2.39 per hundred servings
$\qquad$ or 2.39¢ ($.0239) per individual serving

operator is not likely to count each coffee sale. Instead, he may tabulate his beverage orders over a specified period to determine a fairly reliable average: perhaps 85 percent of his customers order coffee; 10 percent order milk; 5 percent order tea. Thus, the coffee count and its resulting cost can be closely approximated from the customer count alone.

By adding the standard costs for all the items served, a manager can determine his total standard cost for the meal or period. Comparing this figure with the cost of the food actually used provides the difference between his standard and actual cost. Normally, this comparison is made on a daily basis. In Figure 3, the cost of food actually charged to the kitchen

STANDARD FOOD COST REPORT

Date_____

	Sales	Calculated Cost	Cost per Dollar Sale	Sales Ratio to Total Sales (%)
Breakfast				
Combinations	60	25	41.7	12
A la carte	30	10	33.3	6
Total	90	35	38.9	18
Lunch				
Complete	75	25	33.3	15
A la carte	35	10	28.6	7
Total	110	35	31.8	22
Dinner				
Complete	80	25	31.5	16
A la carte	20	6	30.0	4
Total	100	31	31.0	20
Banquets	200	80	40.0	40
Total sales	500			
Standard cost		181	36.2	100
Actual cost		210	42 %	
Less adjustments		18	3.6%	
Adjusted actual cost		192	38.4%	
Variation (from $181)		11		
Percentage of variation			2.2%	

Figure 3

for the day through direct purchases and requisitions was $210. Of this amount, $18 was allocated to employee meals leaving a net actual food cost of $192. The standard cost was $181. (This figure was determined by multiplying the calculated cost of each item by the number served and adding the costs of all items.) The difference or "variation" was $11 or 2.2 percent of the $500 sales. This particular format provides Cost-per-Dollar Sales and Sales Ratio to Total Sales which are helpful for, but not essential to, a Standard Cost System.

Figure 4 shows an application of standard costs for a college dormitory. The budget for food served is $2.50 a day per student, with a daily clientele of 520 students. For the day, the actual cost of food was $1256. Pre-calculated standard costs were $1202 giving a variance of $54, but the amount budgeted for food was $1300 for the day. The result, then, is a favorable budget variance over the actual food cost of $44.

In Figure 4, the actual cost exceeded the standard cost by about 4.3 percent, suggesting that the kitchen operation could be improved even though the actual cost remained under the budgeted amount.

Commodity Groups. Standard food cost systems are based on actual costs compared to the calculated cost of items. The smaller the variation between the estimated and actual costs, the better the control. The investigation of these variations can be made with specific commodity groups. One list of commodity groups for control purposes includes these headings:

Beef	Poultry
Lamb	Seafood
Veal	Vegetable
Pork	"Other"

Actual cost for commodity groups is found by breaking down the food purchases or requisitions for the day or period on a columnar pad according to these headings. These costs are compared to the costs of various items from costed recipes multiplied by the number of portions served. Once the commodity group or groups with abnormal variations are determined, reasons for the variation may be investigated. However, if the variations reflect general weaknesses or breakdowns in control procedures over the physical flow of food through the cost cycle, it is likely that the weaknesses will affect all major commodity groups, thereby negating the analysis since all commodity costs will have variations. In other words, the procedure may be tried to determine the commodity group causing a variance but not necessarily to determine an overall variance.

This system involves many technicalities and considerable detailed planning. It is usual to rely on food consultants for its installation.

STANDARD FOOD COST REPORT FOR AN INSTITUTION
WHOLE DOLLAR ACCOUNTING

Date _Jan. 15, 197–_   Day of Week _Friday_

	Number Served	Calculated Cost ($)	Total Cost ($)
Breakfast			
Items 1	100	$0.45	$ 45.00
2	150	0.50	75.00
3	100	0.30	30.00
4	110	0.40	44.00
Total	460		$ 194.00
Lunch			
Items 1	170	$0.90	$153.00
2	140	0.80	119.00
3	200	0.95	190.00
Total	510		$ 462.00
Dinner			
Items 1	220	1.20	$ 264.00
2	110	1.10	121.00
3	140	1.15	161.00
Total	470		$ 546.00
Total for day	1440		$1,202.00

	Today	To-Date
Actual food cost	$1,256.00	$7,615.00
Standard cost	1,202.00	7,445.00
Variance	54.00	170.00
Budget cost allowance (520 × $2.50)	1,300.00	7,800.00
Budget-actual cost variance	44.00	185.00

Figure 4

The Precost-Precontrol Food Accounting System. "Precost," or the "Precontrol" system as it is often called, is a system that is concerned with the effectiveness of merchandising, with sales analysis, and with the application of this information to planned production. It provides the means whereby an operator can predetermine his food cost and adjust either selling prices, portion costs, or menu servings to achieve the profit he expects.
Precontrol can:

a. Provide sales data which helps merchandising.

b. Coordinate purchasing and preparation with sales data.

c. Reduce overproduction by coordinating production with forecasted sales, thereby reducing waste.

Precontrol will disclose when food costs are excessive, and will indicate whether or not overproduction is one of the causes of the high food cost. As in any other food cost accounting system, a manager must review the purchasing, receiving, storage, issuing and other functions that affect the food cost. Precontrol utilizes historical data—past sales and past data— to help forecast production quotas, current sales, and current cost data. Precontrol requires accurate forecasts on which to base production, so it is essential to compare actual sales and cost data with the previously forecasted data and to analyze the differences.

Precost precontrol is described in detail in the book, *Profitable Food and Beverage Operation* (New York, 1963) written by members of the firm of Harris, Kerr, Forster and Company. The operation of precontrol involves five major steps.

The Restaurant Portion Sales History (Figure 5). The Restaurant Portion Sales History is the record of the number of portions of various entrees sold. An easy way to keep this record is to make tick marks on the menu. (Separate counts should probably be made, one for luncheons and one for dinners, and multicounting machines may be used instead of tick marks.) The number of items sold can also be determined by going through guest checks or by using a checking system in the kitchen.

The Sales Analysis Book (Figure 6). Information from the Restaurant Portion Sales History is entered in the Sales Analysis Book. This form has enough lines to list vertically all of the different entrees served during the month with their respective portion cost and sale prices. (Each entree is listed only once.) The Sales Analysis Book also has a column for each day in the month beginning with the first day and proceeding horizontally along the top of the page. There are blanks for each day to record factors that might affect sales volume. These factors include the weather, the day of the week, special events, the house count (if the food service is in a hotel) and the total number of meals served. Also, the number of each

TODAY'S MENU

HOME STYLE SOUP <u>Cream of Potato Vegetable</u> .30

CHILI _____ .50

HHT HHT I	1. Special - Fish Sandwich, Choice of Soup .75
HHT IIII	2. Apple Dumpling w/ Milk .40
HHT HHT	3. Macaroni + Cheese veg. or Salad 1.00
HHT II	
HHT I	4. Creamed Hamburger on Toast, 2 veg or Salad 1.25

HHT HHT II
HHT HHT Spaghetti, Meatballs, Salad _____ 1.10

HHT III Baked Meat Loaf _____ Choice of 2 Vegetables or Salad 1.35

HHT HHT III
III Fried Chicken—3 Thighs _____ Choice of 2 Vegetables or Salad 1.45

IIII Baked Beef Liver _____ Choice of 1 Vegetables or Salad 1.50

HHT II
HHT HHT Baked Stuffed Cabbage Roll _____ Choice of 2 Vegetables or Salad 1.10

Roll & Butter Served with Dinners

Chef's Vegetable Salad 1.15 Choice of Dressings	Fruit Salad Plate 1.15	Head of Lettuce 50c Choice of Dressings

HHT HHT Sea Food Platters _____ Potatoes, Vegetable or Salad 1.45

HHT II Fried Shrimp (4) _____ Potatoes, Vegetable or Salad 1.35

II
HHT HHT College Diner Crab Meat Cakes _____ Potatoes, Vegetable or Salad 1.20

HHT III Fried Fish Sticks, _____ w/tartar sauce (2)_____ Potatoes, Vegetable or Salad 1.10

JUMBO SHAKES (ALL FLAVORS) 40c

Figure 5   Restaurant portion sales history.

entree sold is recorded. An entree is entered the first time it is served during a month. Each time it is served thereafter the quantity is recorded under the date. Luncheon sales of the item would be recorded above dinner sales in the same blank. If the entree has already been listed,

SALES ANALYSIS BOOK

DATE	10/1	10/31
DAY	Friday	Sunday
WEATHER	Clear	Clear
HOUSE COUNT	241	210
MEALS SERVED	310	245
SPECIAL EVENTS	Night Football	None

Portion Cost	Item	Sales Price	Portions Served	
0.35	Fish sandwich and soup	.75	11/–	11/–
0.30	Macaroni and cheese	1.00	17/31	—
0.40	Creamed hamburger	1.25	6/–	17/–
0.35	Spaghetti and meatballs	1.10	22/43	21/45
0.40	Baked meatloaf	1.35	8/–	—
0.40	Fried chicken	1.45	23/–	–/12
0.40	Baked beef liver	1.50	4/13	—
0.35	Baked stuffed cabbage	1.10	—	5/15
0.55	Seafood plate	1.45	11/17	4/12
0.50	Fried shrimp	1.35	7/21	6/19
0.45	Crab meat cakes	1.20	—	—
0.35	Fried fish sticks	1.10	8/13	—
0.55	Roast sirloin of beef	1.50	—	/31
0.60	Baked Virginia ham	1.50	–/22	/21
0.35	Hot meat-loaf sandwich	1.00	–/21	5/19

Figure 6

only the portions sold are entered under the proper date on the entree line.

With this format, a manager can estimate the sales of an entree in various kinds of weather, judge the relative popularity of an entree in relation to total meals, and determine how one entree sells in combinations with other items. Fried chicken may be a very popular item and ordinarily represent 30 percent of sales. However, if ham steak, another popular item, appears on the menu with fried chicken, the fried chicken may generate only 20 percent of total sales because of competition from the other popular item. Because it indicates the popularity of various items, the Sales Analysis Book is a great help in menu planning and in forecasting future production. It also allows more control in experimenting with menu combinations, pricing arrangements, and in eliminating "slow movers."

Precontrol is concerned not only with analyzing sales but also with analyzing costs. It is very important for menu items to be costed in advance so management knows the raw food cost for the various items. For precontrol to function best, there must be an accurate record of portion costs based on standard recipes, purchase specifications, yield conversion factors, and standard portion sizes.

Forecasting Sales. Using the information from the Sales Analysis Book, the manager forecasts the number of each menu item that will be sold during the meal or day. This forecast usually involves a determination of the total number of people that will be served. He calculates the number of people, or the percentage of the total, that will order each course to determine production quantities.

Menu Precost and Abstract. The sales forecast and the cost information are combined in the Menu Precost and Abstract. By showing the anticipated number of sales, the selling prices and the cost of each item, a manager can readily estimate the total cost and total sales for each item.

The Menu Precost and Abstract is divided into two sections, a "Forecast" section which is filled in before the day or meal and an "Actual" section which shows actual sales of the various items and is completed after the day or meal. Since a major part of control entails an accurate forecast of sales to coordinate purchasing with production, managers are eager to see how the actual sales agreed with the forecasted ones. Large differences would call for closer attention to the forecasting. Figure 7 illustrates the Menu Precost and Abstract.

Two food cost percentages are also supplied on the Menu Precost and Abstract. The first gives the preliminary food cost percentage based on the sales mix resulting from the estimated number of each item that will be sold. The second is based on the actual number of each item sold. This information allows management to revise prices, menu offerings, or portions if the required cost ratio is not being produced.

Summary of Food Cost and Potential Savings. For good management and proper pricing, the various menu items must be costed. Instead of costing every vegetable, cup of coffee, and sweet roll, the main entree may be costed and a "make up cost," or average cost of "surrounding" courses or items, added to it. Figure 8, "Summary of Food Cost and Potential Savings," is prepared on both a daily and a to-date basis. It analyzes sales by meal and by dining area. It also includes what this food should cost on the basis of costing the items. The potential food cost, or food cost on the basis of costing the items sold, is compared with the actual cost of the food used (as determined by direct purchases plus requisitions from stores) with the difference being the area of potential savings.

This procedure can be illustrated by a banquet for 100 people, paying

MENU PRECOST AND ABSTRACT

Menu Item	Selling Price	Cost	Forecast					Actual				
			Number	Revenue	Cost	Cost (%)	Ratio to Total	Number	Revenue	Cost	Cost (%)	Ratio to Total
LUNCHEON												
Fish Sandwich and Soup	$0.75	$0.35	10	$ 7.50	$ 3.50	46.6	02.1%	11	$ 8.25	$ 3.85	46.6	02.4%
Macaroni and Cheese	1.00	0.30	20	20.00	6.00	30.0	05.7	7	7.00	2.10	30.0	02.0
Creamed Hamburger	1.25	0.40	10	12.50	4.00	32.0	03.6	6	7.50	2.40	32.0	02.1
Luncheon total			125	$ 96.00	$ 36.75	38.3	27.5	116	$ 86.50	$ 33.15	38.3	24.7
DINNER												
Macaroni and Cheese	1.00	0.30	25	25.00	7.50	30.0	07.1	27	27.00	8.10	30.0	07.7
Spaghetti and Meatballs	1.10	0.35	50	55.00	17.50	31.8	15.7	49	53.90	17.15	31.8	15.4
Roast Sirloin of Beef	1.50	0.55	35	52.50	19.25	36.7	15.0	31	46.50	17.05	36.7	13.3
Dinner total			225	253.50	86.25	34.0	72.5	239	264.25	89.95	34.0	75.3
Daily total			350	349.50	123.00	35.2		355	350.75	122.10	34.8	

Figure 7

SUMMARY OF FOOD COST AND POTENTIAL SAVINGS

DATE   October 15, 197___
DAY   Friday
WEATHER   Clear

	To-Day				This Month to Date			
	Number Sold	Actual Sales	Calculated Cost	Cost per Dollar Sale	Number Sold	Actual Sales	Calculated Cost	Cost per Dollar Sale
Main Dining Room								
Luncheon	175	$ 325.40	$110.25	33.9	2,580	$ 4,824.25	$ 1,682.50	34.9
Dinner	210	725.50	274.40	37.8	2,894	9,942.75	3,524.80	35.5
Total	385	$1,050.90	$384.65	36.6	5,474	$14,767.00	$ 5,207.30	35.3
Coffee Shop								
Breakfast	85	$ 145.10	$ 50.60	34.9	1,305	$ 2,178.50	$ 725.10	33.3
Lunch	35	93.50	33.55	35.9	580	1,472.35	511.20	34.7
Dinner	111	374.60	138.75	37.0	1,583	5,612.15	2,008.35	35.8
Total	231	$ 613.20	$222.90	36.3	3,468	$ 9,263.00	$ 3,244.65	35.0
Totals	912	$2,471.80	$854.10	34.6	13,628	$36,901.10	$12,935.40	35.1
Actual net cost			875.30	35.4			13,201.65	35.8
Potential savings			21.20	00.8			266.25	00.7

Figure 8

175

$4.50 per platter. The cost of each food item on the menu is costed, or calculated in advance, with the cost-per-person coming to $1.44 multiplied by 100. On this basis, the potential food cost should be $144, or 32 percent of sales. However, after the banquet is served, the total actual net food bills and storeroom issues are $180, or 40 percent of sales. The area of potential savings would be $36 or eight percent.

Potential savings represents the difference between actual net food costs and what the food costs would have been under optimum conditions with no waste, spoilage, or oversized portions.

Precost precontrol systems can also be adapted to indirect food selling operations such as those conducted at hospitals. Forecasting is done for the various meals according to the items served. Dollar sales figures are usually dispensed with and only the number of portions utilized. Comparisons are then made on a "cost-per-cover" or a "cost-per-patient day" basis. At the end of the period, the actual cost of food is compared with what the food should have cost on the basis of precosting. The difference between the actual cost and the cost calculated on a loss-free basis is the area for potential savings.

Standard Costs Compared to Percentage Cost Systems. Some people find it difficult to differentiate between the standard cost systems' purposes and the percentage cost systems' purposes. The difference is this: The basic control factor in the percentage systems is the ratio of costs to sales. If this ratio rises above proper limits, it may be assumed that food costs are too high. The percentage is affected by the items on the menu and menu pricings. An operation may have a food cost of $350 and sales of $1000, which means the food cost is 35 percent. If menu prices are raised 10 percent, and costs and volume remain the same, the new ratio would be $350 divided by $1100. Although the food cost percentage is now a more favorable 32 percent, the actual control of costs is the same as before.

A restaurant may want to sell higher priced items which also have higher food costs. A steak selling for $6 at a 50 percent food cost produces a gross profit of $3. Fried chicken selling for $3 at a 30 percent food cost produces only a $2.10 gross profit. The percentage figure is considerably better for the chicken, but most operators would prefer to sell more steaks.

Institutions such as hospitals, which do not have direct sales, find it difficult to use a percentage system effectively, since their food sales allowance from total income may be very arbitrary.

A standard cost system, on the other hand, does not have to consider sales at all. (They may be included for other analyses, however.) It calculates, using standard costs, what the ideal dollar food cost should be, and then it compares the actual amount spent with this figure. The difference shows by how much food cost could be reduced in dollars under ideal conditions. Standard costs can be readily used by hospitals, since sales are not required. Standard cost systems are only as accurate as the costing of the items, and unless these costings are accurate and the portions correct, the system cannot be truly effective.

COST ANALYSIS SYSTEM

The Modified Cost Analysis System. The Modified Cost Analysis System is a simplification of the cost portion of a Detailed Cost and Sales Analysis System developed earlier by the firm of Laventhol Krekstein Horwath and Horwath. The "Laventhol System," while very effective, required a great deal of clerical work and time, and the cost of implementation became prohibitive. The modified system, a relatively simple method, utilizes a limited sales analysis which can be prepared by the food checker or cashier. It provides for both a daily food cost report and precosting and production control.

The system can be part of a broader system which provides Beverage Cost Control features and a Daily Payroll Cost Report. The food cost accounting portion of the total system is based on a comparison of the ratio of costs to total sales in about twenty food groups. This comparison can reveal which of the food groups show cost discrepancies and adversely affect the food cost.

Daily Food Cost Report. A format for showing the daily food cost or Daily Summary of Food Cost is shown in Figure 9. Listed there are the costs of the various food categories according to kitchen departments for the day or for other appropriate periods. These cost figures are divided by the total food sales for the same period, and the results are shown in the ratio to total sales. The bottom part of the form has space for average check statistics. An operation might use a line each for breakfast, lunch, and dinner. It might use another line for total figures and yet another line for banquets or room service.

Preparation of the Daily Summary of Food Cost. The Cost Analysis Sheet (Figure 10) provides the detailed data for the Daily Summary of Food Cost. Normally, two Cost Analysis Sheets are used each day. The first is used for purchases. The top section lists the purchases, which are sent to the storeroom under "Distribution of Food Issues," and this food will be charged to the daily food cost when it is actually issued, not necessarily on the day it is received. The lower part of the first sheet shows direct purchases of food items that are received and sent directly to the kitchen

Day_____   Date_____ 19____

	This month		To date		Ratio to total sales			
	Today	To—date	Last month	Last year	Today	To date	Last month	Last year
Kitchen & pantry								
Beef								
Veal								
Lamb & mutton								
Pork								
Game								
Poultry								
Seafood								
Vegetables								
Salads & relishes								
Fruits								
Milk & cream								
Eggs								
Cheese								
Butter								
Coffee, tea, cocoa								
Shortening & oil								
Staples								
Bake shop								
Pastry shop								
Ice cream								
D.r. butter								
D.r. groceries								
Freight & express								
Total cost								
Total sales								

Statistics

	Today		To date		Average check			
	Covers	Sales	Covers	Sales	Today	To date	Last month	Last year
Total								

Figure 9   Daily summary of food cost.

for use that day. These appear under the heading, "Distribution of Food Issues." The postings are made from invoices, and the totals of direct and stores purchases should equal the totals found on the Daily Receiving Report. The bottom section of the other "Cost Analysis Sheet" is used to list all issues and charges from the storeroom for a particular day.

The daily direct and issue total figures for the various commodities are posted on the "Daily Summary of Food Cost" (Figure 9) from the "Cost Analysis Sheets." To-date figures are found by adding the daily figures to the accumulated totals.

Commodity ratios for various operations generally follow definite patterns. Deviations from these patterns, especially increases, indicate where attention and perhaps corrective action should be directed.

For storeroom control, two columnar sheets are prepared with the same commodity classifications as the "Cost Analysis Sheet." On one sheet, starting inventory and daily storeroom purchases are posted under the appropriate commodity. The other sheet lists all storeroom issues similarly classified. By subtracting the issues shown on the first sheet, one can establish a daily storeroom inventory. Storeroom shortages can be more readily traced with these records of "inflow" and "outgo," especially where meats are charged to the storeroom and issued by requisition.

The Budgetary Cost Analysis System. The "Budgetary Cost Analysis System," a further adaptation of the original Detailed Cost and Sales Analysis System, can be used as another aid in food cost control.

A form, the "Record of Portions Sold" (Figure 11) is prepared for each principal menu item or entree. The number of portions of the item which were sold can be determined by making "ticks" on the menu card, by using a multicounter or a tally sheet. The estimated and actual numbers of portions sold of each item are recorded daily on the form for each item. The "class" blank in the upper right corner refers to the classification of the entree such as beef, or veal, or poultry. The exact name of the entree as it appears on the bill of fare is entered on the "Menu Item" line. The top block of the form accommodates a description of the various combinations in which the menu item may be sold. For example, on the line marked "a," the entree may be turkey with four ounces of white meat at 12 cents and two ounces of dark meat at five cents; line "b" might indicate a different combination.

In the lower part of the form, an entry is made for each day in which the item appears on the menu. The same letter that appears in the upper part of the form is recorded in the first blank column to indicate in which combination the item appeared on the menu that day. After the day, date, and price (or total cost), the number of portions estimated in advance is entered and, in the next column, the number of portions actually sold.

Distribution of Food Purchases

	Total		Beef		Veal		Lamb and mutton		Pork		Game		Poultry		Seafood	
Total today brought forward total to date																

Distribution of Food Issues

	Total		Beef		Veal		Lamb and mutton		Pork		Game		Poultry		Seafood	
Kitchen and pantry																
Bake shop																
Pastry shop																
Ice cream																
Dr. butter																
Dr. groceries																
Bars																
Total today brought forward total to date																

Figure 10 Cost analysis sheet.

Distribution of Food Purchases

Vegetables	Salads and relishes	Fruits	Milk and cream	Eggs	Cheese	Butter	Coffee, tea, cocoa	Shortening and oil	Staples	Freight & express

Distribution of Food Issues

Figure 10 Cost analysis sheet. (continued)

Class _Poultry_

Menu item _Roast Turkey_

Meal		Check courses included							
		Soup & Appetizer	Garniture & sauce	Vegetable	Potato	Salad	Bread & butter	Dessert	Beverage
a	Turkey 4 oz. White meat @ .12, 2 oz. dark @ .05	✓	✓	✓	✓	✓	✓	✓	✓
b	Turkey 6 oz. White meat @ .12	✓	✓	✓	✓	✓	✓	✓	✓
c	Hot Turkey sandwich 3 oz. White meat @ .12/8 oz dark	✓	✓	✓	✓			✓	✓
d	@ .05								
e									
f									

Lunch

	Date	Day	Price	Number Est.	Number Sold	Factor
c	7/1	Mon.	2.25	68	54	28
c	7/3	Wed.	2.25	70.	70.	32

Supper

	Date	Day	Price	Number Est.	Number Sold	Factor
a	7/1	Mon.	4.00	60	50	18
a	7/3	Wed.	4.00	68	68	16

Date	Day	Price	Number Est.	Number Sold	Factor

Figure 11 Record of portions sold.

The popularity index of the item will be entered in the next column under "Factor." The factor or popularity index is useful in evaluating the appeal of an item, which may be important in deciding whether it should be kept on the menu. It may also be used to help determine production quantities. The first step in the determination of production quantities is forecasting the total number of covers that are likely to be served. The second step, if there is a choice of menu items, is the determination of how much of each item to prepare, since demand will probably not be uniform for all items. By indicating the popularity of an item, the popularity index can be helpful when it becomes time to determine how much of each item to prepare. The popularity index is found by dividing the number of portions sold of a particular item by the total number of portions of all items sold in the period.

The "Record of Portions Sold" may be used in various ways. There are four sets of columns on each side. It is possible to use one block for each day of the week, and one block for special holidays. If the record is used so that the sale of the item on each day of the week is recorded in a separate block, then, of course, a separate sheet must be used for each dining room and for each meal. However, the sheet may be employed so that two blocks may be used for a dining room, one for lunch and one for dinner, which will be sufficient in the case of most items because most of the entrees are not served for breakfast.

The number of portions that should be prepared is estimated on the basis of the actual number sold, as recorded in the "Record of Portions Sold," and on the basis of the popularity index which appears on that record. In estimating the number of portions to be prepared, a manager should give proper consideration to the changing seasons, to the trend of the sales of that particular item in the past, and to the various combinations in which the item has been sold. Taking merely an arithmetical average of the number of portions sold in the past may give very inaccurate results.

The cost of each menu is estimated in advance on the "Menu Cost Sheet" (Figure 12). After entering on this sheet the cost per unit in which that particular item is purchased, the cost accountant calculates the cost per portion. In the column headed "Quantity," the cost accountant enters the quantity of the item used per portion.

Units are used to show where an entree may have more than one component, such as turkey with its white and dark meat, or a mixed grill with its various items.

As for the secondary items that may be included in the price of an entree, in some cases, special cost calculations have to be made to account for them, while in other cases it will be necessary to use standard costs. For example, if the menu item is roast beef with potatoes and fresh aspara-

Dining room ___

Date ___ **Day** ___ **Meal** ___

Item	Principal ingredients					Secondary items								Total direct cost	Unprod. items	Per portion		Total		Cost per and sale	Number of portions	
	Cost	Per	Quantity	Units		Soup and app.	Garn. and sauce	Veget.	Potato	Salad	Bread and butter	Dessert	Bev.			Cost	Selling price	Cost	Selling price		Estim.	Actual
Turkey	40	#	6 oz.	4whiT 4dark	48 10 58	9	8	7	7	12	6	15	8	1 30	13	1 43	4.00	97 24	272 -	357	68	68
Steak	1 50	#	8 oz.		75	9	8	7	7	12	6	15	8	1 47	15	1 62	5.00	72 90	225 -	324	45	43
Spaghetti and Meat Ball	80	#	6 oz.		30	9					7	15	8	69	7	76	2.00	22 80	60 -	380	30	30
Trout	80	ea.	1		80	9	8	7	7	12	6	15	8	1 52	15	1 67	4.50	66 80	180 -	371	40	36
																		259 74	737 -	352	183	177

Figure 12   Menu cost sheet.

184

gus, a manager should calculate the cost of the asparagus, particularly if it is served during a season when asparagus is very expensive. On the other hand, if the customer is given a choice of vegetables and a potato, or if the roast beef is part of a whole dinner, including a beverage and dessert for which one price is charged, general average costs will have to be used for all items listed under "Secondary Items." In some operations, a standard total cost for make up items is added rather than breaking them down into the separate items. Once the total cost of the item is determined and entered, a manager must add the cost of unproductive items, a cost which would not be included in the preceding cost calculation. (Often ten percent is used.) The total cost of the items and the selling price are entered in the two columns headed "Per Portion." After these two columns are filled in, the number of portions estimated to be sold is entered in the column provided for that purpose. Then the total cost and the total selling price of this menu item, which means the cost and selling price per portion multiplied by the number of portions estimated to be sold, is entered in the "Total" column, and the cost per dollar sale is calculated and entered.

After the costs and the selling prices for the whole menu are determined, the "Total" columns are added and the estimated cost per dollar sale for all entrees of that meal is calculated. If this combined total cost ratio is higher than the operation permits, or allows, or wants, a cost accountant must go over the menu, perhaps in consultation with the chef, and make substitutions which will bring the whole menu cost within the limit prescribed by the management. Also, each completed "Menu Cost Sheet" can be used to determine the relative popularity of an entree based on the other selections offered.

When the day or period for which the cost sheet was prepared has passed, the number of each entree sold is entered on the menu cost sheet. The estimated and actual portions and the popularity index are also posted to the "Record of Portions Sold" (Figure 11).

Since actual costs and standard costs are not compared, it should be noted that all items on the menu need not be analyzed. However, it is best to control all main menu entrees. Sandwiches can be included in one total figure in order to determine the popularity index. Salads and a la carte items may also be handled in the same way.

chapter 12

Financial Statements and Their Analysis

FINANCIAL STATEMENTS

In order to comprehend the financial status and progress of its operation, management must be able to understand and evaluate its financial statements. Financial statements are also necessary for preparing tax forms, arranging loans or credit, and determining how much can be withdrawn from the business. If one is thinking of buying an operation, he would certainly want to examine its financial records.

There are two basic accounting statements. One, the Profit and Loss Statement, or the Income Statement as it is sometimes called, shows whether the operation has made or lost money over a specific period. From sales or income are subtracted the cost of food and the costs of every other expense item. The difference between the total sales or income and the total costs is the profit, or the loss.

The second major statement is the Balance Sheet which portrays the financial condition of a business at a particular time. One part of the balance sheet shows all the assets, all the things of value, owned by the operation. The other half lists all the liabilities, all the debts, of the operation. The difference between the assets and liabilities is the operation's net worth, or its equity. How much money an operation is making or losing during a period is found by examining the Profit and Loss Statement. The financial condition or value of an operation on one particular day (December 31 is most commonly used) is found on the Balance Sheet.

Although accounting should be numerically correct, the statements cannot be entirely accurate in all respects. It is, for example, impossible to say at what precise rate a piece of equipment will actually depreciate or what its exact salvage value will be. Inventories may have values considerably different from the original costs. A value given to such an intangible asset as good will, for example, is strictly an estimate. Financial statements cannot show such things as employee morale or patron satisfaction, which are no less important to success for their imprecise value. There is truth in the saying that "the devil can quote figures in his own behalf," and although figures are vital for information, one should not rely entirely upon financial statements for his information. Since there is considerable leeway in the preparation of statements, it is often important to know who prepares them. A good accountant does not have to be a Certified Public Accountant, but the letters "C.P.A." after his name indicate that he has had to fulfill certain requirements to gain this status and must adhere to the rules and regulations as prescribed by the American Institute of Certified Public Accountants.

There is no one accounting system universally applicable to all industries, since each has different sales or expense classifications. Restaurants are fortunate, however, in having a *Uniform System of Accounts for Restaurants* that has been prepared by the Laventhol Krekstein Horwath and Horwath firm of Certified Public Accountants, under the auspices of the National Restaurant Association. This system, which can be used by both large and small food service operations, has been developed specifically for these operations. It specifies how various expenses and income items should be treated; it allows comparisons among all operations using the system; and by using the system, any accountant can have the benefit and experience of specialists in food accounting.

An example of a Profit and Loss Statement is shown in Figure 1. This statement lists sales and other income. It then deducts all expenses to find the profit before taxes. For better interpretation, each item is also calculated as a percentage of sales. The operation has earned a profit of $12,229, or 6.1 percent of its sales. *Cost of Food Consumed* is calculated in the following manner.

Inventory of food on hand at beginning of period	$ 3,000
Plus purchases of food during period	72,900
Total value of available food	75,900
Inventory of food on hand at end of period	2,500
Value of food used during period	$73,400

To find out how much food has been used, it is necessary to conduct an opening and a closing inventory. Otherwise, an operation could show an unrealistically low food cost by using inventory on hand; or if the operation accumulated a higher inventory during the period, it would show an inaccurately high food cost and a lower profit.

The following list includes the most common Profit and Loss statement terms.

PROFIT AND LOSS STATEMENT
Year ended December 31, 19_____

	Amounts	Percentages
Food sales	$200,000	100.0%
Cost of food consumed	73,400	36.7
Gross profit	$126,600	63.3%
Other income	1,600	.8
Total income	$128,200	64.1%
Controllable expenses		
Payroll	$ 63,000	31.5%
Employee benefits	7,200	3.6
Direct operating expenses	10,200	5.1
Music and entertainment	200	.1
Advertising and promotion	2,200	1.1
Utilities	4,600	2.3
Administrative and general	5,400	2.7
Repairs and maintenance	3,800	1.9
Total controllable expenses	$ 96,600	48.3%
Profit before rent	$ 31,600	15.8%
Rent or occupation costs	12,000	6.0
Profit before depreciation	$ 19,600	9.8%
Depreciation	2,922	1.5
Profit before interest	$ 16,678	8.3%
Interest expense	1,000	.5
Profit before income tax	$ 15,678	7.8%
Income tax (22%)	3,449	1.7
Net profit	$ 12,229	6.1%

Figure 1

Gross Profit is the profit shown after a deduction of the cost of raw food from sales and before consideration of other expenses.

Other Income includes income from such nonfood items as cigarette or candy sales and concessions.

Controllable Expenses are those that are the direct responsibility of the management and can be influenced and controlled by competent management and efficiency.

Payroll is the salaries and wages paid to service, preparation, and administrative personnel.

Employee Benefits include such items as social security taxes, workman's compensation insurance, medical insurance programs, and any expenses furthering employee good will.

Direct Operating Expenses are items directly involved in the service to the customer. Included would be such costs as uniforms, laundry, china, glassware, silver, flowers, licenses, decorations, and parking fees.

Administrative and General Expenses are overhead expenses which are not connected directly with the service and comfort of the customer. Included in this category are office supplies, the telephone, postage, insurance, dues, and professional fees.

Profit Before Rent is sometimes called operating profit and shows how much profit has been made from the operation before the cost of the facilities has been considered.

Rent or Occupation Costs are the costs necessary to present the premises to the management ready to operate. Included in this category are rent, real estate taxes, and insurance. These costs are usually beyond the control of active and current management. The dollar cost of the physical assets, the financing arrangements, the interest rates, or the rent, all result from the type of structure built or acquired. These costs are considered fixed overhead and cannot be readily changed.

Depreciation. Every physical object incurs wear and tear; many become obsolete. If this expense is not considered, profits are overstated since they are an actual cost and the operator would be forced to supply replacements without funds set aside for them.

An example of a Balance Sheet is shown in Figure 2. The top section of Figure 2 shows the assets, all the things of value owned by the operation. The lower section lists the liabilities along with the overall worth of the business. This balance sheet represents December 31 only; it could be considerably different if it showed any other day.

Current Assets are those assets that can be converted into cash in a short time. They commonly include cash, the accounts and notes receivable, and the inventory. Prepaid items are services, taxes, insurance, interest, and other items for which money has been paid in advance.

Fixed Assets are those assets of a permanent nature which will not be sold as long as they serve the needs of the business. Since they usually lose value during their lifetime, their book value is found by subtracting their depreciation from the original cost.

Leasehold Improvements indicates that the operation leases its premises but has spent its own money improving them. If the building were

BALANCE SHEET
Year ended December 31, 19_____

ASSETS

Current Assets			
Change funds	$ 1,100		
On deposit, First National Bank	12,100		
Total cash		$13,200	
Accounts receivable—customers		2,000	
Advances—employees		550	
Deposits—utilities		400	
Inventories			
Food	$2,500		
Supplies	900		
Total inventories		$ 3,400	
Prepaid insurance, taxes, etc.		900	
Total current assets			$20,450
Fixed Assets			
Furniture and fixtures	$20,500		
Deduct accumulated depreciation	6,100	$14,400	
Air conditioning	7,200		
Deduct accumulated depreciation	3,514	3,686	
Leasehold improvements	4,000		
Deduct accumulated depreciation	1,200	2,800	
Operating equipment—china, glass and silver		2,000	
Total fixed assets			22,886
Total assets			$43,336

LIABILITIES AND CAPITAL

Current liabilities			
Accounts payable—trade		$ 7,000	
Accrued taxes payable		920	
Accrued expenses payable		2,528	
Total current liabilities			$10,448
Equipment contracts payable			9,800
Notes payable—long term			8,000
Total liabilities			$28,248
Capital (owner's equity)			
Proprietor's Account December 31, 19_____		$14,859	
Profit for 19_____ (from Figure 1)		12,229	
Total		$27,088	
Cash drawings		12,000	
Proprietor's Account			$15,088
TOTAL LIABILITIES AND CAPITAL			$43,336

Figure 2

owned by the business, its cost, together with accumulated depreciation, would be shown.

Current Liabilities are obligatons that will become due within one year. Accounts Payable usually make up the bulk of this item.

Fixed Liabilities shown on Figure 2 are Equipment Contracts Payable and Notes Payable Long Term. They are defined as obligations or parts of obligations that will not be paid within the current year.

Capital Account shows the value or the worth of the business. In the example shown, the business is owned by one person, the proprietor. It shows that between December 31, 19___, and December 31, 19___, the proprietor withdrew $12,000 of the $12,229 profit so the worth of the business increased $229. If the business were a corporation, capital stock and surplus would be shown instead of the Proprietor's Account; and if it were a partnership, each partner's share and withdrawals would appear.

Other common accounting terms follow.

Auditing. A review of the general accounting to confirm its validity. This is often done by an outside accountant.

Current Ratio. The ratio of current assets compared to current liabilities. In Figure 2 it is $20,450 divided by $10,448, or 1.96, which is rather high for a restaurant.

Journal. The daily record of itemized business transactions usually known as books of original entry. From the journal, the transactions are posted to a ledger under such typical headings as "cash receipts," and "cash disbursements".

Ledger. Sheets that are used to show monthly transactions classified according to a system of accounts. There may be a ledger sheet for sales, purchases, payroll, and cash, among many others. Every Profit and Loss Statement and Balance Sheet item has a ledger sheet.

Working Capital. The excess of current assets over current liabilities. This is the amount of money the operation has available to finance its daily operations. Insufficient working capital prohibits the operation from paying bills or meeting current obligations. In Figure 2, working capital is $20,450 less $10,448, or $10,002.

ANALYZING FINANCIAL STATEMENTS

Financial statements may be examined by different analysts for different purposes. A banker may analyze the statements to see if there will be potential earnings to repay a loan or if there are sufficient assets to provide security for a loan. An investor may analyze the statement to estimate the rate of return on his investment, the chances for appreciation of his investment, and the projected earnings. A purveyor may check statements before extending credit. Management looks at the statements to determine the profitability of its operation. Management may also use the financial statement to judge the efficiency of its operation, to determine where its costs have gotten out of line, and to make basic decisions.

Analyzing financial statements is basically a comparison process. The periodic statements of the same operation may be compared in order to locate trends. (The figures are often converted into ratios; expense amounts, for example, may be expressed as a percentage of sales. These percentages may then be compared with prior percentages, projected percentages, general industry percentages, percentages released by trade associations or specialized accounting firms, and budgeted percentages.

Such nonpercentage ratios as the current ratio or inventory turnover may often be used. These again may be compared with general industry experience or with the historical data of the same operation. Ratios are especially useful in analyzing balance sheet items.

ANALYZING THE PROFIT AND LOSS STATEMENT

For analysis purposes, the Profit and Loss Statement can be divided into three parts. The first part shows sales or the amount of business. The second shows expenses, which are subtracted from sales to provide the third category, profit. Although the three parts are related, each can be analyzed separately.

Analyzing Sales. In analyzing sales, the operator wants to determine several things. Are sales increasing or decreasing and, if so, why are they increasing or decreasing? He may also want to know if the sales are appropriate to the value of the physical facilities or the number of seats for the operation—or to the size of his investment in it.

A yearly sales increase or decrease is shown by comparative figures. It is important to know the make up of sales. If alcoholic beverages are sold, total sales should be broken down to show them. If other merchandise is handled, it should be separated for analysis purposes. An operator may want to break down sales into the different meal periods so that each meal can be examined separately. Total sales for the current year and past years can be shown in this way.

Although dollar sales have shown an increase each year in the following example, the amount is small and probably reflects higher selling prices due to higher costs. There may have been a decrease in real volume.

	1972		1973		1974	
	Amount	Ratio to Sales	Amount	Ratio to Sales	Amount	Ratio to Sales
Net food sales	$105,600	56.1	$107,900	56.8	$107,900	56.5
Net beverage sales	82,500	43.9	82,000	43.2	83,100	43.5
Net sales	$188,100	100.0%	$189,900	100.0%	$191,000	100.0%

Sales may be compared on a monthly basis. (The current month could be compared with the past four months, or with any other appropriate period.) Such a sales comparison appears below.

The table on page 196 presents a form for comparing Food, Beverage, and Net Sales for a given month with the same month of the previous year. This form also compares this year to date sales with the sales of the previous year to the same date. Two important items in this form are the columns headed "Amount of Increase or (Decrease)" and "Percent of Increase or (Decrease)." These call attention to the variations in sales for a given month as compared to the same month of the previous year, and for a given date in the current year as compared with the same date in the previous year.

If food sales are increasing, it is desirable to know why they are increasing. Increases can be due to one or both of two factors: more covers served or higher prices received per cover. An operation may be showing an increase in sales while serving fewer customers. Dollar volume may rise while customer volume declines. This information is determined by recording the number of covers served. Dividing this number into sales will give the price of the average check, a very significant figure. The

	Current Month			Last Month		
	Food Sales	Covers	Average Check	Food Sales	Covers	Average Check
Breakfast	$1,400	1,068	$1.31	$1,385	1,108	$1.25
Lunch	6,170	2,210	2.79	6,320	2,194	2.88
Dinner	9,250	2,020	4.57	9,244	2,045	4.52
Total	$16,820	5,298	$3.17	$16,949	5,347	$3.16

average check figure indicates whether prices have increased enough to absorb costs. If costs increase 10 percent, the average check should rise

	February 1974	Ratio to Sales	March 1974	Ratio to Sales	April 1974	Ratio to Sales	May 1974	Ratio to Sales	June 1974	Ratio to Sales
Net food sales	$20,000	72.7	$20,600	73.8	$21,100	74.0	$21,700	74.4	$24,150	75.4
Net beverage sales	7,500	27.3	7,300	26.2	7,400	26.0	7,450	25.6	7,900	24.6
Net sales	$27,500	100.0%	$27,900	100.0%	$28,500	100.0%	$29,150	100.0%	$32,050	100.0%

	February 1974	February 1973	Amt. of Inc. or (Dec.)	Percent Inc. or (Dec.)	Sales to Date 1974	Sales to Date 1973	Amt. of Inc. or (Dec.)	Percent Inc. or (Dec.)
Net food sales	$18,720	$18,350	$370	2.08	$37,370	$36,670	$700	1.98
Net beverage sales	6,430	6,670	(240)	(3.74)	12,730	12,920	(190)	(1.47)
Net sales	$25,150	$25,020	$130	.58	$50,100	$49,590	$510	1.07

proportionately. Unless it adversely affects the volume of covers, the higher the average check, the better. This optimum return may be accomplished by increasing prices, by introducing higher priced menu selections, by changing the menu compositions, and by promoting and merchandising more imaginatively. Prices and menu changes can be increased only if the patrons will accept them. Unwarranted increases could mean higher individual average checks, but smaller sales if fewer customers patronize the establishment.

If sales are decreasing, it is most important to discover why. Perhaps one segment of the business, such as breakfast, is unprofitable. Discontinuing it may lower sales, but the profit may nevertheless rise. Generally, decreasing sales are, of course, serious in a period when all costs are rising.

It is sometimes helpful to relate sales to the value of fixed assets. Money must be spent on fixed assets to produce sales. More money spent on fixed assets should generally be expected to produce more in sales. The Fixed Asset Ratio relates net sales to fixed assets:

$$\text{Fixed Asset Ratio} = \frac{\text{Net Sales}}{\text{Net Book Value of Fixed Assets}}$$

If net sales are $200,000 and net fixed assets are $22,886, for example, the Fixed Asset Ratio would 8.7.

The higher the ratio, the more money in sales that is being generated by the fixed assets. The ratio will vary considerably according to the type of operation; it can best be used in analyzing similar operations or in analyzing different periods in the history of the same operation. The Fixed Asset Ratio will also be affected by the large scale leasing of equipment, by an advantageous building rental agreement, and by various methods of calculating depreciation.

Another ratio that is sometimes used to analyze sales places net sales over net working capital. Working capital is the difference between current assets and current liabilities, the money available for running the business. The ratio calculation would be as follows.

$$\frac{\text{Net Sales}}{\text{Net Working Capital}} \quad \frac{\$200,000}{10,002} = 20{:}1$$

The ratio also tends to vary drastically from period to period and from operation to operation. Analyzing sales by the number of times each dollar of working capital is turned over in sales has only limited applicability in the food industry.

Sales can also be analyzed in terms of turnover per seat, or the dollar amount of sales produced by each seat. For turnover per seat, it is usually desirable to break down sales into different meal periods. Such an analysis could be made on a daily, weekly, monthly, or yearly basis (see Figure 3).

The higher the turnover the better. If it is lower than management thinks reasonable, more promotion, or some menu or price changing might be in order. It is very helpful to compare the turnover per seat for the present period with past periods, since the ratio would not be affected by inflation, the way it is for the average check figure.

The amount of an investment in a food service operation is directly related to the size of the operation; the size of the operation, in turn, is generally directly reflected in the number of patrons' seats. Ideally, the more seats available, the greater the number of sales; and some operators have very definite feelings on how much in sales each seat should produce. This yield per seat can be calculated for any period from a meal to a whole year. If the net food sales per year of an operation were $200,000 and it had 36 seats, the sales per seat would be calculated in this way:

$$\text{Sales per seat} = \frac{\text{Net Sales}}{\text{Number of Seats}} = \frac{\$200,000}{36} = \frac{\$5555}{\text{per year}}$$

Analyzing Expenses. Since controllable expenses are related to sales, the normal procedure in analyzing an expense is to calculate the expense item as a ratio to sales. The sales figure is considered 100 percent, and

	Yearly Covers	Seats	Turnover per seat
Breakfast	12,801	36	355.6
Lunch	24,607	36	685.2
Dinner	24,444	36	679.0
	Monthly Covers	Seats	Turnover per seat
Breakfast	1,068	36	29.7
Lunch	2,210	36	61.4
Dinner	2,020	36	56.1
	Daily Covers	Seats	Turnover per seat
Breakfast	36	36	1.0
Lunch	75	36	2.1
Dinner	68	36	1.9

Figure 3

the amount of the expense divided by the sales figure will give the expense percentage. So if food sales are $200,000 and food costs are $73,400, the food cost percentage is 36.7.

$$\frac{\text{Cost of Food Sold}}{\text{Food Sales}} = \frac{73,400}{200,000} = 36.7\%$$

The amounts of various expense items are difficult to analyze by themselves, but as a percentage of sales they become more meaningful. If one particular expense rose considerably over a previous period, there could be cause for concern. However, if sales had increased proportionately there would probably be no cause for alarm.

The cost percentages of the various expense categories can be compared with percentages for past periods in the history of the same operation, with budgeted percentages, with goals that have been set, or with industry averages. Figure 4 supplies industry data that might be used for these comparisons.

In comparing the cost category percentage figure of the present period with past periods, an operator should notice all trends, especially the upward ones. These might indicate lack of control in the area under analysis. Sharp variations both upward and downward should be resolved. If utility costs have remained a constant percentage for a period of time, a sudden increase or decrease calls for an immediate explanation.

Expense categories may be classified as variable, semivariable, and fixed. Variable dollar expenses should change more or less directly with volume. Food cost is an excellent example. Such semivariable expenses, as some types of labor costs, change with sales volume, but not as proportionately as the variable food cost. Fixed expenses such as "Administration and General" remain relatively constant despite changes in volume. The more variable the expense, the more significant its percentage figure as related to sales.

The two largest expense categories are "Salary and Wages" and "Cost of Food Sold." These two are sometimes referred to as "prime costs." Management should have a definite idea of what percentage of labor expense to sales it considers comfortable for its operation. If the percentage should rise above the desired one and selling prices are adequate, the rise could indicate the need for better labor cost analysis and control. (Chapters 1 to 3 should be helpful here.) The use of work production standards can show where the increase is occurring. If, on the other hand, the labor cost percentage is significantly lower than planned, the operation may be understaffed, and as a result, it may be providing substandard food and service to its patrons. Quality control is equally important with labor and food cost control.

RESTAURANT OPERATIONS (Summary Profit and Loss Statements)

	1971 All Restaurants	1971 Food Only	1971 Food and Beverage Restaurants				1970 All Restaurants	1970 Food Only	1970 Food and Beverage Restaurants			
			Total	Neighbor-hood	Center City	Suburban			Total	Neighbor-hood	Center City	Suburban
Sales												
Food	80.2%	100.0%	72.9%	70.7%	76.3%	71.5%	79.8%	100.0%	72.2%	70.6%	76.0%	70.2%
Beverages	19.8		27.1	29.3	23.7	28.5	20.2		27.8	29.4	24.0	29.8
Total sales	100.0	100.0	100.0	100.0	100.0	100.0	100.0	100.0	100.0	100.0	100.0	100.0
Cost of sales												
Food*	37.4	33.6	39.3	40.7	37.6	40.0	37.3	33.9	39.0	40.2	37.3	39.8
Beverages*	30.3		30.3	29.3	28.5	32.1	29.9		29.9	29.9	28.0	31.2
Total cost of sales	36.0	33.6	37.0	37.4	35.4	37.7	35.8	33.9	36.5	37.1	35.1	37.3
Gross profit	64.0	66.4	63.4	62.6	64.6	62.3	64.2	66.1	63.5	62.9	64.9	62.7
Other income	1.0	.5	1.2	.7	.8	1.8	1.1	.8	1.1	.4	.9	1.8
Total income	65.0	66.9	64.6	63.3	65.4	64.1	65.3	66.9	64.6	63.3	65.8	64.5
Controllable expenses												
Payroll	29.2	32.1	28.3	29.1	27.6	28.0	29.7	32.5	29.0	29.1	29.4	28.0
Employee benefits	3.9	3.9	4.0	3.3	4.9	3.4	3.5	3.7	3.7	3.2	3.7	3.4
Direct oper. exp.	5.6	5.0	5.9	5.4	6.9	5.4	5.5	4.8	5.9	5.5	6.2	5.4
Music and enter.	1.4	.1	1.4	2.3	1.2	1.4	1.3	N	1.5	2.1	1.0	1.5
Adver. and prom.	1.7	1.8	1.7	1.6	2.1	1.2	1.7	1.7	1.9	1.6	2.5	1.3
Utilities	2.1	2.5	2.0	2.0	1.8	2.2	1.9	2.2	1.9	1.8	1.5	2.0
Admin. and genrl.	4.9	4.2	5.4	5.5	6.3	4.4	5.5	4.9	4.6	5.3	6.9	5.0
Repairs and maint.	1.7	1.6	1.8	1.7	1.9	1.9	1.6	1.5	1.8	1.5	1.7	1.7
Tot. control. exp.	50.5	51.2	50.5	50.9	52.7	47.9	50.7	51.3	50.3	50.1	52.9	48.3
Income before occupation costs	14.5%	15.7%	14.1%	12.4%	12.7%	16.2%	14.6%	15.6%	14.3%	13.2%	12.9%	16.2%

* Ratios based on individual department sales. Food costs are before credit for employees' meals.

Figure 4. Abstracted from "Restaurant Operations: 1971," Norman Katz and Kenneth I Solomon in Laventhol, Krekstein, Horwath and Horwath, eds., *Restaurant, Country Clubs, and City Clubs, 1972 Edition Reports on Operations* (Phila., 1972), pp. 6-7.

Food cost, as already mentioned, is one of the most variable of expenses. As the number of meals changes, the total cost of food used should also change. The chapters on the various aspects of food cost control should be helpful in combating an excessive food cost.

Although the prime costs, food and labor, account for the major portion of total costs, the other categories are worthy of examination. One way to keep from spending money in the short run is to defer needed repairs and upkeep and maintenance. These savings will have to be made up later, perhaps at considerably higher cost. Thus, an unusual decline of expenses in this category may be suspicious.

In analyzing the cost percentages, care must be taken not to compare the percentage in question with a "standard" one only. An operation that uses a great many convenience and prepared foods may have a high food cost that is more than offset by low labor costs. An operation may be willing to have a higher than normal food cost if it believes that its low menu prices can bring in more than enough additional business to provide a higher dollar profit despite a higher food cost ratio. The same may hold true of relatively high entertainment and advertising costs.

In comparing the cost percentages of two operations, it is most important that they be of similar types. The percentages for a hamburger stand and a luxury restaurant will vary considerably. It is also very important that each operation use the same accounting classifications. (Once again, the Uniform System of Accounts for Restaurants permits excellent comparisons.) The volume of sales will also affect the cost percentages, especially those in a fixed category. The Administration and/or General expenses may make up a certain percentage of sales. If sales double, and no new expenses are incurred, that percentage figure should be cut in half.

The controllable expenses are the most important indication of the proficiency of a manager. There may be little the manager can do about occupation or depreciation expenses, but there is always a great deal he can do about controllable expenses.

Analyzing Profit. The third area of the Profit and Loss Statement is profit, what is left when expenses are deducted from sales. What is an appropriate profit? Apart from any ratio analysis, profit must be sufficient for the business to continue and to satisfy the operators. Ratios might indicate a favorable profit, but if the operator is not satisfied with his profit and could do better in another endeavor, his profit is simply insufficient. Three ratios are often used to analyze profit: the net profit to net sales, the net profit to total net worth, and the net profit to total assets.

The net profit to net sales is often called the Operating Ratio or the Operating Margin of Profit Ratio. It is found by dividing the net profit before taxes by the net sales.

$$\frac{\text{Net Profit}}{\text{Net Sales}} = \text{Operating Ratio} \frac{\$\ 15{,}678}{\$200{,}000} = 7.8\%$$

Adaptations of this ratio include the substitution of gross profit, or operating profit, or net profit after taxes for net profit before taxes. Generally though, this ratio is the most important one used by food service operators, since it shows the profitability of the operation based on the amount of sales. The higher the ratio, the more effective management has been in controlling costs. Like other ratios, the operating ratio may be used to compare different financial periods and to compare the operation's performance to that of other operations.

Net profit (usually after taxes) to net equity represents the owner's return on his investment. Equity investment is the difference between assets and liabilities, or theoretically, the equity amount that is invested in the business. A return is expected from any investment, and the higher the investment risk, the higher the expected return. If the operator could take the money he has invested in the business and invest it in another business that offers a higher return with the same risk, or less of a risk, his inclination would be to do so, assuming the first investment could be readily liquidated. In some fast food operations with high volume sales compared with a relatively small percentage of investments to sales, it is possible to have a low operating ratio but a high net profit to equity investment percentage. The calculation of the ratio of net profit to net worth, or equity investment is:

$$\text{Net Profit to Net Worth} \frac{\text{Net Profit}}{\text{Net Worth}} = \frac{\$12{,}229}{15{,}088} = 81.05\%$$

The ratio of net profit to total assets is sometimes called the Management Proficiency Ratio. It shows how much profit management can make with the total assets (not just the investment of net worth) at its disposal. The greater the percentage, the more proficient the management, at least this is the assumption. Calculations for the ratio are:

$$\text{Management Proficiency Ratio} \frac{\text{Net Profit (after taxes)}}{\text{Total Assets}} \frac{\$12{,}229}{43{,}336} = 28.21\%$$

ANALYZING THE BALANCE SHEET

Cash. The average operation has two cash accounts. One is the cash on hand used for change and petty cash. The other is cash on deposit for payment of expenses and reserve funds. There must be enough cash available to meet expense demands, but amounts over this can be used to provide interest income, among other purposes. Each operation must determine the amount it should keep on hand and on deposit, and different operations may have considerably different cash needs. Depending on the financing, purchasing, and withdrawals, the cash balances may fluctuate considerably. A cash budget, like the ones discussed in Chapter 14, can help show in advance when there may be a scarcity or overabundance of cash so that appropriate planning and action can be pursued. Whenever a new manager is employed, one of the first things he should do is count the money on hand and determine the amount on deposit.

Accounts Receivable. Accounts receivable are amounts owed to the operation by customers. Operations with sales strictly on a cash basis will probably have no accounts receivable. Others, to serve their patrons more conveniently, allow them to charge meals. This, of course, is an added expense to the operation as it does not have immediate use of the money owed to it, and often does have bookkeeping costs, interest expenses, and bad debts. Operations have to determine if these costs outweigh the increased sales to be gained by providing this service. The increased use of credit cards has greatly affected the accounts receivable of many operations. A large banquet or function business will often vastly increase accounts receivable. Accounts receivable can be evaluated in terms of their turnover, average collection period, percentage to sales, and the number of sales days tied up in accounts receivable. The following formula is for accounts receivable turnover:

$$\text{Accounts Receivable Turnover} = \frac{\text{Total Sales}}{\text{Average Accounts Receivable}}$$

If total sales are $200,000 for the period and accounts receivable are $2000, the calculations would be $200,000 divided by $2000 or 100. The period can be for a week, a month or a year.

The average collection period formula follows:

$$\text{Average Collection Period} = \frac{365 \text{ Days}}{\text{Accounts Receivable Turnover}}$$

If the turnover is 100, the average collection period would be 365 divided by 100, or 3.65.

Sometimes an analysis is made in terms of the number of days of sales tied up in accounts receivable. An operation that averages $500 in daily sales and has $2000 in accounts receivable would have four days of sales tied up in its accounts receivable. Sudden and marked changes in the character of the accounts receivable are as important as the amount of money in the accounts receivable total. If the percentage of accounts receivable to sales, or the number of days of sales represented by accounts receivable should increase suddenly or considerably, there is cause for immediate investigation. The "quality" of the receivables is defined by the willingness of the ones owing to pay promptly. The quality may be determined by aging the receivables. Assume total accounts receivable are $2000; this chart helps establish the quality of these accounts receivable.

Normally, the longer the accounts are past due, the less the chance of eventual collection. It is often desirable, then, to create a reserve for doubtful accounts so the net accounts receivable figure will be more accurate.

Accounts receivable from established credit card operations normally do not present a problem except for commissions paid to the credit card companies. Accounts receivable from employees usually are individual situations and are, therefore, another matter entirely.

AGING ACCOUNTS RECEIVABLE

Classification by Due Date	Balance in Each Classification Summarized from Individual Accounts	Expected Percentage Uncollectable	Estimated Uncollectable Amount
Not yet due	$1,200	60.0%	1%	$12.00
Less than 30 days past due	350	17.5%	5%	17.50
31–60 days past due	300	15.0%	10%	30.00
61–120 days past due	150	7.5%	10%	15.00
Over 120 days past due	—	—	—	—
Total	$2,000	100.0%	—	$74.50

Inventories. Food operations should differentiate among the values of the food, beverage, and supplies inventories. The value of food on hand depends on the type of operation. A fast service, limited menu operation, may turn over its inventory every few days, while an operation that has a very varied menu and delivery problems may have an extremely slow inventory turnover. Food inventory turnover is determined by dividing the value of the food inventory into the cost of the goods sold. If the food inventory figure is $2500 and the cost of goods sold is $73,400 per year, the inventory turnover is 29.4 per year. A turnover of three to five times a month is usual for many operations. Too high a turnover may mean that the operation is living from hand to mouth, which may be expensive. If cash is short, for example, too high a turnover may indicate that the operation cannot afford to buy in sufficient quantities; it may also signify that the operation cannot secure credit from purveyors, which limits its competitive buying power.

Too slow an inventory turnover can indicate that management is not turning over this asset fast enough to attain its highest profitability potential but is, instead, incurring the extra costs involved in protracted storage. It may also indicate that the inventory is loaded with old merchandise that cannot be moved. It is helpful to examine the storeroom shelves to see if there is a large quantity of old, unusable merchandise still carried at purchase value.

Alcoholic beverage inventory turnover must also be evaluated. The rate of turnover will be affected by the overall volume of business, the amount of slow moving "show" merchandise, and the volume of beer sold. Six to seven times a year is a good alcoholic beverage turnover figure for most operations.

Current Ratio. The ratio of current assets to current liabilities is known as the current ratio. If current assets are $20,450 and current liabilities are $10,448, the ratio is 1.96 to 1. The current ratio indicates how well an operation can pay off its short term creditors and is therefore, an indication of financial strength. In many businesses a ratio of 2 to 1 is considered desirable. However, in food service operations it is often closer to 1 to 1. Factors causing this lower ratio are lack of accounts receivable, relatively small inventories, and a fast inventory turnover. By living on the credit of their purveyors, some operations exist on a less than 1 to 1 ratio, but this practice can hardly be recommended.

The current ratio can be misleading. By incurring long term debt, an operation may receive more cash and improve its current ratio; but its overall financial position has not changed. Too high a current ratio may indicate that management is not turning over its current assets or utilizing them in other ways to the best advantage.

The dollar difference between current assets and current liabilities is the working capital. If this amount is limited, there will be a high turnover. (Turnover is determined by dividing the amount of working capital into sales.) Excessive turnover indicates a shortage of working capital that could cause severe problems in a financial emergency and that limits purchasing capability. A slow turnover indicates that working capital may be excessive and is, therefore, not being used to its best advantage.

Fixed Assets. Analyzing the fixed assets of two different operations, even though they may be the same size and generally the same type, presents problems. One operation may own its location while the other rents its facilities. One operation may purchase all of its equipment while another leases much of its equipment. Different depreciation policies and the different ages of the facilities and equipment often make comparisons difficult. The Equipment Ratio, or the ratio of net sales to fixed assets, is sometimes used to make these comparisons. This ratio, which has already been discussed in the sales analysis section, shows how much money in sales is generated by each dollar invested in fixed assets. An operator contemplates some new equipment. Should he purchase it or not? He calculates that the new equipment will bring in two dollars in yearly sales for each dollar invested. However, the present ratio is three dollars of sales for each dollar represented by his present equipment. On this basis the purchase may seem unfavorable, but there could be other factors in other situations which might suggest the advisability of the purchase.

Sometimes fixed assets investments are expressed as the "cost per seat." An operator may calculate that with his anticipated volume and profit he can afford to spend, say, $3000 per patron seat (his total cost divided by number of seats). If the projected cost exceeds $3000 per seat, he would not consider the investment feasible.

Liabilities. Liabilities are the amounts owed by the operation to others. If they are excessive, the operation is obviously in trouble. Employee wages are the first claim on the resources of an operation, and wage payments are usually, of necessity, current. The other major expense is payment to food purveyors. Dividing the yearly Cost of Food Consumed by 12 will provide an average monthly amount to be paid to purveyors. An accounts payable figure higher than this could indicate that the operation is slow to pay (assuming its sales are about the same each month). High accrued expenses are also significant. The Current Ratio gives an indication of the operation's ability to pay off its current creditors. One refinement of the Current Ratio is the "Quick Ratio" or "Acid Test." This ratio eliminates inventory value from the current assets and includes only cash and assets readily transformed into cash as marketable securities and quality accounts receivable. A ratio of 1 to 1 indicates that theoretically the operation has current assets available to pay off its short term liabilities.

Liabilities may also be compared to the net worth or equity investment. Liabilities of the operation are protected, or cushioned, by the investment of the ownership. The lower the ratio of debt to equity the more secure are the creditors of the operation. The debt to worth ratio shows this, and a low ratio enhances the chances of getting additional credit.

A number of ratios have been presented in this section. Not all are appropriate for every operation and there must be some selectivity in their use. A ratio or percentage figure may be somewhat misleading by itself, but used with other ratios or percentages, it may give a better picture of the whole financial condition of an operation and its financial progress. Care must be used in employing the so-called standard percentages and ratios. Every operation is different, and because of its special circumstances, a standard ratio or percentage figure might not be appropriate. The same difficulty arises in comparing one operation with others. The percentages and ratios are most helpful in determining trends and their direction. However, trends use only historical data; actual figures in the near future can be considerably different. Percentages and ratios can help predict progress and future conditions, but they depend on accurate forecasts.

The analysis of financial statements using ratios and percentages is a most helpful tool to management in decision making. It is, however, only a tool. Decisions should not be made routinely on the analysis of financial statements alone.

chapter 13

Electronic Data Processing

Control can be greatly helped by the computer. Not only may more control procedures be employed, but the results can become available in time to take corrective action. The exception principle—which dictates that the machine single out only deviations from the norm—may also be used, since deviations demand management attention. Some aspects of information systems that can be handled by a computer include guest check averages, breakdowns of menu sales, hourly sales figures, sales forecasts, employee payrolls, employee activity rates, inventory levels, issues, customer reactions, and budgeting and financial statements.

It must be remembered that although computers may not make mistakes, erroneous data given them will produce erroneous calculations ("garbage in, garbage out"). Therefore, an error in programming will negate the helpfulness of the computer. Computers are also very expensive to operate, so careful consideration must be given to whether their benefits will offset their cost.

DATA PROCESSING APPLICATIONS

Business in general has been quick to utilize the computer for much of its paperwork. With its capacity for rapid calculations and quick data retrieval, the computer provides information faster, more completely, with more accuracy, and at a lower cost for many business operations. Where a procedure involves a great deal of routine work, as in payroll calculations or maintaining records for receivables or payables, Electronic Data Processing (EDP) can be the most feasible approach. The greater the number of transactions, the greater the benefits of EDP. In the past, many food service operations, being relatively small, did not have the volume of paper work to use EDP effectively. However, the decreasing costs involved with EDP have allowed many food service organizations to computerize parts of their operations.

Financial Statements. Financial statements can be prepared manually or by EDP; either means provides the same information. Preparing a financial statement, like a Profit and Loss Statement, manually, is usually a time consuming procedure, and the statement is often not available until some time after the end of the period being considered.

EDP provides a statement in a matter of minutes—or even seconds—and the interval before it is available depends only on the time necessary to get the input into the machine. EDP, then, makes it possible to take corrective action or make decisions on the basis of very current information.

An operation using a computer to calculate food and labor costs can produce an abbreviated Profit and Loss Statement each day, or even after each meal if need be. For other costs, normal percentages or prorated amounts can be used in an abbreviated statement. The headquarters of chain operations can secure statements on any particular unit whenever necessary.

Besides the speed and ease with which it provides statements, the computer can also very easily include other information that can aid in interpreting the statement. This additional information might include percentages, figures for comparable past periods, ratio calculations, and special printouts when figures deviate from predetermined standards or norms. (These are the "exception reports" already discussed.)

Payroll. EDP can be utilized to record employee labor hours; calculate payrolls (including deductions); prepare payroll registers, checks and statements; reconcile cashed payroll checks; prepare government reports, and analyze labor costs.

Departmental supervisors normally turn in a daily attendance record to the payroll control center. If hours have already been scheduled, only exceptions to scheduled hours need to be reported, a procedure which cuts down on paperwork. Exceptions might include overtime, gratuities, and temporary or casual employees like banquet waiters.

The computer updates each employee's time and payroll records with the new daily data, and a daily payroll cost distribution report, like the one depicted in Figure 1, may be prepared. At the end of the payroll period, any changes in payroll calculations, such as increases in the pay rates or special deductions, are fed to the computer. The payroll is then calculated, taxes are computed, deductions are determined, and the pay checks and employee earnings statements are printed. A payroll register and deduction and bond register, if desired, may also be printed with all

DAILY LABOR COST DISTRIBUTION REPORT

Depart-ment	Description	Labor Cost				Month to Date			
		Regular	Overtime	Other	Total	Regular	Overtime	Other	Total
1	Main kitchen	xxx.xx	xxx.xx	x.xx	xxxx.xx	xxx.xx	xxx.xx	xx.x	xxxx.xx
2	Bake Shop	xxx.xx	xxx.xx	x.xx	xxxx.xx	xxx.xx	xxxx.xx	xx.x	xxxx.xx
3	Salad	xxx.xx	xxx.xx	x.xx	xxx.xx	xxx.xx	xxxx.xx	xx.x	xxx.xx
4	Dining room	xxx.xx	xxx.xx	x.xx	xxx.xx	xxx.xx	xxx.xx	xx.x	xxx.xx
5	Coffee shop	xxx.xx	xxx.xx	x.xx	xxx.xx	xxx.xx	xxx.xx	xx.x	xxx.xx

Figure 1

the information updated. Data for quarterly and annual government reports are maintained in the master payroll records and can easily be transcribed to the required report forms when necessary.

The labor cost distribution breaks down hours and labor costs by various cost centers. This information can appear in a separate report or be part of a daily management report.

Accounts Payable. Besides recording invoices and the amounts due creditors, the computer can perform other functions in the accounts payable area. Different analyses such as statements showing amounts purchased from various vendors, distribution of purchases by cost centers, and trial balances of payables, may be made from purchase records.

EDP can keep track of discount dates, compute discount amounts, and give notice when payments are necessary to earn the discount. The computer can prepare a Cash Requirements Statement showing the amount of cash necessary for payments by due dates; it can also address and prepare the necessary checks and remittance statements for vendors (Figure 2). It automatically correlates payments with cash disbursements and cash balances.

One procedure for handling accounts payable starts at the receiving area where items received are checked against the invoice and entered on the receiving report. After being approved, the purchase information is punched on cards which have been prepunched with the vendor's name and code. At the same time, another card could be punched with the purchase information to adjust inventory records. The computer can extend items, verify the totals of invoices, provide a control figure to compare with an adding machine tape of purchases for the periods, calculate purchase discounts, update vendor files, and prepare control reports. Inventory figures can also be updated by the purchases, and an analysis of purchases may also be prepared.

CASH REQUIREMENTS STATEMENT

Purveyor	Number	Due Date	Invoice Amount	Discount	Net Amount

Figure 2

Accounts Receivable. Most food service operations have limited accounts receivable, since payment at the time of service is the general custom. If customer accounts receivable are a major factor, however, they may be handled by a computer. Besides maintaining records of individual and total accounts receivable, the computer can age the accounts, follow up delinquent accounts, prepare statements when required, and audit the accounts. Information from the receivables file may also be used for sales analysis purposes.

Figure 3 depicts one format for aging the accounts receivable. Each account is given a credit limit and the computer records any balance in excess of this limit.

Menu Planning. Computers can help cost menus, analyze nutritional content, and write special diets, and computers save time that is normally spent writing out menus manually.

The computer can be fed such menu information as the food cost per serving, nutritional values, and customer preferences. Using this information it can then print out a number of menus all contained within the desired cost and nutritional limitations. The manager or dietitian can choose the menu considered most desirable, but may make changes, for example, to balance colors or to make use of leftovers. The computer can then recalculate costs and nutritional qualities incorporating the changes. The computer can also be programmed to limit the frequency with which items will appear on the menu.

For a commercial operator with a varied and regularly changing menu, the main advantage in using computers for menu planning is their ability to cost the menus.

For the dietitian or hospital food service manager, the computer not only offers its menu costing potential but also plays a beneficial role when it comes to nutritional calculations. It can perform a nutritional analysis for every regular diet, and it can readily prepare diets with special nutritional constraints.

Menu Precosting. Costing the items served is desirable for both menu pricing and control, but it is very difficult to keep cost records current. Changes in the purchase prices of items and recipe ingredients· occur frequently, and many operations cannot keep their cost calculations up to date. When provided with purchase price changes, the computer with standard recipes in memory can readily record these changes and keep item and recipe costs current. When a requisition is processed through the computer, it can be automatically priced. Recipes can be similarly priced; moreover, they may be specifically priced for the quantity to be produced even though it may not conform to the standard recipe yield.

AGED ACCOUNTS RECEIVABLE TRIAL BALANCE

Account Number	Customer Name	Balance	Current	30–60 Days	60–90 Days	Over 90 Days	Credit Limit	Credit Excess
1234	Abrams, Levi	220.00	220.00				500.00	
1235	Adams, Louis	500.00	150.00	150.00	100.00	100.00	450.00	50.00
Total		5,675.00	3,750.00	1,600.00	400.00	200.00		275.00

Figure 3

With this ease of costing it becomes considerably more feasible to use standard costs as a control rather than just a food cost percentage. The latter measures only the relationship between cost and sales. The former allows comparison of actual costs with the costs that were determined by precosting. The difference indicates how much money could be saved with better control.

The ease of precosting also aids menu pricing. Too often menu prices are based on cost "guestimates" rather than on the more exact food costs that can be determined by a computer.

With more exact menu precosting and an average labor cost determination, it would be possible to determine the approximate profit for every meal or for any other fiscal period. (A certain amount or percentage would, of course, have to be allocated for overhead and other expenses.)

Another advantage of the computer's ability to precost menus is that menus can be readily precosted ahead of the serving date. If costs are out of line for budget standards or selling prices, it is then possible to make corrections before actually serving the menu. Instead of being forced to take correctional action later, the cost problems can be minimized before they occur.

Controlling Purchasing. For purchasing, the computer may be programmed to print out a list of items needing reordering when the amounts on hand reach predetermined reorder points. It is possible to use the computer to determine the most effective reorder point on the basis of usage and times required for delivery. Instead of a par stock approach, the computers can print out purchase lists indicating replacement only of the goods consumed. If desired, the computer could print out a record of past orders for the item indicating the purveyor and price paid. The computer may also be programmed to prepare and address an actual purchase order for the item. Perhaps in the future all purchasing may be accomplished by allowing an operation's computer to "talk" with its purveyor's computer, thereby eliminating manual operations or fallible human judgment in deciding purchase orders.

Computers may be instructed to print out a list of items that have not been requisitioned from the storeroom for a month or for any other period. This practice is helpful in indicating possible loss from items that are kept in storage too long.

With a computerized perpetual inventory, it is possible to determine the amount and value of any inventory item or class of items, and the total inventory. Computerization should help in determining the optimum inventory level for every item, and better purchasing should be possible in terms of size and frequency of purchases.

If perishable items are needed in constantly changing amounts that

DAILY REPORT

Meal	Sales	Food Cost	Percent	Direct Labor Cost	Percent	Gross Margin Amount	Percent	Overhead Amount	Percent	Profit (Before Taxes) Amount	Percent
Breakfast	xxx.xx	xxx	xx.x	xxx.xx	xx.x	xxx.xx	xx.x	xxx.xx	xx.x	xxx.x	xx.x
Lunch	xxx.xx	xxx	xx.x	xxx.xx	xx.x	xxx.xx	xx.x	xxx.xx	xx.x	xxx.x	xx.x
Dinner	xxx.xx	xxx	xx.x	xxx.xx	xx.x	xxx.xx	xx.x	xxx.xx	xx.x	xxx.x	xx.x

must often be ordered at the last minute, the computer's purchasing function is limited. However, once the food is purchased, the computer can be helpful in analyzing the costs of these items and in maintaining the inventory records.

Controlling Food Inventory. A more positive control of food inventory records has long been desired by food service operators. Perpetual inventories using manual techniques to provide better control have been used by some organizations. However, the amount of work and financial cost involved has greatly limited the feasibility of such systems. Human errors in posting reduce the accuracy of the records. Even if a current inventory count is maintained, it is difficult to correlate this information with purchasing requirements. Unless inventory records are current, they are useless.

Electronic data processing can process inventory data and prepare current, meaningful reports quickly. To accomplish this, a unit of requisition would first be determined. This unit of requisition is the smallest unit of the amount that is ever issued—pounds or ounces or the size of the container or box. The requisition unit could be different from the purchase unit. Flour, for example, could be purchased in 100-pound bags, but requisitions could be in pounds or even ounces. Canned goods are usually purchased by the case, but issues could be by the can or even by a portion of a can. A conversion factor makes it possible for the computer to convert purchase costs into requisition costs so the value of both incoming purchases and outgoing issues can be considered in updating current inventory value. Each item in stock or every numbered item could have its own supply of prepunched computer cards. These could be kept with the item at the place of storage. When an item is requisitioned, the quantity, date, and requisitioning department would be filled in on the card that had been prepunched to identify the item. These cards are fed into the computer which automatically reduces the quantity and value of the item's inventory in its memory unit. When purchases are received, the amounts of each item are put on cards that accordingly increase the inventory figures in the memory unit. For pricing purposes, the computer could use the latest cost, original purchased cost, or an average cost, which is determined from the costs of a predetermined number of the latest purchases of the various items.

Input devices other than punched cards, like programmed keyboards, may be used to send the information to the computer. Necessary input information could also be taken from the receiving report or requisitions.

Only quantities need to be given to the computer, which, by having purchase prices in its memory, can calculate the value of merchandise on hand. However, even with a computerized perpetual inventory, it is desirable to take periodic physical inventories. Material differences between the computerized and physical inventory should be investigated.

In determining the cost of goods sold for the profit and loss statement, the value of issues from the computer could be used rather than opening and closing inventories.

If a physical inventory is taken, the computer may still be helpful in consolidating quantities stored in different areas and in calculating the values of the various items and of the total inventory.

Figure 4 gives the format for one type of inventory report. Not only does it take into account amounts on hand in the ending inventory figures, it also shows amounts that have been used in the cost of sales figures.

Food Issuing. Much supervisory time can be spent on the clerical job of preparing requisitions. The requisitions are often based on recipe yield amounts instead of on exact amounts that should be prepared based on forecasted consumption. This practice can lead to over- or underproduction.

Requisitions function as a control device, over food items issued, only when they are valid. However, controlling requisitions can cause a great deal of trouble. Quantities can be altered on them, and unauthorized requisitions can be filled.

EDP can eliminate much of the clerical work by producing requisitions using only the number of portions desired and the recipe number, if the recipes are stored in memory. It can designate the requisition for specific production items and quantities or combine all similar items required in one requisition. While it may be easy to falsify a written requisition form, it is more difficult to do so with a dated computer printout.

Food Production Control. A computer can be used in many ways to provide more effective control in food production, and the benefits may be both direct and indirect. One of the biggest potential benefits lies in the freeing of managerial and supervisory personnel from many routine time-consuming clerical duties. Rid of these duties, they may spend more time in production and patron areas; time previously spent on paper work may now be used to manage and supervise more effectively.

An indirect benefit in the installation of EDP comes from the systems analysis necessary for implementation of the system. Searching questions have to be asked about the operation that often suggest more efficient ways of accomplishing production.

For any EDP system to function properly in food production, standard recipes and standard portions must be used. Insistence on their use can, by itself, make an operation more efficient.

The computer can supply more information than was available previously, and it can also have it available in time to make production

INVENTORY REPORT

Item No.	Code	Description	Purchase Unit	Stock Unit	Begin Inventory Units	Begin Inventory Dollars	Purchases (Units)	Purchases (Dollars)	End Inventory Units	End Inventory Dollars	Cost of Sales (Units)	Cost of Sales (Dollars)
89	1	8 oz. Filet steak	lb.	lb.	12.00	24.00	40.00	100.00	22.00	55.00	30.00	69.00

Figure 4

changes. Instead of management's guessing production amounts, the computer can evaluate the basic factors that determine consumption and produce a more exact forecast. Instead of the old practice of requisitioning by standard recipe amounts, the computer can make requisitions for the exact amount necessary to be prepared.

Computer input can include forecasted production, menus, and recipes. (The computer may have earlier written the menu and determined production quantities.) The computer can print out requisitions for the production quantities of the menu items and their recipes. If a recipe produces 100 portions, and forecasted consumption is 168, the computerized requisition will be for quantities sufficient for 168. In many noncomputerized operations, probably twice the standard recipe of 100 portions would have been ordered, and the extra food for 32 patrons would present problems of usage.

Many operators determine production quantities in large measure by past experience. The resulting amount is usually based on considerations such as the day of the week, the consumption during the same period last year or last month, any external factors that might influence consumption, an allowance for general trends (such as sales being up or down), or the house count, if the operation is a hotel. There is no reason why these factors cannot be programmed for computerized forecasts. If food consumption is stable, like that in an institution, the computer can determine production quantities of each item on the basis of the past history of menu item usage.

An ingredient room system (which is thoroughly discussed in Chapter 7) can easily take advantage of EDP, since it combines the advantages of greater efficiency, control, and specialization with better forecasting and scheduling.

Because the recipes are already in the computer's memory, it is very easy for it to print copies when the food is being issued.

The computer can also keep in its memory the times required for preparation; moreover, it can schedule production and specify the times when it should begin and end. The computer could probably determine staffing requirements for each menu as well.

One food production report format is shown in Figure 5.

Food Cost Accounting Systems. From a food cost accounting system, management wants to determine if food costs are in line with the volume of business, the current selling prices, and budgetary constraints. The reports generated within a system must be current so that corrections can be made before unnecessary costs accumulate. (Food cost accounting is a system interdependent with other systems and subsystems such as precosting, inventory control, portion control, pricing, and menu writing.)

FOOD PRODUCTION REPORT

Menu Item Code	Menu Item Description	Number of Portions Sold	Number of Portions Prepared	Number of Portions Leftover	Cost of Leftover
10	Fresh fruit cup	48	50	2	.24
64	Roast turkey	59	65	6	1.56

Figure 5

Manual food cost accounting systems have several drawbacks. Producing the most complete and helpful reports requires a great deal of clerical time that many operations cannot afford. Even if this labor cost can be absorbed, there is usually a delay before the meaningful reports reach management and action can be taken. EDP can process food cost data cheaply and produce timely reports from it.

There are several types of general food cost accounting systems. A percentage system compares the cost of food to sales to produce a percentage food cost. The standard costs system precosts the food and determines what the food cost should be on the basis of the precosting. Actual costs are compared with the precosted or standard ones, and the difference or variance indicates the amount of potential savings. Another type of food cost accounting system can take the form of a budget where actual food costs are compared to a budgeted amount.

Percentage systems are most frequently utilized, probably because of their relative simplicity of operation. However, they show only the comparison of costs to sales, while standard costs provide a more effective control by showing the actual differences between projected costs and actual costs. But standard cost systems require a considerable amount of work to keep purchase prices current, in addition to the calculation of the standard costs themselves. EDP can be used to implement standard cost systems.

Formats for food cost accounting statements can be developed specifically for the individual operation depending on the type of information desired. Percentage systems often break down food costs into food categories. It is possible to calculate not only the total food cost percentage but the percentage for each of the categories as well. This extra calculation can be helpful in determining which category or categories of food items are pushing total costs out of line. A format for such a report analyzing the fish category is shown in Figure 6.

FOOD SALES
Fish Category
Period 11-21-7___ to 11-30-7___

L O C	G R P	C A T	Item No.	Description	On Hand	Unit Cost	Cost Extended
1	01	06	1001	Anchovies Canned	25.00	0.20	5.00
1	01	06	3002	Catfish Frozen	9.00	0.45	4.05
1	01	06	20935	Rainbow Trout	19.00	0.99	18.81

	10-DAY PERIOD	MONTH-TO-DATE
Beginning inventory	422.84	190.95
Purchases	103.60	1,107.93
Ending inventory	266.47	266.47
Cost of sales	259.97	1,032.41
Sales (group)	10,848.35	36,476.60
Ratio of cost to sales	2.3	2.8

Figure 6

This format, developed by Dr. Thomas Powers, shows that the ratio of fish costs to sales was 2.3 percent for the current 10-day period, and 2.8 percent for the month to-date. The number of food categories to be analyzed depends on the needs of the operation. Fourteen categories are sometimes used. Inventories are taken every 10 days, and reports are prepared every 10 days. The 10-day period allows corrective action to be taken in time to prevent any accumulation of losses. Similar reports are prepared for the other categories, and a combined percentage is also prepared.

The preceding format necessitates a physical inventory. Although EDP can expedite pricing, extending, footing, and preparing the inventory statement, the items must still be actually counted. For daily statements, or for other frequent statements, food costs may be calculated on the basis of food issued or food sent to the preparation units. Of course, this calculation will not show if food is being wasted on a daily basis, but it can indicate if food costs are in line with sales. Figure 7 gives a format for this type of statement.

In this example, prime units are the total number of the prime ingredient that have been used: 1480 ounces of roast beef. Other costs refer to the nonprime food ingredients that are included in the selling price, such as the potato, other vegetables, and the salad.

SUMMARY OF SALES AND POTENTIAL COST

Menu Item	Selling Price	Code	Total Servings	Total Sales	Total Prime Units	Total Prime Costs	Total Other Costs	Total Cost	Cost per Dollar of Sale
Prime ribs	5.50	30	80	440.00	1480	96.00	36.00	132.00	30.00¢
Chopped steak	2.80	42	40	112.00	320	18.00	12.00	30.00	26.79¢
Total food sale				1,000.00		200.00	100.00	300.00	30.00¢

Figure 7

223

Standard cost systems require that a periodic value of inventory be determined so actual food costs can be compared to the projected costs, which are determined by multiplying standard costs per item by the number of items served. It is possible to derive totals of actual costs and standard costs for all foods served during a period and also standard and actual costs for each specific food item. The inventory determines how much of the food item was utilized from this figure, and the resulting actual cost may be calculated. Figure 8 provides one possible format for utilizing standard costs.

It would also appear to be feasible to develop a food cost accounting system based on the sales value of food. Every food or recipe item would have a sales value, and actual sales could be compared to the sales values of the foods used. One complexity to overcome, however, is that a food item may be used in different menu items and have a different sales value for each item.

Another approach to food cost accounting is the quantity approach, where the quantity of various items issued is compared with the quantities of the items sold as shown by guest checks. This approach has been attempted manually, but the voluminous record keeping usually proves to be too cumbersome. EDP should be able to surmount the difficulties encountered by the manual methods. First, management must analyze guest checks to determine the quantities of the various items sold. In some cases different size portions may be served, like a smaller one for lunch compared to dinner, or a larger portion for a la carte. However, the percentage of lunch, dinner, a la carte, and other type portions should be fairly consistent. A weighted standard portion could then be determined. All portions served would be converted to the standard ones, and the number of these standard portions could be compared to the number of standard portions issued as determined through an analysis of requisitions and menu item recipes. A difficulty may arise with food issued one day but kept in the kitchen inventory for an additional day. This discrepancy

STANDARD COST ANALYSIS

Menu Item	Code	Total Servings	Total Prime Units	Total Prime Costs	Total Actual Cost	Variance (Over)	Variance (Under)
Prime Ribs	30	80	1480	96.00	101.00	5.00	
Chopped Steak	40	40	320	18.00	19.00	1.00	

Figure 8

in issues and consumption can be handled by comparing the issues and consumptions for a number of days. If the specified number were seven, the computer would keep totals for seven days. Every day it would add the latest, or current, day's figure into the counts and drop the figures from the last, or eighth, day. Not only would this system provide a positive control by showing discrepancies between issuing and consumption, but the issues could also be compared and reconciled with purchases (with inventory fluctuations), and consumption could be compared and reconciled with sales figures as well.

Guest Check Control. Guest check control under manual conditions often consists of auditing for missing checks, occasionally spot checking arithmetic, and comparing the total of guest check sales with cash register readings. In some operations, guest check control is one of the first items to be neglected when the office staff is busy.

EDP can be used to provide faster and more complete guest check control with only a little labor. While using the data on checks for cost and sales analysis, the computer can determine if any checks are missing. A report, such as that shown in Figure 9, lists the numbers of missing checks. If the numbers on the checks issued to serving personnel are recorded, it is easy to determine the person who lost a check.

In analyzing the sales value of menu items served, it is possible to see if there are mathematical errors, errors in pricing, or items omitted, since the sales values recorded by the computer for each serving person should equal the total of his or her guest checks. If there is a significant difference, the checks can be audited to find the nature of the variance, whether it be an addition error, a price transcription error, or an error of omission.

The computer can also calculate the sales tax on food and beverage sales, provide sales totals for each server, and provide a total for all servers to compare with amounts actually received or charged.

By comparing the totals of the guest checks with the sales value of

CHECK SEQUENCE AUDIT	
Check Number	**Status of Check**
10001	Start
10064	Missing
10089	Void
10184	Missing

Figure 9

food issued from the kitchen, cash register readings and, if desired, the amount of the daily bank deposit, EDP can provide a most effective control over guest checks.

Figure 10 shows a format for a restaurant check audit using EDP. Each check is shown by number, and if it involves a charge, the charge group is indicated. The serving person, the number of covers on the check, and the total figure of the check are also shown. The computer will calculate the appropriate sales tax. The sales tax and the tip are added to the total to produce a settlement figure. The actual settlement, whether cash or charge, is shown, and any difference is noted. This format is very useful in comparing check totals with the sales value of the items on the checks, which are given to the computer and shown on the settlement column. Any discrepancy in pricing is revealed. The cashier's report of sales tax should agree with the computer's amount. This comparison may be helpful regarding sales tax reports. If a mistake is made in arithmetic, it would show up in a difference in the settlement amounts. The form can also be used to verify cash sales to bank deposits and charge sales to accounts receivable.

Sales Analysis (For Personnel); Personnel sales analysis is helpful in determining:

a. Whether the proper number of personnel are on duty at the proper time.
b. Who the best sales personnel are in terms of the sales volume they generate.
c. Whether standards of service, as judged by personnel on duty, are being maintained.
d. What the sales output per labor cost input is.

A "Daily Period Analysis," which shows dollar sales and customers for various periods, is very helpful in personnel analysis. The periods chosen are those appropriate for the operation: every half hour, or every two- or three-hour periods, for example. Once a definite average sales figure per employee-hour is chosen as a goal, it is very easy to determine the number of employees that should have been on duty by dividing sales by the sales per employee-hour figure. This calculation can be done automatically by the computer with the format shown in Figure 11. This analysis could show whether personnel time was appropriate for the sales volume from the standpoints of both cost and adequacy of service. The operation utilizing a Daily Period Analysis wants every employee hour to yield $12 in sales. It has broken 12 hours down into 12 hourly periods.

It is possible for the computer to forecast volume in advance of the period. At the same time, it could determine hourly labor requirements. These, in turn, could guide the scheduling of employees.

RESTAURANT CHECK AUDIT

Check Number	Accounts Receivable	Waitress Number	Covers	Sales	Tax	Tip	Required Settlement	Actual Settlement Cash	Actual Settlement Charge	Difference
10001	Diners	12	6	21.00	1.26	4.00	26.26		26.26	
10002		12	4	24.00	1.44		25.44	25.40		(.04)
Total diner sales			100	350.00	22.96	40.00	412.96	211.00	200.00	(1.96)

Figure 10

227

DAILY PERIOD ANALYSIS

Period	Sales per Period	Hourly Sales Goal	Desired Employee (Hours/Period)	Actual Employee (Hours/Period)	Variance Over	Under
1	80	12.00	6.67	6.25		0.42
2	60	12.00	5.00	5.75	0.75	
12	900	12.00	75.00	77.50	2.50	

Figure 11

Figure 12 represents another form of the Daily Period Analysis. It shows hourly sales for a 12-hour day in dollars and in number of customers along with the number of checks, the check average, and the hourly seat turnover. Labor costs are broken down into the classifications of service, preparation, and sanitation. It is possible to compare sales with these costs to determine sales output per labor cost input, and it would be possible to compare these actual labor costs with labor cost percentages desired for these categories.

Another operation might desire a form such as a "Server Production Report" for its personnel sales analysis. A sample format is shown in Figure 12A.

With this report, which in this case has been prepared for an operation serving both food and beverages, but could be used for one serving only food, it is possible to see which personnel are doing the best selling jobs in terms of the highest average check (in this case per-cover, not per-party) for both food and beverages. The number of covers informs management whether its scheduling of waitresses correlates with its desired service standards. In using this format, one must recognize that the rotation of stations and the particular shift the server works may be reflected in different average checks and numbers of customers served.

EDP can also produce an analysis of the menu items served by each waitress, sales for each waitress per man-hour worked, and the percentage of her sales compared to total sales for the period.

Sales Analysis. It is usually desirable to have immediate information on the numbers of each item sold. This information is useful for forecasting, ordering, and cost control. EDP can provide many variations in menu sales analysis and provide the specific information desired by the opera-

DAILY PERIOD ANALYSIS

Period	Sales per Period	Customers per Period	Checks per Period	Average Check	Seat Turnover	Labor Cost per Period		
						Service	Preparation	Sanitation
1	80.00	40	20	4.00	.20	7.00	12.00	6.00
2	60.00	24	12	5.00	.12	6.00	11.00	6.00
12	50.00	30	15	3.00	.15	5.00	4.00	8.00
Total	900.00	480	300	3.00	2.45	90.00	140.00	80.00

Figure 12

SERVER PRODUCTION REPORT

Waitress Number	Covers	Food Sales	Beverage Sales	Average Food Check	Average Beverage Check
1	40	120.00	40.00	3.00	1.00
2	36	117.00	40.00	3.25	1.11
10	30	75.00	24.00	2.50	0.80
Total	300	900.00	360.00	3.00	1.00

Figure 12A

tion. Often the sales analysis report has cost data incorporated in it. One type of report showing the appetizer items is illustrated in Figure 13.

This example depicts the sales breakdown for appetizers (Type A), but the same analysis could be performed on entrees, vegetables, salads, desserts, breads, beverages, or any other food category.

If desired, it is possible to include in the sales analysis the number of servings of a particular item sold in prior periods and also the percentage of that item sold compared to the total items in the same menu.

SALES ANALYSIS

Item Number	Description	Price	Type	Portion Cost	Item Sales	Sales Total	Number Served
01	Chicken soup	0.30	A	0.20	9.00		30
02	Fruit cup	0.50	A	0.30	14.00		28
03	Tomato juice	0.30	A	0.10	3.60		12
04	Shrimp cocktail	1.00	A	0.45	14.00		14
						40.60	84

Figure 13

Kitchen Planning. The layout of the kitchen is critical to the success of a food service operation. Not only does the physical equipment represent a considerable investment, but built-in labor costs due to a poor layout can also be a constant drain on potential profits. Moreover, poor arrangement of equipment may cause slow service to patrons. A kitchen layout is by nature rather fixed, and it is difficult to make major changes once the equipment is installed. Thus, a trial and error approach to kitchen design simply will not do.

Computers are now being used to solve problems concerned with work analysis and design that must be surmounted to produce an efficient kitchen layout. It is possible to program information on the production sequence into the computer and have it produce a layout design that reduces to a minimum the movement of employees between the various pieces of equipment.

A prime tool for layout planning is a work flow chart showing the flow of work between stations. Work flow may be considered in two parts: one is the movement of employees between work stations; the other is the flow of materials between work areas. The less movement of either employees or materials, the more efficient the work area. Information regarding the number of times a menu item is produced each month, the production sequence (or, the order of movement of materials from one piece of equipment to another for the menu item in question), the frequency of movement of employees from the various pieces of equipment, and possible arrangements of equipment is collected. From this information, the computer can determine the best travel index (the product of the frequency of movement of employees and materials times the distance moved). The lower the travel index, the greater the kitchen efficiency.

General industry has evolved computerized techniques for developing and evaluating alternative layouts. Input data can consist of flow information, frequency of materials handling calculations, cost data, and the existing (or proposed) block layout of equipment or work production centers. Costs of various arrangements can be determined to aid in the selection of the layout to be used. Since different arrangements can be evaluated, the final plans can be based on a careful analysis and comparison of a large number of alternative layouts. This approach makes possible more experimentation than has been practical before, and this experimentation can be performed before detailed plans are produced. More effort can then be spent on preparing final plans at lower costs.

Computers can also be used to calculate the cost for various types of fuels. These calculations can indicate not only which fuel is most economical but will also aid in the selection of cooking equipment.

FAST FOOD OPERATIONS

Franchised, fast food operations can often utilize EDP effectively. Their characteristics—limited menus, uniformity of operation, high volume, many outlets, and limited on-site management—lend themselves to computerized control and supervision.

For example, it may be possible for a fast food operation to eliminate regular guest check procedures. An attendant, who may also be the cashier, stations himself at a keyboard with buttons for each menu item offered. While the customer places the order, the cashier pushes the appropriate button on the keyboard. This system can produce an order for the preparation section and a bill or receipt for the customer. When the item button is pushed, the machine automatically prices and extends the various items and provides a total charge for the order. Taxes and the customer's change can also be calculated automatically. Provision can be made to accommodate transactions that cannot be accomplished by pushing item buttons.

As the order is recorded, the computer deletes the item from inventory. Purchase orders or requisitions can readily be prepared on a replacement basis by the machine. Since every menu item has a sales value, a very positive control is obtained by comparing total sales value for all items served with the actual cash receipts. A difference indicates that some food escaped, unpaid for. Inventory shortages become apparent when the amount on hand differs from the computerized inventory balances. Provisions in the processing programs allow for consideration of waste and nonsales usage.

Information from the computer may be transmitted through telephone wires, or by punched paper tape, or on cards to a central headquarters. If the information is transmitted by telephone wires, printouts of reports can be had whenever they are needed.

Since the computer can handle much of the bookkeeping, the manager can spend more time working with customers and personnel, unburdened by paper work. Such a system appears to offer considerable benefits in the areas of fast service, friendly management, comprehensive information, vigilant control, and cost savings.

chapter 14

Budgetary Control

The primary purpose of any commercial food operation is to earn the largest profit possible, while the nonprofit organization wants to provide for its patrons the best food and service that its financial resources permit. Good financial management is necessary to both goals, and a budget is a basic tool for proper financial management. Without some form of budgeting or financial planning, problems arise quickly: costs are excessive; the cash drain becomes too heavy for a balanced cash flow; the operation is liable to be caught in a profit squeeze when costs are rising without a compensatory selling price increase; or provisions for major or capital improvements do not get made. A planned budget is vital to anyone considering the feasibility of a new operation, as well as to anyone interested in maintaining a going business.

WHAT IS A BUDGET

There are many definitions of the term "budget." Here is a convenient one: "An organized plan of operation for a specified period of time which forecasts activity and income, determines expenses and other disposition of funds, and concludes with an estimate of an overall financial position at the end of the specified period." A budget is a plan, often in chart form, of how one expects to perform during a specified period. It coordinates financial factors, sales, and operating results. It forecasts (for a commercial operation) the amount of money that will be coming in; it determines how much should be disbursed; and it predicts what will be available at the end of the period. For an institution or operation without direct sales, a budget estimates expenses and, therefore, the necessary cash appropriation.

Besides being a plan for business operation, a budget is an important control device. It provides a basis for comparing actual operations with planned or desired results.

There are many kinds of budgets. One is the *overall financial budget* that coordinates every aspect of the operation. Components of this are *operating budgets*, which forecast, for example, sales activity and such expense categories as food and labor. A *cash budget* shows merely the inflow and outgo of funds and the amount on hand. An *equipment budget* indicates when it is financially feasible to purchase equipment, and it helps in deciding the priority of purchases. A *renovation, remodeling, and repair budget* provides for, surprisingly enough, renovation, remodeling, and repair.

Budgets are not limited to dollar expressions only. A *sales budget* can specify the number of meals an operator expects to serve as well as his dollar volume. A *labor budget* may be expressed in terms of the number of personnel, man-days, or man-hours required, as well as labor dollar costs.

ADVANTAGES OF BUDGETS

Budgets offer many advantages. From a practical standpoint they:

a. Provide a goal. (An operation that should do a $250,000 volume per year is not achieving its potential if it does only $220,000. In the budget process, a realistic goal is determined to provide incentive for both individuals and departments. If these goals do not exist, there may be little that will cause the individuals to go beyond routine performance or enable management to gauge performance.)

b. Provide a control device. (Expenses and needs have been determined in advance. Comparing actual costs with the predetermined ones reveals deviation from the predetermined standards.)

c. Establish a yardstick. (A budget allows you to plan your operation and measure the results. It is much better, for example, to discover, through your budget, a possible loss situation than to have the loss become apparent later when you are close to bankruptcy.)

d. Coordinate the organization. (To prepared a budget, one must consider all the aspects of his operation. Sales, expenses, personnel, and equipment needs must be coordinated. With an effective budget there is direction and less possibility of the interdepartmental confusion that occurs when departments work independently.)

e. Provide responsibility. (Besides providing goals for individuals and departments, the budget also places a responsibility on personnel to generate sales and to control costs. Everyone must do his part in conforming to the budget if it is to be effective.)

f. Help in planning. (By definition, a budget is a plan for the future. Forecasting the volume of activity helps determine what must be provided to meet this level of activity. Knowing the anticipated financial status of your operation is essential to planning future policies.)

g. Solve problems. (Besides the broad considerations, a budget is very helpful in many down-to-earth, pragmatic ways. Such problems as whether a disbursement can be afforded by the operation, what changes should be made in staffing, whether selling prices should be changed, and whose responsibility is a particular task are all answered in part by a good budget.)

DISADVANTAGES OF BUDGETS

Budgets have their price, however; and here are some of their disadvantages.

a. A good budget requires time to prepare, and time costs money. The preparation time can also take personnel away from their necessary management functions. Workable budgets are usually not a one-man job but require cooperation and coordination.

b. Budgets are based on forecasting, and the future cannot always be told readily. Factors may occur that were impossible to predict and that affect the budget and plans based on it considerably.

c. To be truly effective, the budget and budgeting process must have the support of the organization. Going through the motions of preparing and working with a budget, without really trying to utilize it, often results in a false sense of security. Sometimes the allocation of resources in the budget can cause difficulties within the organization, when, for example, various factions compete against one another for allocations.

d. A budget also requires that management make known its plans and goals, which, for various private reasons, it may not wish to do.

FACTORS TO CONSIDER IN BUDGET PREPARATION

Many budgets do not work well because of poor preparation and planning. Using a previous budget, or operating figures borrowed from the previous period with only casual hopeful adjustments for a new budget, can be more damaging than having no budget at all. Or, if a casual forecast of business volume is made and expenses are determined with pre-established percentages based on the sales, trouble can result. It is implied that these ratios are static, cannot be improved upon, and are not to be changed. But they are often misleading and sometimes overlook actual facts.

In larger operations, there is a budget officer, someone from operations research or the controller's office who is familiar with budget preparation and who is assigned this responsibility. Although the budget may require work and cooperation from many people, there should be one person assigned the responsibility (and authority) to carry through the budget preparation. In some operations there may even be a budget committee working with the budget project officer.

The first step in budget preparation is to ascertain the general level of income or activity—by individual departments, if there is more than one contributing to this activity. Once the level of activity is determined, appropriate costs for this level can be established. Various departments may prepare their own cost estimates, and the budget official may participate in these deliberations. Then the budget official combines and coordinates the estimates from the various sections. He also prepares the cash budget that covers the whole operation and depends on the general budget. He submits the combined budget to top management or to the owners; and they may demand changes. Their desires must be resolved, and the completed budget must, of course, be finally approved by them.

It is very helpful to have a budget timetable indicating when budget work should start and when the deadlines for the various phases occur. Otherwise, preparation may be put off until the last minute. A budget developed under the pressure of time may not be well thought out or reflect the desired cooperation and coordination among those affected by it. The results often create disappointment or discontent. It is better for the completion of a yearly budget to occur several months before the beginning of the budgeted year.

Budgets may cover various periods, but the budget prepared for a forthcoming fiscal, or business, year is most common. It is usually preferable to break down the year by weeks and/or months first, and then add the periods together to determine a total budget for the whole year. In a yearly budget, some fixed expenses and some fixed income may be divided by 12 (or whatever the periods of activity) for the breakdown. But other budget categories will vary according to the number of days or weekends or holidays in the month, and these should be calculated separately for each month.

It is possible to make appropriate changes in the budget once the budget period has begun to increase the budget's accuracy over the remainder of the period. A steep rise in food purchase costs, for example, may necessitate higher menu selling prices, and the budgeted sales and food costs would have to be adjusted.

Budgets may be fixed or flexible. The fixed budget is based on a definite level of sales or activity, while a flexible budget provides cost information for differing levels of sales activity. The cost percentages may differ for different sales volumes. Thus, labor costs might be 28 percent of sales at a monthly sales volume of $15,000 but 26 percent at $25,000 monthly sales volume.

In order to provide accurate forecasts of sales and expenses, it is necessary to know the operations of the particular department thoroughly. Some useful knowledge to collect while budget making follows.

The department's actual operating and budget variance figures from previous years.

The department's goals.

The department's sales experience, sales reports, and sales statistics.

The department's future operating policies.

National and local economic conditions.

Sales and expense trends.

Menu prices, customer selection, portion sizes, and food cost per portion.

Such payroll statistics as the number of employees, their duties, their hours, and their wage rates.

Figure 1 shows a budget format for a seaside restaurant, owned by two partners, that has considerable seasonal and monthly fluctuations. Monthly food sales range from $2640 in December to $20,460 in July, and they total $113,520 for the budget year. Beverage sales range from $884 in December to $6851 in July, and they total $38,013 for the year. Factors influencing the forecasting of beverage sales include past percentages of beverage sales to food sales, the number and dollar value of drinks served per food cover, and seasonal fluctuations in beverage consumption. This operation wants food and beverage costs to be 40 and 30 percent of food and beverage sales, respectively. There are both cost and merchandising factors to be considered in determining these percentages. The cost considerations involve how much food the partners can provide for the desired selling price and whether this amount will be commensurate with the quality and quantity their customers want. Merchandising considerations involve determining the highest price patrons will readily pay for the food and service provided. In the expense categories, some items, such as payroll and direct expenses, vary according to sales. To determine the payroll cost, it is necessary to estimate the number of employees needed and their cost for various customer volumes. In Figure 1, this cost works out, on a percentage basis, this way.

Payroll Cost Percentage	Sales Dollar Volume per Month
32 percent	less than $6000
30 percent	$6000 to $12,000
28 percent	over $12,000

SEASHORE RESTAURANT BUDGETED PROFIT AND (LOSS)

	January	February	March	April	May	June
Sales						
Food	3,300	4,950	6,600	8,250	9,900	13,200
Beverage	1,105	1,658	2,210	2,763	3,315	4,420
Total sales	4,405	6,608	8,810	11,013	13,215	17,620
Cost of sales						
Food	1,320	1,980	2,640	3,300	3,960	5,280
Beverage	332	497	663	829	995	1,326
Total cost of sales	1,652	2,477	3,303	4,129	4,955	6,606
Gross profit	2,753	4,131	5,507	6,884	8,260	11,014
Controllable expenses						
Payroll	1,410	1,982	2,643	3,304	3,700	4,934
Direct	264	396	529	661	793	1,057
Utilities	250	250	250	250	250	250
Advertising	100	100	100	100	100	100
Repairs and maintenance	200	200	200	200	200	200
Administrative	200	200	200	200	200	200
Total controllable expenses	2,424	3,128	3,922	4,715	5,243	6,741
Operating profit	329	1,003	1,585	2,169	3,017	4,273
Noncontrollable expenses						
Occupation expenses	500	500	500	500	500	500
Interest expenses	32	43	54	54	54	54
Profit before depreciation	(203)	460	1,031	1,615	2,463	3,719
Depreciation	360	360	450	450	450	450
Amortization	200	200	200	200	200	200
Profit before taxes	(763)	(100)	381	965	1,813	3,069

Figure 1

Such expenses as repairs and maintenance or administration may be spread out equally during the year. Although different amounts for these expenses may have to be paid during different months, it is often impractical to break these costs down to correlate directly with sales.

Figure 2 shows the cash budget for the Seashore Restaurant. It shows only the amount of money coming in and the amount that has to be dis-

SEASHORE RESTAURANT BUDGETED PROFIT AND (LOSS) (cont.)

July	August	September	October	November	December	Total
20,460	20,460	13,860	6,600	3,300	2,640	113,520
6,851	6,851	4,641	2,210	1,105	884	38,013
27,311	27,311	18,501	8,810	4,405	3,524	151,533
8,184	8,184	5,544	2,640	1,320	1,056	45,408
2,055	2,055	1,392	663	332	265	11,404
10,239	10,239	6,936	3,303	1,652	1,321	76,812
17,072	17,072	11,565	5,507	2,753	2,203	94,721
7,647	7,647	5,180	2,643	1,410	1,128	43,628
1,639	1,639	1,110	529	264	211	9,092
250	250	250	250	250	250	3,000
100	100	100	100	100	100	1,200
200	200	200	200	200	200	2,400
200	200	200	200	200	200	2,400
10,036	10,036	7,040	3,922	2,424	2,089	61,720
7,036	7,036	4,525	1,585	329	114	33,001
500	500	500	500	500	500	6,000
54	54	51	49	46	44	589
6,482	6,482	3,974	1,036	(217)	(430)	26,412
450	450	450	450	450	450	5,220
200	200	200	200	200	200	2,400
5,832	5,832	3,324	386	(867)	(1,080)	18,792

Figure 1 (continued)

bursed (the cash flow). The difference between inflow and outflow of funds is usually not the same as the profit figure for the period. Depreciation cost, for example, is an expense item, but it does not require an immediate outlay of cash. The restaurant depicted in the example has suffered from a severe shortage of working capital. It will, however, start its fiscal year with a line of credit that will allow it to borrow necessary funds. The

SEASHORE RESTAURANT CASH BUDGET

	January	February	March	April	May
Opening balance	520	1,009	1,029	1,080	1,715
Sources of cash					
Sales	4,405	6,608	8,810	11,013	13,215
SBA loan	6,400	2,200	2,100	–	–
Total	11,325	9,817	11,939	12,093	14,930
Applications of cash					
Food	5,528	1,320	1,980	2,640	3,300
Liquor	332	497	663	829	995
Payroll	1,410	1,982	2,643	3,304	3,700
Direct	264	396	529	661	793
Repairs and maintenance	500	500	140	140	140
Other controllable	550	550	550	550	550
Other	–	–	–	–	–
Mortgage amortization	–	–	600	–	–
Mortgage interest and taxes	500	500	500	500	500
SBA interest	32	43	54	54	54
SBA principle	–	–	–	–	–
Equipment loan	–	–	2,000	500	500
To partners	1,200	1,200	1,200	1,200	1,200
Total	10,316	8,788	10,859	10,378	11,732
Closing balance	1,009	1,029	1,080	1,715	3,198

Figure 2

budget was very helpful in obtaining the line of credit, since it demonstrated that loans could be easily repaid with cash generated.

An operation that makes an overall profit may still be short of cash and need additional funds at some period or other. In January, our Seaside Restaurant generated $4405 in sales and received $6400 in loan proceeds. These two amounts, with the opening balance of $520, made $11,325 in cash available. Applications of $10,316 in cash—including $600 to each partner— leave a cash balance of $1009 at the end of the month. Repairs and maintenance expenses of $2400, which were divided into twelve equal monthly amounts, are now budgeted to show when the $2400 actually will be disbursed. Cash payments are shown when they actually will be paid, not when the obligation was incurred. Thus, if food bills are paid the month after the food purchase, the cash paid will be shown for that following month. In the general budget, the food cost was shown the month it was incurred, rather than when it actually was paid, to provide a true profit and loss figure.

SEASHORE RESTAURANT CASH BUDGET (cont.)

June	July	August	September	October	November	December
3,198	4,997	12,743	17,585	16,179	31,171	9,494
17,620	27,311	27,311	18,501	8,810	4,405	3,524
20,818	32,308	40,054	36,086	24,989	17,576	13,018
4,960	5,280	8,184	8,184	4,544	2,640	1,320
1,326	2,055	2,055	1,392	663	332	265
4,934	7,647	7,647	5,180	2,643	1,410	1,128
1,057	1,639	1,639	1,110	529	264	211
140	140	140	140	140	140	140
550	550	550	550	550	550	550
—	—	—	—	—	—	—
600	—	—	600	—	—	600
500	500	500	500	500	500	500
54	54	54	51	49	46	44
—	—	—	500	500	500	500
500	500	500	500	500	500	500
1,200	1,200	1,200	1,200	1,200	1,200	1,200
15,821	19,565	22,469	19,907	11,818	8,082	6,958
4,997	12,743	17,585	16,179	13,171	9,494	6,060

Figure 2 (continued)

Usually the most difficult problem in preparing a budget is forecasting sales. This estimated sales figure is extremely important, since it is not only the largest figure and the basis for many other budget calculations, but it is also the goal for the period and the motivation for the whole operation. The planned sales figure should be realistic, but it should also provide the incentive to improve on the past. Therefore, past sales records showing the number of covers and average charge per cover must be examined. One should also discover what might be done within the operation itself to increase volume. For example, would advertising changes, renovations, better merchandising, and different pricings help? Outside influences, like local population and general prosperity levels, inflation trends, and new competition, can be equally important. All factors that influence volume must be appropriately weighed to estimate how the volume will change. This change is usually expressed as a percentage of the current year's level. However, one should hesitate to conclude that this volume, throughout the new year, will increase over the last year by a certain—say 5 percent. It would be better to expect the volume to be 7 percent higher in the budgeted year during the winter months and 2 percent higher during the summer months, even though the overall result may be the desired 5 percent.

It is also important to remember that sales dollar volume is composed of two factors: the number of covers and the average price per cover. In forecasting, one must estimate the number of covers that he can expect to serve. These estimates should be broken down according to meal periods (breakfast, lunch, and dinner), and the average check price should be determined for each meal period. Multiply the number of covers per meal period by the average check and add the meal periods together to find the sales volume. (The process is demonstrated in Figure 3.)

Sales volume may be calculated on a weekly basis and then on a monthly basis, as in Figure 4. Or instead of 12 months, 13 periods of four weeks may be used. The four-week periods allow the use of whole weeks, each with seven equal operating days; monthly calculations require the division of the last week. The four-week periods also permit accurate com-

BREAKDOWN OF SALES

Date	Meal	Number of Covers	Average Check	Total
Week of				
January 2	Breakfast	1,200	$1.25	$1,500
	Lunch	2,200	1.40	3,080
	Dinner	1,800	2.70	4,660
				$9,240

Figure 3

BREAKDOWN OF SALES

Month	Covers Last Year	Forecast Covers Budget Year	Food Sales Budget Year	Beverage Sales Budget Year	Total Sales Budget Year
January					
February					
December					

Figure 4

parison with the same four weeks from previous periods. Despite theoretical advantages of the four-week period, however, some operations have trouble converting from a monthly period to a four-week period.

ADDING FLEXIBILITY TO THE BUDGET

A budget should be a plan, a guide and a control, but not a rigid program; a budget which becomes unrealistic is quickly ignored. Forecasts may have to be changed despite the fact that they are basic to the plan of operation. It is easier to change your weather forecast than it is to change the weather. Supplemental figures may be prepared to show operations at other levels that are related to the forecasted ones. Sales, for example, can be calculated this way:

	90% of Budget	Budget	110% of Budget
Sales	$9000	$10,000	$11,000

Expense categories can then be correlated with the adjusted sales. Since the budget is really a goal, every effort should be made to reach (or surpass) its estimates.

An amended budget may be prepared during the budget year that offers realistic goals under current conditions, and a breakeven chart is especially helpful in determining costs at different sales volumes.

Figures 5 to 8 present a short, simplified method of preparing sales, food cost, and payroll budgets. Budget sales figures, shown in Figure 5, are determined partially on the basis of sales for the last four years. (Consideration, of course, has to be given to external and internal factors affecting the operation during the budget year.) Food cost ratios to sales for the four years are analyzed and potential and budget cost ratios determined in Figure 6. (The basic staff for additional business is also predetermined here.) Figure 8 permits actual figures to be compared with budgeted figures.

PROJECTION OF RESTAURANT SALES

Actual Sales

	Four Years Ago	Three Years Ago	Two Years Ago	Last Year	Budget
January	$ 48,300	$ 48,000	$ 48,700	$ 48,200	$ 48,500
February	50,800	50,900	50,300	50,700	51,000
March	52,700	53,200	52,700	52,800	53,000
April	55,200	54,900	55,600	55,500	56,000
May	57,900	58,100	58,200	57,900	58,500
June	51,300	51,500	51,600	51,400	52,000
July	47,300	47,900	48,100	46,000	48,000
August	42,600	42,900	43,000	45,000	44,000
September	47,700	47,800	47,100	47,600	48,000
October	50,100	50,900	51,100	50,700	51,000
November	52,300	52,600	52,900	53,200	54,000
December	55,400	55,900	55,100	57,100	56,000
Annual Sales	$611,600	$614,600	$614,400	$616,100	$620,000

Figure 5

ANALYSIS OF FOOD COST RATIO TO SALES

Food Cost Ratio to Sales

	Four Years Ago	Three Years Ago	Two Years Ago	Last Year	Budget
January	41.1%	40.3%	40.0%	40.4%	40.0%
February	39.8	39.8	39.7	40.1	39.5
March	39.3	39.3	39.4	39.7	39.5
April	39.1	39.6	39.1	39.3	39.0
May	38.7	38.8	38.5	38.7	39.0
June	39.5	39.7	39.9	39.4	39.5
July	40.3	41.8	40.2	40.1	40.0
August	42.0	42.8	41.9	41.2	41.0
September	39.1	40.1	41.0	40.0	40.0
October	39.6	39.6	39.1	39.5	39.5
November	39.8	39.4	39.5	39.2	39.5
December	39.2	38.8	39.1	38.7	39.0
Annual ratio	39.3%	39.7%	39.6%	39.7%	39.6%

Figure 6

PROJECTION OF PAYROLL

Position	Number of Employees	Average Month Wage	Total Month Payroll	
Manager	1	$1,400	$1,400	
Assistant Manager	2	750	1,500	
	3			$2,900
Preparation				
Chef	1	700	700	
Cooks	3	500	1,500	
Pantry Girls	3	320	960	
Potwasher and Porter	2	320	640	
	9			3,800
Sanitation				
Dishwashers	7	320	2,240	
	7			2,240
Service				
Hostesses	1.5	400	600	
Waitresses	14	250	3,500	
Bus Girls	4	250	1,000	
		19.5		5,100
General				
Storeroom	1	425	425	
Office Clerks	1	400	400	
Cashiers	1.5	400	600	
	3.5			1,425
		Total monthly payroll		$15,465

SALES	TOTAL MONTHLY PAYROLL		
Under $45,000	$15,465—Basic staff required Add:		
$45,000–50,000	16,035	1 dishwasher at	$320
		1 waitress at	250
$50,000–55,000	16,785	1 cook at	500
		1 waitress at	250
$55,000–60,000	17,605	1 dishwasher at	320
		1 waitress at	250
		1 bus girl at	250

Figure 7

COMPARATIVE SALES, FOOD COST, AND PAYROLL BUDGET

Month	Sales		Food Cost				Labor Cost			
			Budget		Actual		Budget		Actual	
	Budget	Actual	Amount	Ratio	Amount	Ratio	Amount	Ratio	Amount	Ratio
January	$48,500		$19,400	40.0%			$16,035	33.06%		
February	51,000		20,145	39.5			16,785	32.91		
March	53,000		20,935	39.5			16,785	31.66		
April	56,000		21,840	39.0			17,605	31.43		
May	58,500		22,815	39.0			17,605	30.09		
June	52,000		20,540	39.5			16,785	32.27		
July	48,000		19,200	40.0			16,035	33.40		
August	44,000		18,140	41.0			15,465	34.36		
September	48,000		19,200	40.0			16,035	33.40		
October	51,000		20,145	39.5			16,785	32.91		
November	54,000		21,330	39.5			16,785	31.08		
December	56,000		21,840	39.0			17,605	31.43		
	$620,000		$245,530	39.6%			$200,310	32.3 %		

Figure 8

chapter **15**

Management Decisions in Acquiring New Equipment

CAPITAL BUDGETING

Many subsidiary decisions present themselves when management decides to acquire new equipment. Should an expensive or inexpensive model be bought? Should new equipment be bought if some equipment is still functioning well? Should all of it be replaced? Will the new equipment pay for itself? If funds permit only one purchase, which piece of equipment should be secured? A new dishwasher? New ranges? How much money should be spent on modernization projects?

Efficient management decision making techniques can help with these problems. Economy studies, anticipated pay-back periods, anticipated rate of return analyses, and time value of money considerations can be employed to help place the proposed expenditures in a better perspective. However, these techniques can help only from the financial point of view; they cannot gauge such factors as customer satisfaction and employee cooperation. Anticipated results from using the techniques are only as accurate as the data used to calculate them, and this data may be hard to determine accurately. Furthermore, some money outlays do not lend themselves to this type of evaluation. A broken pavement, for example, must be repaired even though it will neither bring in new business nor cut costs.

ECONOMY STUDY

An economy study is a comparative analysis of the financial factors of two or more alternative programs to determine which would be economically advantageous. An economy study is often used to compare an existing procedure with possible innovations.

Figure 1 depicts an economy study for the replacement of rack-conveyer-type dishwashing equipment with flight-type equipment. An average of three workers, instead of four, could operate the new equipment, which has an expected life of 10 years, costs $12,000, installed, and has no expected salvage value at the end of the 10 years. The present equipment is still in good condition, has a net book value of $5000, and could be expected to last five more years. It could probably be sold now for $2000. The economy study considers fixed expenses like interest, depreciation, taxes, and insurance. These total $1275 for the present machine and $1860 for the proposed new machine. Operating expenses, which are largely labor, total $20,120 for the present machine and would total $15,940 for the proposed one.

ECONOMY STUDY
PROPOSED PURCHASE OF FLIGHT TYPE
DISHWASHING EQUIPMENT

	PROJECT A		PROJECT B
	Present Rack Conveyor		Proposed Flight Conveyor
Fixed Expenses			
Interest, 6% of $2,500			
(average value)	$ 150	6% of $ 6,000	$ 360
Depreciation, 20% of $5,000	1,000	10% of $12,000	1,200
Taxes and Insurance,			
5% of $2,500	125	5% of $ 6,000	300
	$1,275		$ 1,860
Operating Expenses			
Direct labor	$16,000		$12,000
Related labor costs 12%	1,920		1,440
Power and water	1,200		1,800
Supplies	600		600
Repairs and maintenance	400		100
	$20,120		$15,940
Total cost	$21,395		$17,800

A. Net annual savings before income taxes $ 3,595
B. Net annual savings after taxes (48% + 4.8 = 52.8%) 1,697
C. Net capital investment ($12,000 cost minus $2000 salvage) 10,000
D. Annual return on initial cash investment ($1,697 ÷ $10,000) 17%
E. Annual return on average investment ($1,697 ÷ $5,000) 34%

Figure 1

Based on these computations, the new machine would save, after income taxes, $1697 annually. This represents 17.1 percent annual return on the net capital investment of $10,000 ($12,000–$2000) in the new machine. Using the average investment figure of $5000 over 10 years, the annual return would be 34.0 percent.

Management should make studies of this nature continually, in order to remain competitive and maintain its annual earnings. In this example, the economy study was used to compare the replacement of equipment with a newer product. However, other factors, such as the ability of the new equipment to handle any increased sales, must be evaluated separately.

It is necessary to forecast future costs in preparing an economy study. All operating expenses for the various options should be included: payroll and related costs, utilities, interest on equipment, and maintenance and supplies. Depreciation presents a problem, since it is always difficult to estimate an actual effective life or the actual salvage value. A conservative approach is to ignore any salvage value and use instead, straight line depreciation, which is determined by dividing the value of the equipment by the number of years of useful life to give the depreciation per year. The value of the investment is usually decreasing constantly during its useful life, and in an economy study it is better to use the average value of the investment for interest cost considerations instead of the initial value. Here is a formula for computing the average value of the investment.

$$A = \frac{\text{Initial investment minus salvage value}}{2}$$

In Figure 1, the existing rack dishmachine has a book value of $5000 and should have five more years of useful life with no salvage value. Substituting the figures in the formula, the average value of the investment for interest computations becomes:

$$A = \frac{\$5000}{2}$$

$$A = \$2500$$

Dividing the expected useful life of five years into the present value of $5000 provides the straight line depreciation figure of $1000 a year.

The average cost of the new equipment would be:

$$A = \frac{\$12,000}{2}$$

$$A = \$\ 6000$$

The actual cost of the new equipment less any salvage value is used in

determining depreciation. The rate of depreciation is one over the anticipated useful life, which in this case is 10 years. On $12,000, this amounts
to $1200 per year.

Properly interpreted and used, the economy study can be very valuable in bringing the economic variables inherent in acquiring new equipment into focus. However, it should be used only as a guide and not as
the sole determinant since there may also be noneconomic intangibles.

ANTICIPATED PAY-BACK PERIOD

A technique for evaluating capital expenditures is to determine the
length of time it will take to recover the expenditure. Generally, the
shorter the pay-back period, the better the investment. An operation can
set standards for captal expenditures, such as requiring that they pay for
themselves within two, three, five, or some other specified number of
years. However, larger expenditures often require longer pay-back periods
than smaller ones, and a different standard should often be applied to
them. (It may be reasonable to expect a wash basin to pay for itself in
three years, but a new building will probably take far longer.) One formula for determining the pay-back period follows:

$$\text{Pay-back period} = \frac{\text{Cash or Cash Outlay for project}}{\substack{\text{Annual net income (or savings) from project} \\ \text{before depreciation but after taxes}}}$$

Using the net savings figure of $1697 from Figure 1, and adding back
net depreciation ($1200–$1000, or $200), one reaches the figure $1897.
Dividing this into the net cash outlay of $10,000, a pay-back period of
5.27, or about five years and three months emerges.

The actual cost of the project is sometimes used, but using only the
actual cash required is often a more practical approach. A project may
not be feasible if the entire cost must be paid when the equipment is
acquired. If the cost can be financed through savings from the project
itself and comparatively little cash is required for the initial payment, the
installation may then become both feasible and very desirable.

Tax considerations also influence the desirability of expenditures. If
additional income or profit must, in large part, be given up in taxes, the
new equipment may be less desirable and less justifiable than the old.

If the project brings in additional sales, this amount of additional sales
would be used to calculate the pay-back period; if the project cuts costs,
the amount saved would be used.

It is often hard to place dollar values on the benefits accrued from
improvements. What is redecorating the dining room worth in sales
potential? What is a remodeled employee lounge worth in employee satis-

faction? Both of these projects may be very desirable—even necessary—but it is difficult to put a quantitative value on such intangibles as these.

Income or savings may vary from year to year, and it is necessary to add up dissimilar amounts to determine the pay-back figure. The higher the immediate gain, the more desirable the project. A dollar received or saved today is worth more to the operation than a dollar received or saved two years from now. Also, a project may pay for itself in a short period but then produce comparatively little more profit. Another project may take longer to pay for itself, but it may continue after paying for itself to reap profits over a long period. The second project may be more desirable in the long run, but—on a pay-back period basis—the first project could be rated higher because of its performance during the first years.

ANTICIPATED RATE OF RETURN

A proposed capital expenditure may be evaluated by comparing the savings (or additional income) to the amount expended. One formula for making this comparison follows.

$$\text{Anticipated rate of return} = \frac{\text{Average additional income or savings generated by project (after taxes and depreciation)}}{\text{Average amount invested in project}}$$

Income taxes and depreciation reduce the true return from an investment, and they must be subtracted from the income, or the savings, figure. The value of the acquisition will generally decline during its life, so an average value should be used rather than the initial one. A new piece of equipment costs $10,000 and will last 10 years with no salvage value. Management expects to earn (or save) $1000 more (after taxes and depreciation) during each year of the useful life of the new equipment. than it would have earned (or saved) by operating the old equipment. The rate of return calculated on the initial outlay would be $1000/$10,000, or 10 percent. The average value of the equipment is $5000, and the rate of return on the average value of the equipment over its lifetime would be $1000/$5000, or 20 percent.

COST CATEGORIES

For management decision making, costs may be categorized differently than in conventional accounting or financial reporting. These different categories help provide a better understanding and evaluation of costs involved in decision making and can provide a broader cost perspective. Some of the categories used to analyze costs follow.

Relevant Costs. Relevant costs are those costs that are relevant to the proposed decision. If a cost is not changed by a possible alternative, it should not be considered in the analysis. If, for example, the labor cost remains the same under different options, it would not have to be considered. However, if an option affects the labor cost, it would then be relevant.

Sunk Costs. "Sunk costs" is the term denoting costs that have already been incurred and cannot be recouped by a new decision or alternative. Normally, sunk costs should not be considered in decision making. A common example is an installation cost that would have to be duplicated if the equipment, already installed, is subsequently replaced. The original cost of installation would be a sunk cost. Sunk costs can also be thought of as costs that will not be changed by a decision and are therefore irrelevant costs.

Opportunity Costs. Opportunity costs are the costs of the profit foregone when an opportunity is rejected. For example, a food service establishment may need both new kitchen and new dishwashing equipment, but may have resources enough to acquire only the kitchen equipment. The savings (or the profit) sacrificed by not securing the dishwashing equipment would be considered an opportunity cost. Often a decision depends on a choice between alternatives. One alternative may be selected over another because the anticipated profit or saving is greater than the opportunity costs of the other alternatives. This difference between chosen profit and the remaining opportunity costs is called the "incremental cost."

Incremental Cost. Incremental cost then is the difference in cost between one alternative and another. Considering two projects, A and B, the incremental cost would be the difference between profits or savings resulting from Project A and the profits or savings that would have been realized by implementing Project B. The decision maker may handle this calculation as Project A minus Project B or Project B minus Project A, as long as he is consistent and handles all cost items in the same manner. Incremental costs may thus be either positive or negative. In the example in Figure 2, all costs are handled on an incremental basis, Project B minus Project A.

TIME VALUE OF MONEY

We would all prefer to receive a sum of money today instead of the same amount at some future date. This is because a dollar possesses an earning

INCREMENTAL APPROACH
PROJECT B MINUS PROJECT A

	Project B	Project A	Incremental
Fixed expenses			
Interest expense	$ 360	$ 150	$ 210
Depreciation	1,200	1,000	200
Taxes and insurance	300	125	175
Total incremental fixed expenses			$ 585
Operating expenses			
Direct labor	$12,000	$16,000	$(4,000)
Related labor costs	1,440	1,920	(480)
Power and water	1,800	1,200	600
Supplies	600	600	—
Repairs and maintenance	100	400	(300)
Total incremental operating expenses			$(4,180)
Total net incremental expenses			$(3,595)

The ($3585) indicates a negative value to our incremental costs; in effect Project B will cost $3595 less than Project A, which agrees with our Net Annual Savings before income taxes (Line A) in Figure 1.

Figure 2

power that it exercises over a period of time, and the interest a dollar earns over a period adds to its value over that period. If the dollar is invested in a business asset, that interest income is sacrificed because the money is not earning interest. This lost interest income becomes an opportunity cost. When expressed as a percentage, this opportunity cost figure is often used as a minimum cost of capital, or the minimum return expected on the investment for an investment decision. The reason for considering this percentage as a minimum desired return on the investment is that the income (the return on investment) comes from a very low risk investment, in which both the return of the principàl and the interest income are largely assured. Business investments are usually not so free of risk, since future events can cause a business to suffer and negatively affect the investment. With these two factors in mind, an investor would normally choose a low risk investment, such as a savings account or bank certificates or even high grade bonds, unless the business investment promised a return commensurate with the risk involved.

The next two sections consider the time value of money. In both sections, the cash inflows and outflows are considered along with the timing of these inflows and outflows. This approach contrasts with the economy study approach, which used a financial accounting analysis. Figure 3 takes data used in the economy study presented in Figure 1 and handles it on a cash flow basis.

Tax Considerations. In the cash flow method, taxes have a considerable effect on business decision making. A basic role of thumb for determining the effect of taxes might to multiply a noncash expense by the tax rate to get the impact of the cash flow (the profit and depreciation expense) on your decision, and multiply a cash expense by one minus the tax rate (1−tax rate) to get the cash flow impact. A noncash expense has the effect of reducing taxable income; therefore, if an operation had such a noncash expense as a depreciation of $1000 under a particular alternative and a tax rate of 40 percent, the cash flow impact would be $1000 times 40 percent, or $400. This figure represents the increased cash available over the amount of the noncash expense because of the reduction in taxable income. A cash expense has the effect of reducing taxable profits by the amount of the expense times the tax rate. However, since it is a cash expense, where cash must be paid, the net cash flow effect is the expense less the tax reduction. For example, a cash expense of $1000 and a tax rate of 40 percent would yield $1000 times 40 percent, or a $400 reduction in taxes. However, since the firm has to pay the $1000 expense, the net effect is $1000 minus $400, or $600. This is equivalent to $1000 times (1−.40), or $600.

Another important aspect of the tax structure is the special tax rate that is applied to long term capital gains from the sale of capital assets. A business asset not held primarily for resale to customers in the ordinary course of business is considered a capital asset, and a gain on the sale of this asset is considered a capital gain. In a restaurant, the equipment used in the kitchen and dining room would be two examples of capital assets. The food inventory, on the other hand, would not be a capital asset, since it is resold to customers in the course of ordinary business transactions.

Cash Flow Example. Figure 3 depicts the yearly cash flows of Projects A and B. The first item is the interest expense, a cash expense, that has the effect of reducing taxable income and, in effect, reducing the actual amount of the expense. For example, the interest expense on Project A, which is $150, is reduced to $150 times (1−tax rate) or ($150×.472) or $70.80. Depreciation, the next expense item, is a noncash expense and has the effect of an inflow of cash, since it reduces taxable income and thus taxes but does not require any cash outlay. In Project A, depreciation of $1000 reduces taxes by $1000 times the tax rate, or ($1000×.528) or $528. The remainder of the expenses require cash outlays and are handled in the same manner as the interest expense. (It might be noted that the

PROJECT "A"

	Inflows	Outflows
Interest $150 × 0.472[a]		$ 70.80
Depreciation $1000 × 0.528[b]	$528.00	
Taxes and insurance $125 × 0.472		$ 59.00
Operating Expenses		
Direct labor $16,000 × 0.472		$7,552.00
Related labor costs $1920 × 0.472		$ 906.24
Power and water $1200 × 0.472		$ 566.40
Supplies—not a relevant cost		
Repairs and maintenance $400 × 0.472		$ 188.80
	$528.00	$9,343.24
Net Outflows		$8,815.24

PROJECT "B"

Interest $360 × 0.472		$ 169.92
Depreciation $1200 × 0.528	$633.60	
Taxes and insurance $300 × 0.472		$ 141.60
Operating Expenses		
Direct labor $12,000 × 0.472		$5,664.00
Related labor cost $1440 × 0.472		$ 679.68
Power and water $1800 × 0.472		$ 849.60
Supplies—not relevant cost		
Repairs and maintenance $100 × 0.472		$ 47.20
	$633.60	$7,522.00
Net Outflows		$6,918.40

Net outflows of costs for Project "A" minus net outflows of costs for Project "B" equals cash saving per year; if Project "B" is selected.

$$\$8,815.24 \text{ minus } \$6,918.40 = \$1,896.84$$

[a] 1 minus tax rate of 52.8 percent = 47.2 percent
[b] tax rate = 52.8 percent

Figure 3

cost of supplies is no longer included in the analysis, since that cost remains the same under both alternatives and is, therefore, not a relevant cost.) The analysis shows that the net outflows (outflows minus inflows) are greater in Project A ($8815.24) than in Project B ($6918.40) and thus, on a cash flow basis, Project B would save the firm $1896.84 and appears to be the better alternative. However, in order to receive this $1896.84 saving in each of the next 10 years, the firm must spend $12,000 now, and this expenditure involves a consideration of the time value of money. One approach for handling this consideration is the net present value method.

Net Present Value Method. The net present value of money can be determined by calculations or by using tables. The basic formula for finding the present value of a sum of money received at the end of number of years is

$$PV = \frac{FV}{(1+i)^n}$$

where:

PV = the present value of a future return
FV = the amount of the return received at the end of n years
  i = the desired return on the investment
  n = the number of years which will pass before the future return will be received.

Calculations using the formula can become complex if "n" becomes large. Tables have been calculated that give a factor that when multiplied by the future return will give its present value.

Table 1 gives these factors for common desired returns over a varying number of years. For example, an investor may wish to know the present value of a future payment of $500 to be received at the end of five years, with a desired return of 10 percent on the investment. By looking at Table 1, under the 10 percent column and along the row marked five years, he can find the present value factor. of .621. Multiplying .621 by the $500 gives a present value of $500 of $310.50. Thus, an investment of $310.50 now, giving an annual return on the investment of 10 percent, would equal the sum of $500 offered at the end of five years.

In the dishwasher economy study in Figure 3, Project B yielded a cash savings of $1896.84 per year on a cash flow basis. These savings would continue for five years or until the rack-type dishwasher wears out. However, if Project B (showing the flight-type dishwasher) is selected, there would still be five more years of useful life left after the rack-type dishwasher has been worn out. In order to decide whether the present value of the cash savings in Project B are greater than the investment cost, the decision maker must make some assumptions regarding the value of the remaining five years of life for the flight-type dishwasher. These decisions could be made in several ways; the decision maker could (1) assume that the rack-type dishwasher is replaced at the end of five years with a similar model and that the cash savings would therefore continue in the same amounts for another five years; or (2) use some estimated salvage value at the end of five years discounted back to its present value. For simplicity's sake, it is assumed in Figure 4 that the rack-type dishwasher (Project A) is replaced at the end of its life with another rack-type machine yielding equal savings and that these savings continued over the entire 10-year life of Project B.

The decision maker must also determine a desired rate of return on investment. This rate of return normally would be greater than the rate of return available from low risk investments and would be affected by the risk involved in the proposed investment and any effected loss in value from inflation. (For a more complete discussion on determining the cost of capital—desired rate of return—the reader is referred to a book on capital budgeting.)*

In Figure 4, the analysis of the purchase of the flight-type dishwasher is presented using the present value method and a desired rate of return of 10 percent. The purchase of the new dishwasher is an outflow at the beginning of the first year and has a present value factor of 1.0, yielding an outflow of 12,000. At this point, the cash received for the sale of the old dishwasher must be considered. Two thousand dollars is received at the beginning of the first year (present value factor 1.0). The loss on the sale of the old machine (its book value of $5000 minus the sale price of $2000) must also be considered. This reduces taxes, thus in effect, it is an inflow of $3000 times the tax rate of 52.8 percent, or $1584. The savings of Project B ($1896.84 per year) must be discounted to present value. This is done by multiplying $1896.84 times each of the present value factors for years 1 through 10, thus a discounting of each year's savings to the present value is accomplished. These savings represent a reduction in expenditures and may be considered an inflow of cash. The total for the inflows is $15,238.19; $12,000 equals the outflow. Since the total present value of the inflows is greater than the total present value of the outflow, Project B seems to be a better choice. The net present value (inflow minus outflow) is $3238.19.

Other alternatives, like keeping the rack-type dishwasher for five more years and then replacing it with the flight-type dishwasher, should also be analyzed, and the decision maker should then be able to pick the alternative having the greatest net present value.

In Figure 4, the calculations for the present value of the cash savings of Project B required a large amount of repetitive calculating that can be avoided since the $1896.84 is a constant payment received at the end of each year. Such a payment is called an annuity. Table 2 gives the present value of $1 received annually for "n" years. If one wished to know the present value of $500 received at the end of each year for, five years with

---

* Bierman, Harold and Seymour Smidt, *The Capital Budgeting Decision* 2nd ed. (New York 1966), for example.

TABLE 1
PRESENT VALUE OF $1

Years Hence	1%	2%	4%	6%	8%	10%	12%	14%	15%	16%
1	0.990	0.980	0.962	0.943	0.926	0.909	0.893	0.877	0.870	0.862
2	0.980	0.961	0.925	0.890	0.857	0.826	0.797	0.769	0.756	0.743
3	0.971	0.942	0.889	0.840	0.794	0.751	0.712	0.675	0.658	0.641
4	0.961	0.924	0.855	0.792	0.735	0.683	0.636	0.592	0.572	0.552
5	0.951	0.906	0.822	0.747	0.681	0.621	0.567	0.519	0.497	0.476
6	0.942	0.888	0.790	0.705	0.630	0.564	0.507	0.456	0.432	0.410
7	0.933	0.871	0.760	0.665	0.583	0.513	0.452	0.400	0.376	0.354
8	0.923	0.853	0.731	0.627	0.540	0.467	0.404	0.351	0.327	0.305
9	0.914	0.837	0.703	0.592	0.500	0.424	0.361	0.308	0.284	0.263
10	0.905	0.820	0.676	0.558	0.463	0.386	0.322	0.270	0.247	0.227
11	0.896	0.804	0.650	0.527	0.429	0.350	0.287	0.237	0.215	0.195
12	0.887	0.788	0.625	0.497	0.397	0.319	0.257	0.208	0.187	0.168
13	0.879	0.773	0.601	0.469	0.368	0.290	0.229	0.182	0.163	0.145
14	0.870	0.758	0.577	0.442	0.340	0.263	0.205	0.160	0.141	0.125
15	0.861	0.743	0.555	0.417	0.315	0.239	0.183	0.140	0.123	0.108
16	0.853	0.728	0.534	0.394	0.292	0.218	0.163	0.123	0.107	0.093
17	0.844	0.714	0.513	0.371	0.270	0.198	0.146	0.108	0.093	0.080
18	0.836	0.700	0.494	0.350	0.250	0.180	0.130	0.095	0.081	0.069
19	0.828	0.686	0.475	0.331	0.232	0.164	0.116	0.083	0.070	0.060
20	0.820	0.673	0.456	0.312	0.215	0.149	0.104	0.073	0.061	0.051
21	0.811	0.660	0.439	0.294	0.199	0.135	0.093	0.064	0.053	0.044
22	0.803	0.647	0.422	0.278	0.184	0.123	0.083	0.056	0.046	0.038
23	0.795	0.634	0.406	0.262	0.170	0.112	0.074	0.049	0.040	0.033
24	0.788	0.622	0.390	0.247	0.158	0.102	0.066	0.043	0.035	0.028
25	0.780	0.610	0.375	0.233	0.146	0.092	0.059	0.038	0.030	0.024
26	0.772	0.598	0.361	0.220	0.135	0.084	0.053	0.033	0.026	0.021
27	0.764	0.586	0.347	0.207	0.125	0.076	0.047	0.029	0.023	0.018
28	0.757	0.574	0.333	0.196	0.116	0.069	0.042	0.026	0.020	0.016
29	0.749	0.563	0.321	0.185	0.107	0.063	0.037	0.022	0.017	0.014
30	0.742	0.552	0.308	0.174	0.099	0.057	0.033	0.020	0.015	0.012
40	0.672	0.453	0.208	0.097	0.046	0.022	0.011	0.005	0.004	0.003
50	0.608	0.372	0.141	0.054	0.021	0.009	0.003	0.001	0.001	0.001

TABLE 1 (continued)

18%	20%	22%	24%	25%	26%	28%	30%	35%	40%	45%	50%
0.847	0.833	0.820	0.806	0.800	0.794	0.781	0.769	0.741	0.714	0.690	0.667
0.718	0.694	0.672	0.650	0.640	0.630	0.610	0.592	0.549	0.510	0.476	0.444
0.609	0.579	0.551	0.524	0.512	0.500	0.477	0.455	0.406	0.364	0.328	0.296
0.516	0.482	0.451	0.423	0.410	0.397	0.373	0.350	0.301	0.260	0.226	0.198
0.437	0.402	0.370	0.341	0.328	0.315	0.291	0.269	0.223	0.186	0.156	0.132
0.370	0.335	0.303	0.275	0.262	0.250	0.227	0.207	0.165	0.133	0.108	0.088
0.314	0.279	0.249	0.222	0.210	0.198	0.178	0.159	0.122	0.095	0.074	0.059
0.266	0.233	0.204	0.179	0.168	0.157	0.139	0.123	0.091	0.068	0.051	0.039
0.225	0.194	0.167	0.144	0.134	0.125	0.108	0.094	0.067	0.048	0.035	0.026
0.191	0.162	0.137	0.116	0.107	0.099	0.085	0.073	0.050	0.035	0.024	0.017
0.162	0.135	0.112	0.094	0.086	0.079	0.066	0.056	0.037	0.025	0.017	0.012
0.137	0.112	0.092	0.076	0.069	0.062	0.052	0.043	0.027	0.018	0.012	0.008
0.116	0.093	0.075	0.061	0.055	0.050	0.040	0.033	0.020	0.013	0.008	0.005
0.099	0.078	0.062	0.049	0.044	0.039	0.032	0.025	0.015	0.009	0.006	0.003
0.084	0.065	0.051	0.040	0.035	0.031	0.025	0.020	0.011	0.006	0.004	0.002
0.071	0.054	0.042	0.032	0.028	0.025	0.019	0.015	0.008	0.005	0.003	0.002
0.060	0.045	0.034	0.026	0.023	0.020	0.015	0.012	0.006	0.003	0.002	0.001
0.051	0.038	0.028	0.021	0.018	0.016	0.012	0.009	0.005	0.002	0.001	0.001
0.043	0.031	0.023	0.017	0.014	0.012	0.009	0.007	0.003	0.002	0.001	
0.037	0.026	0.019	0.014	0.012	0.010	0.007	0.005	0.002	0.001	0.001	
0.031	0.022	0.015	0.011	0.009	0.008	0.006	0.004	0.002	0.001		
0.026	0.018	0.013	0.009	0.007	0.006	0.004	0.003	0.001	0.001		
0.022	0.015	0.010	0.007	0.006	0.005	0.003	0.002	0.001			
0.019	0.013	0.008	0.006	0.005	0.004	0.003	0.002	0.001			
0.016	0.010	0.007	0.005	0.004	0.003	0.002	0.001	0.001			
0.014	0.009	0.006	0.004	0.003	0.002	0.002	0.001				
0.011	0.007	0.005	0.003	0.002	0.002	0.001	0.001				
0.010	0.006	0.004	0.002	0.002	0.002	0.001	0.001				
0.008	0.005	0.003	0.002	0.002	0.001	0.001	0.001				
0.007	0.004	0.003	0.002	0.002	0.001	0.001					
0.001	0.001										

	P.V. Factor	Inflows	Outflows
Purchase of flight type dishwasher			
$12000 × 1			$12,000.00
Proceeds from sale of old dishwasher		$2,000.00	
Tax advantage of loss on sale of			
old dishwasher $3000 × 0.528^a × 1		$1,584.00	
Cash Saving^b			
Year 1	$1,896.84 × .909	$1,724.23	
Year 2	1,896.84 × .826	1,566.79	
Year 3	1,896.84 × .751	1,424.53	
Year 4	1,896.84 × .683	1,295.54	
Year 5	1,896.84 × .621	1,177.94	
Year 6	1,896.84 × .564	1,069.82	
Year 7	1,896.84 × .513	973.08	
Year 8	1,896.84 × .467	885.82	
Year 9	1,896.84 × .424	804.26	
Year 10	1,896.84 × .386	732.18	
		$15,238.19	$12,000.00

^{a} Tax rate of 52.8 percent.

^{b} Cost savings of Project B over Project A per year after tax considerations (from Figure 3).

Figure 4

a desired return of 10 percent, he could go to Table 1 and calculate the present value of $500 for each of the years one to five and add these present values (Example 1), giving a total present value of $1895. An easier way to do this would be to multiply $500 times the present value factor from Table 2, for 10 percent over five years, 3.791, giving a figure of $1895.50 (Example 2).*

Applying the present value factor from Table 2 for a 10 percent return received over a 10-year period to $1896.84 (Figure 4), one derives $1896.84 times 6.145, or $11,656.08, for the present value of the cost savings, as opposed to the $11,654.19 he derives by using the present value factors of Table 1.† It is important to note that the present value factors of Table 2 may *not* be applied if the payments are not the same for each year.

So far we have assumed a desired rate of return and have then decided whether or not the total net present value of the inflows was greater than

* The 50 cents difference comes from a rounding error in the calculation of these tables.

† Again, the slight discrepancy is due to a rounding error.

Example 1

**Present Value
Factor (Ten Percent)**

Year 1	$500	×	0.909	=	$ 454.50
Year 2	500	×	0.826	=	413.00
Year 3	500	×	0.751	=	375.50
Year 4	500	×	0.683	=	341.50
Year 5	500	×	0.621	=	310.50
					$1895.00

Example 2

$500 × 3.791 = $1895.50

the net present value of the outflows. Next, we will examine a method for calculating a rate of return on the investment that considers the time value of money. This method is called "The Discounted Rate of Return" or, more commonly, "The Internal Rate of Return" (IRR).

In the IRR method, the objective is to find a rate of return such that the present value of the return equals the amount of the investment. Using the dishwasher problem (Figure 4), we see that the investment was $12,000 in year zero (at the beginning of the first year) with inflows at this same time of $2000 and $1,584 from the sale of the old dishwasher and considering the tax advantage deriving from the loss on the sale of the old dishwasher. Since both of these inflows occurred at the beginning of year one, their present values are $2000 and $1584. The total of these amounts may be subtracted from the investment ($12,000), giving a net investment figure of $8416. The question then becomes: what rate of return applied to $1896.84 over ten years would fix a net present value for the return of $8416? By using a trial and error method, one can get a close approximation that for most purposes would be sufficient. A first guess might be a 10 percent return as is used in Figure 5 (a) to calculate the present value of $1896.84 received over 10 years. This, however, turns out to be $11,654.19, which is greater than $8,416, and indicates that the return on the investment is greater than 10 percent.

Using a higher return, such as 18 percent in Figure 5 (b), and the present value factor from Table 2 (since equal payments are involved) of 4.494, one calculates a present value of $8524.39 for the return of $1896.84 per year over 10 years. (The present value factor from Table 2 could have been used for Figure 5 (a) instead of the longer method involved in using Table 1.) The $8524.39 is greater than $8416, indicating that the return is greater than 18 percent.

Figuring the present value of $1896.84 over 10 years at a return of 20 percent, as in Figure 5 (c), one derives $7,951.55, which is less than

TABLE 2

PRESENT VALUE OF $1 RECEIVED ANNUALLY FOR N YEARS

Years (N)	1%	2%	4%	6%	8%	10%	12%	14%	15%	16%
1	0.990	0.980	0.962	0.943	0.926	0.909	0.893	0.877	0.870	0.862
2	1.970	1.942	1.886	2.673	1.783	1.736	1.690	1.647	1.626	1.605
3	2.941	2.884	2.775	2.674	2.577	2.487	2.402	2.322	2.283	2.246
4	3.902	3.808	3.630	3.465	3.312	3.170	3.037	2.914	2.855	2.798
5	4.853	4.713	4.452	4.212	3.993	3.791	3.605	3.433	3.352	3.274
6	5.795	5.601	5.242	4.917	4.623	4.355	4.111	3.889	3.784	3.685
7	6.728	6.472	6.002	5.582	5.206	4.868	4.564	4.288	4.160	4.039
8	7.652	7.325	6.733	6.210	5.747	5.335	4.968	4.639	4.487	4.344
9	8.566	8.162	7.435	6.802	6.247	5.759	5.328	4.946	4.772	4.607
10	9.471	8.983	8.111	7.360	6.710	6.145	5.650	5.216	5.019	4.833
11	10.368	9.787	8.760	7.887	7.139	6.495	5.937	5.453	5.234	5.029
12	11.255	10.575	9.385	8.384	7.536	6.814	6.194	5.660	5.421	5.197
13	12.134	11.343	9.986	8.853	7.904	7.103	6.424	5.842	5.583	5.342
14	13.004	12.106	10.563	9.295	8.244	7.367	6.628	6.002	5.724	5.468
15	13.865	12.849	11.118	9.712	8.559	7.606	6.811	6.142	5.847	5.575
16	14.718	13.578	11.652	10.106	8.851	7.824	6.974	6.265	5.954	5.669
17	15.562	14.292	12.166	10.477	9.122	8.022	7.120	6.373	6.047	5.749
18	16.398	14.992	12.659	10.828	9.372	8.201	7.250	6.467	6.128	5.818
19	17.226	15.678	13.134	11.158	9.604	8.365	7.366	6.550	6.198	5.877
20	18.046	16.351	13.590	11.470	9.818	8.514	7.469	6.623	6.259	5.929
21	18.857	17.011	14.029	11.764	10.017	8.649	7.562	6.687	6.312	5.973
22	19.660	17.658	14.451	12.042	10.201	8.772	7.645	6.743	6.359	6.011
23	20.456	18.292	14.857	12.303	10,371	8.883	7.718	6.792	6.399	6.044
24	21.243	18.914	15.247	12.550	10.529	8.985	7.784	6.835	6.434	6.073
25	22.023	19.523	15.622	12.783	10.675	9.077	7.843	6.873	6.464	6.097
26	22.795	20.121	15.983	13.003	10.810	9.161	7.896	6.906	6.491	6.118
27	23.560	20.707	16.330	13.211	10.935	9.237	7.943	6.935	6.514	6.136
28	24.316	21.281	16.663	13.406	11.051	9.307	7.984	6.961	6.534	6.152
29	25.066	21.844	16.984	13.591	11.158	9.370	8.022	6.983	6.551	6.166
30	25.808	22.396	17.292	13.765	11.258	9.427	8.055	7.003	6.566	6.177
40	32.835	27.355	19.793	15.046	11.925	9.779	8.244	7.105	6.642	6.234
50	39.196	31.424	21.482	15.762	12.234	9.915	8.304	7.133	6.661	6.246

TABLE 2 (continued)

18%	20%	22%	24%	25%	26%	28%	30%	35%	40%	45%	50%
0.847	0.833	0.820	0.806	0.800	0.794	0.781	0.769	0.741	0.714	0.690	0.667
1.566	1.528	1.492	1.457	1.440	1.424	1.392	1.361	1.289	1.224	1.165	1.111
2.174	2.106	2.042	1.981	1.952	1.923	1.868	1.816	1.696	1.589	1.493	1.407
2.690	2.589	2.494	2.404	2.362	2.320	2.241	2.166	1.997	1.849	1.720	1.605
3.127	2.991	2.864	2.745	2.689	2.635	2.532	2.436	2.220	2.035	1.876	1.737
3.498	3.326	3.167	3.020	2.951	2.885	2.759	2.643	2.385	2.168	1.983	1.824
3.812	3.605	3.416	3.242	3.161	3.083	2.937	2.802	2.508	2.263	2.057	1.883
4.078	3.837	3.619	3.421	3.329	3.241	3.076	2.925	2.598	2.331	2.108	1.922
4.303	4.031	3.786	3.566	3.463	3.366	3.184	3.019	2.665	2.379	2.144	1.948
4.494	4.192	3.923	3.682	3.571	3.465	3.269	3.092	2.715	2.414	2.168	1.965
4.656	4.327	4.035	3.776	3.656	3.544	3.335	3.147	2.752	2.438	2.185	1.977
4.793	4.439	4.127	3.851	3.725	3.606	3.387	3.190	2.779	2.456	2.196	1.985
4.910	4.533	4.203	3.912	3.780	3.656	3.427	3.223	2.799	2.468	2.204	1.990
5.008	4.611	4.265	3.962	3.824	3.695	3.459	3.249	2.814	2.477	2.210	1.993
5.092	4.675	4.315	4.001	3.859	3.726	3.483	3.268	2.825	2.484	2.214	1.995
5.162	4.730	4.357	4.033	3.887	3.751	3.503	3.283	2.834	2.489	2.216	1.997
5.222	4.775	4.391	4.059	3.910	3.771	3.518	3.295	2.840	2.492	2.218	1.998
5.273	4.812	4.419	4.080	3.928	3.786	3.529	3.304	2.844	2.494	2.219	1.999
5.316	4.844	4.442	4.097	3.942	3.799	3.539	3.311	2.848	2.496	2.220	1.999
5.353	4.870	4.460	4.110	3.954	3.808	3.546	3.316	2.850	2.497	2.221	1.999
5.384	4.891	4.476	4.121	3.963	3.816	3.551	3.320	2.852	2.498	2.221	2.000
5.410	4.909	4.488	4.130	3.970	3.822	3.556	3.323	2.853	2.498	2.222	2.000
5.432	4.925	4.499	4.137	3.976	3.827	3.559	3.325	2.854	2.499	2.222	2.000
5.451	4.937	4.507	4.143	3.981	3.831	3.562	3.327	2.855	2.499	2.222	2.000
5.467	4.948	4.514	4.147	3.985	3.834	3.564	3.329	2.856	2.499	2.222	2.000
5.480	4.956	4.520	4.151	3.988	3.837	3.566	3.330	2.856	2.500	2.222	2.000
5.492	4.964	4.524	4.154	3.990	3.839	3.567	3.331	2.856	2.500	2.222	2.000
5.502	4.970	4.528	4.157	3.992	3.840	3.568	3.331	2.857	2.500	2.222	2.000
5.510	4.975	4.531	4.159	3.994	3.841	3.569	3.332	2.857	2.500	2.222	2.000
5.517	4.979	4.534	4.160	3.995	3.842	3.569	3.332	2.857	2.500	2.222	2.000
5.548	4.997	4.544	4.166	3.999	3.846	3.571	3.333	2.857	2.500	2.222	2.000
5.554	4.999	4.545	4.167	4.000	3.846	3.571	3.333	2.857	2.500	2.222	2.000

	(a)		P.V. Factor (10%)—Table 1		
Year 1	$1,896.84	×	.909	=	$ 1,724.23
Year 2	1,896.84	×	.826	=	1,566.79
Year 3	1,896.84	×	.751	=	1,424.53
Year 4	1,896.84	×	.683	=	1,295.54
Year 5	1,896.84	×	.621	=	1,177.94
Year 6	1,896.84	×	.564	=	1,069.82
Year 7	1,896.84	×	.513	=	973.08
Year 8	1,896.84	×	.467	=	885.82
Year 9	1,896.84	×	.424	=	804.26
Year 10	1,896.84	×	.386	=	732.18
					$11,654.19
	(b)		(18%)—Table 2		
	$1,896.84	×	4.494		$ 8,524.39
	(c)		(20%)—Table 2		
	$1,896.84	×	4.192		$ 7,951.55

Figure 5

$8,416, indicating a rate of return less than 20 percent. We know, then, that the rate of return must lie somewhere between 18 and 20 percent.

A quick method for calculating Internal Rate of Return, which may be used only with equal returns for each year, is to divide the net investment by the annual return. The factor derived this way can be compared with the factors in Table 2 in the row equal to the length of time over which these returns will be received. It is calculated in this way:

$$\frac{\$8,416.00}{\$1,896.84} = 4.437 \ (\text{Factor})$$

The annual returns extend over a 10-year period, thus going across Table 2 on the 10-year row and by reading the percentages from the headings for the columns containing 4.494 and 4.192, we see that 4.437 would lie between these figures, and we conclude that the Internal Rate of Return lies between 18 and 20 percent.

BORROWING

Availability of funds (or lack of their availability) can affect cost control. The operation that is financially pressed cannot take advantage of cash discounts or install new features. An inordinate amount of time and energy must be spent trying to cope with the financial crises, time and energy which could have been spent improving the operation. On the other hand, operations have also run into trouble when funds become too easily available: overexpansion and the temptation to acquire unneeded assets are two obvious problems connected with a too-easy access to funds. Many operators owe a debt of gratitude to that banker who returned an unsympathetic "no" to a loan request.

Over and above the normal cash flow (profits plus depreciation allowances) and sale of assets, there are two general methods a commercial operation can use to gain funds. It can acquire equity capital by stock sales or by taking in partners; this, of course, dilutes ownership and divides profits. Or it can borrow, that is, it can negotiate direct loans, issue bonds, lease premises or equipment, or use a purveyor's money either by paying bills slowly or defaulting entirely. Purveyors may also decide to make direct loans to an operation, sometimes for the privilege of doing business with the operation.

Established financial institutions like banks provide the usual source of direct loans. Normally loans can be made if one or both of two conditions are met. Security is the first condition. If collateral is pledged or if the note is cosigned by a financially responsible person, the chance of loss for the lending institution is diminished. Among other things, collateral can include stocks, bonds, inventories, accounts receivable, cash surrender value of life insurance, or real property.

The other important condition is a means of repayment. Commercial loans normally are made to finance operations that will generate funds sufficient to repay the loan, so a lender will usually want to know where the money to repay his loan will come from. An intangible but important factor in the granting of a loan is the reputation of the borrower for honesty, fair dealing, and promptness.

The federal government can be of assistance. Through the Small Business Administration, it sometimes secures loans that banks would normally not grant. These loans may be used to purchase equipment, facilities, and supplies, or simply as working capital. There are two types of S. B. A. loans: a borrower might deal either with the S. B. A. alone, or with the S. B. A. in conjunction with another financial institution. A direct loan to the operation by the S.B.A. cannot be made if the loan can be arranged in conjunction with a private institution. On these participatory loans, the S. B. A. may agree to purchase from the bank a certain percentage of the principal at the outset of the loan, or it may agree to purchase a certain percentage of the loan during the life of the loan if the participating bank requests it. In either case, the loan becomes more desirable for the lending bank since the possibility of loss is reduced by the amount of S. B. A. participation. Besides its loan function, the S. B. A. can act as an adviser or consultant to small business firms.

Loans must, of course, be repaid with interest. There are a number of methods by which interest is calculated. Interest costs on installment repayment loans can vary considerably despite apparent similarity in interest rates. The method of calculating the interest cost can be more important than the rate itself. Assume $1000 is borrowed for one year at a rate of 6 percent, payable in 12 equal monthly payments. The interest on $1000 at 6 percent for one year would be $60.

If the loan is offered on a discount basis, the lending operation would subtract the $60 from the $1000 at the outset and actually pay out only $940. Sixty dollars interest has been charged for $940—really a rate of about 6.4 percent.

However, remember that the loan is being repaid throughout the year. At the outset of the loan, the full amount is outstanding, but at the last payment only one-twelfth of the full amount is oustanding. The average amount of money outstanding during the year is one-half of $940, or $470, for which $60 of interest has been received. This produces a true interest rate of approximately 12.8 percent.

Smaller interest costs are incurred when interest is charged only on the balance outstanding. If the payments are made on a monthly basis and the interest cost of 6 percent is calculated on the basis of 30 days for the amount of the unpaid balance, a true 6 percent interest rate is provided. The first interest payments are higher than later ones, since there is more money outstanding.

The constant payment method divides the total interest cost and total principal to be amortized by the number of repayment periods. All payments, which include both interest and principal are equal, but the amount of the payment for interest will be highest in the first payments and will be reduced in each succeeding one, the difference being added to repayment of the principal. The constant payment method can allow for a true rate of interest.

LEASING

For an operation short on funds, and having a difficult time securing loans from the usual sources, and requiring new equipment, leasing may provide a satisfactory solution.

The practice of leasing equipment in the food service field has been increasingly rapidly. The leasing of equipment is a comparatively recent practice, but it is gaining popularity.

Food industry leasing usually follows one of two patterns: Small pieces of operating equipment or supplies combined with services (like linen rental and its laundering; kitchen knives together with their periodic sharpening) or straight lease of items such as banquet china, glassware, and silver; or such heavy equipment as ranges, cars, trucks, tables, chairs, or complete kitchens.

Under certain conditions, it may be more desirable and cheaper for an operation to lease equipment than to purchase it. For an operation with a shortage of working capital and no means of securing a loan, leasing can be an avenue of intermediate financing, a way to secure the equipment that could reduce operating costs, increase potential sales, or merely maintain the present profit level.

Leases cannot be "called in" by the bank as a loan can. Problems of loan renewal are also eliminated by leasing. Finally, the interest rates cannot be increased when an operation leases, and there are no requirements for "compensating balances" (a deposit of a certain percentage of a loan, often required by a bank as a condition of the loan).

The rental terms of a lease usually specify higher costs than the costs of a direct loan, but the actual costs may be less in some cases, since lease payments can reduce taxable income and promote greater after-tax profits. Rentals or lease expenses for real estate, buildings, or equipment are direct costs against current income, and they provide higher deductions during the shorter lease period. The depreciation on purchased equipment is usually based on a useful life that is longer than the leasing period, and even accelerated depreciation may not provide as high a deduction during the first few years as lease rentals. So while both lease payments and depreciation reduce taxable income, lease payments may provide greater tax advantages in the first years.

Other advantages claimed by proponents of leasing appear on this list.

a. Equipment financing may be secured without diluting ownership or equity.

b. It is not necessary to wait until capital has accumulated through retained earnings and depreciation to secure new items; leasing allows acquisition of equipment without down payments or loan restrictions.

c. It is possible to increase profits without correspondingly increasing capital investment.

d. A company specializing in leasing certain types of equipment may save on the purchase and maintenance of its equipment and may pass these savings on to the lessee. An automobile leasing company can, for example, purchase and maintain a fleet of vehicles more cheaply than a nonauto operation. A lessee becomes the beneficiary of these savings when he leases trucks and cars.

Opponents of leasing point out these facts.

a. The dollar cost of leasing may be higher than the purchase price of the same equipment.
b. At the end of the lease period, the equipment remains the property of the leasing company. There may be a provision in the lease for the lessee to continue to use the equipment, but this will involve additional cost.

A Leasing Procedure. A food service operation specifies the equipment it wants and supplies its needs and the price it can afford to pay. A leasing firm buys the equipment to these specifications and delivers it to the operation.

After acceptance, the food service operation makes regular payments to the leasing company tailored to its capabilities. (The usual lease payment period runs from three to eight years.)

At the end of the lease payment period, the equipment may be turned in, the lease may be renewed on lower terms, a trade-in on new equipment (with a new lease) may be arranged, or the equipment may be purchased outright by the operation. The purchase option may be included in the original lease agreement.

chapter 16

Break-Even Analysis

INTRODUCTION TO BREAK-EVEN ANALYSIS

Successful management requires an awareness of those relationships between costs and sales that determine profit or loss. A break-even chart can plot these relationships and help answer such questions as:

At what sales volume will the operation make money?

What should the profit (or loss) be at a particular sales volume?

How much should expenses be at a particular sales volume?

How will changing menu selling prices (and possibly changing, thereby, the number of covers served) affect profit?

It is feasible to incur cost designed to increase sales, for example, additional advertising?

Should the operation expand (or begin)?

A break-even chart shows in graphic form the relationship between the volume of business produced (that is, the number of meals) and the resulting sales income, expenditures, and profits or losses. In doing so, it shows at what sales volume the operation will cover its expenses and begin making a profit. It can portray the anticipated effect of menu price changes: It could help determine whether higher menu prices would more than offset a predicted lower customer volume (or number of sales), or whether lower menu prices could be balanced by a customer increase.

Sales and cost categories are shown in graphic form on a breakeven chart. And the chart is, in effect, a visual and variable budget. It allows one to see preplanned costs for any volume. By indicating profits as well as sales, it encourages concentration on profits as well as on sales. Potential financial troubles may be revealed before they are incurred, allowing action to be taken before the difficulty arises, rather than after it has eaten into profits. The portrayal of costs and sales in graphic form makes it easier for some to assimilate the information than if it had been presented in conventional tabular or statistical form. A break-even chart may be used to illustrate past performance, or it may be prepared as a budget or a forecast of future performance.

PREPARING A BREAK-EVEN CHART

The format for a break-even chart is an "L" shaped graph. Usually, the vertical line on the right is used to indicate dollar amounts, and the horizontal bottom line indicates the number of units or meals. One-thousand meals sold at an average price of $2 would be plotted at the point where lines running perpendicular to the bottom scale mark of 1000 and perpendicular to the side figure of $20,000 converge (Point B, Figure 1).

In preparing the chart, it is necessary to consider costs as either fixed or variable. The fixed costs remain constant regardless of volume. These might include such items as rent and insurance. Such variable costs as food costs or linens vary more or less directly with the volume. Some costs may be semivariable since they fluctuate with volume, but not in direct

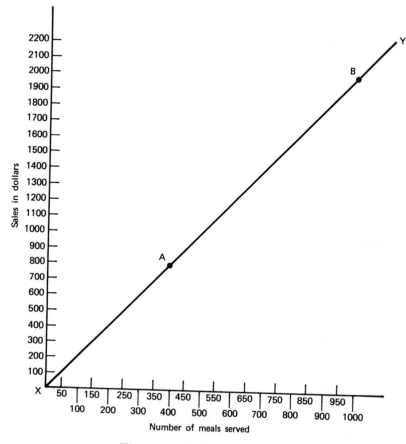

Figure 1   Plotting a sales line.

proportion to the volume change. Labor may be a semivariable cost because a certain basic staff is always required and rather resembles a fixed cost. However, as volume increases, more staff is needed, although a 50 percent increase in volume would probably not require a 50 percent increase in personnel.

Except in the case of fixed costs, where an unchanging dollar amount regardless of volume can be plotted, it is necessary to have two or more points in order to draw sales and cost lines on the chart. Of course, a straight line may be drawn between two points. But if more points that do not fit on a straight line are used, a line may be drawn that represents the points, even though it does not quite intersect them. If enough points are plotted, curves may be drawn. If changes at specific volumes are unusually sharp, a staggered or plateau type may be used.

For illustrative purposes, consider an operation that has an average charge of $2 per meal and is presently serving 800 meals at a daily profit of $90. The following information is given for two levels of activity on a daily basis.

	Low Volume	High Volume
Number of meals sold	400	1,000
Income at $2 per meal	$ 800	$ 2,000
Fixed charges	$ 200	$ 200
General administrative	$ 160 (20%)*	$ 320 (16%)*
Food cost	$ 280 (35%)*	$ 700 (30%)*
Labor cost	$ 280 (35%)*	$ 600 (30%)*

*Percentage of sales

Using these figures, it is easily determined that the operation will lose about $120 at the low volume and will earn about $180 at the higher volume. With a break-even chart, it is possible to determine what the profit or loss would be at any level and what the various expense categories should cost for any level of activity.

The sales figure is found by plotting the low point sales of 400 meals on the bottom scale and $800 on the side scale (Point A, Figure 1). The high volume point is plotted at 1000 meals and $2000 (Point B, Figure 1). The sales line or curve is then Line XY on Figure 1.

The fixed expense of $200 would be a horizontal line at the $200, since it does not vary with volume (Line CD, Figure 2). (Daily fixed expenses are found by dividing the total fixed expenses for the year by the number of days of operation.)

General administrative expenses of $160, at 400 meals volume, and

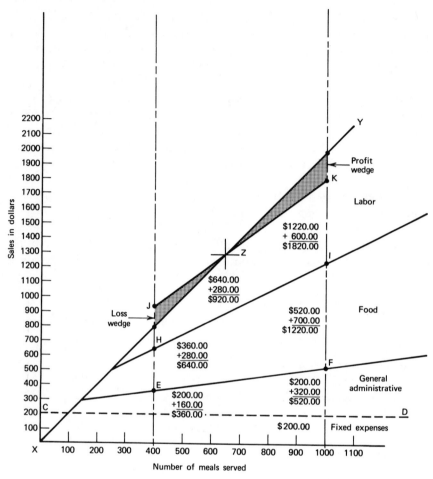

Figure 2   Showing profit or loss.

$320, at 1000 meals volume, are added to the fixed cost making total costs so far $360 and $520 for their respective volumes. These points are plotted allowing Line EF to be drawn. Food costs of $280 and $700 are added to the cost totals accumulated so far, making new totals of $640 and $1220 (line *HI*). Labor costs are then added, making new totals of $920 and $1820 and Line JK, which is also the total expense line. The point where the line crosses the sales line, at 640 meals and $1280 sales volume, is the breakeven point. The wedge to the left of the point shows the loss at any level of volume, while the profit may be read off at any volume to the right of the point. A break-even chart can be prepared on a daily basis to show what volume is necessary to produce a profit as well as what the costs should be at any volume.

A 10 percent increase in selling prices is being considered. However, it is expected that the number of covers sold will be reduced by 5 percent by the price increases. Is the proposed increase feasible? A 10 percent menu increase would make the average check $2.20, and at 400 covers sales would be $880 (Point A, Figure 3) and $2200 at 1000 covers (Point B, Figure 3), or Line XY. Total costs, Line JK, remain the same. If the 800 daily covers are reduced 5 percent because of the price increase, the new average number of covers would be 760. The profit at 760 covers (Wedge Q-R) is $220, a very desirable increase.

Assume the operation is still serving 800 meals with a profit of $90

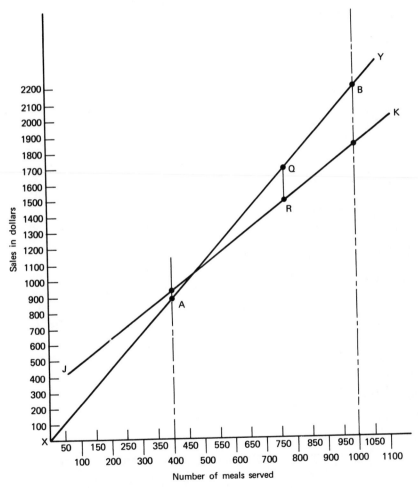

Figure 3   Effect of 10 percent menu selling price increase.

(Figure 2). What greater sales volume would be required to allow a menu selling price reduction of 5 percent but still maintaining the $90 profit? The average price per cover is now $1.90. Four hundred covers would produce sales of $760 (Point A, Figure 4) at the low volume, and $1900 at 1000 cover level (Point B). The chart shows that about 1000 meals (or a gross of $1900) instead of 800 meals (a gross of $1600) would have to be achieved (wedge B-C) for a $90 profit (the reading between income and cost lines) with the lower selling price.

The previous examples have been based on a daily break-even chart. The charts may be prepared for a month, a year, or for any other period. A yearly break-even chart may be very helpful in determining the feasibility of expanding the operation, or projected figures may be used in planning the feasibility of a new operation.

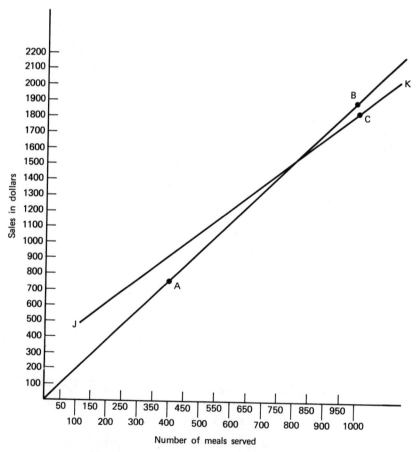

Figure 4   Effect of lower selling price.

It is possible to determine the break-even point of an operation mathematically. One formula is $FC + SVC + VC =$ Total costs of break-even, where:

$$FC = \text{fixed costs}$$
$$SVC = \text{semivariable costs}$$
$$VC = \text{variable costs}$$

This formula adds all costs to determine the total cost. When total costs exactly equal sales, the operation is neither making nor losing money, it is at the break-even point. Assume that an operation has fixed costs (FC) of \$200, semivariable (SVC) costs of \$500, and variable costs (VC) of 50 percent of sales. Inserting these figures into the formula, one can see that \$1400 is the break-even point:

$$
\begin{array}{ccccl}
FC & SVC & VC & & \\
\$200 & + \ \$500 & + \ 50\% \ TC = TC & \text{(Total Costs) or Break-even} \\
& & \$ \ 700 = 0.50 \ TC & \\
& & \$1400 = TC \ \text{or break-even} &
\end{array}
$$

Use of this formula, however, does not permit one to allow for differences in semivariable and variable expenses at different volumes, which in fact, is often the case. The percentage of labor cost to sales, for example, may change considerably at different volumes.

Disadvantages of Break-even Analysis. Break-even analysis can be a helpful tool in analyzing the volume-cost-profit relationship. It can also portray the information in a very desirable graphic form. There are, however, complicating factors in their use by food service (or other) organizations that the reader should be aware of.

A break-even chart is most effective when there is one product. The menu of a food service establishment usually contains many items or products. The markups and profit percentages of these various items may vary considerably, making it difficult to apply a general price increase or decrease to the whole menu, since the same adjustments would probably not be made for each of the items. To overcome this, it is possible to consider weighted or average changes in the break-even calculations. It is also possible to use a break-even analysis for a major menu item. If a steak selection, for example, is one of your major sales items, break-even analysis could be used to determine the optimum selling prices. Of course, assumptions would have to be made for the proportion of fixed and other expenses that should be alloted to the steak sales.

Another complication in utilizing break-even charts is the relevant range of the data portrayed. Straight lines, if used, extend from the vertical axis to the opposite edge. These may be misleading, especially for variable costs, since the cost line may not have the same unit cost-times-volume relationship over the whole length of the line. At different volumes, the unit costs may change due to different utilization of resources. Different unit costs at different volumes cannot be reflected in a straight line. Curves or staggered lines may then be used to show this information if supporting data is available.

Because of the nature of its construction, a break-even chart cannot provide exact information. It is helpful as a first step in developing the basic data for pricing or other financial decision making. Before the final decisions are made, however, other analyses should also be employed.

Contribution Margin. Helpful in the study of cost-volume profit relationships is the analysis of the contribution margin. This may be defined as the excess of revenue of a product over the variable costs of producing it. It is, therefore, the contribution to the recovery of fixed costs and profits. Assume a menu item sells for $2 and variable expenses are $1.20. The contribution ratio, or amount available for fixed costs and profit, is 80 cents or 40 percent of sales. This can be illustrated.

	Per Meal	Percentage
Selling price of meal	$2.00	100%
Variable costs	1.20	60
Contribution Margin	$0.80	40%

Some application of the contribution margin can be found in the following formulas.

$$\text{Sales revenue required to break even} = \frac{\text{Fixed Costs}}{\text{Contribution margin expressed as a percentage of sales revenue.}}$$

If the contribution ratio is 40 percent (for all sales, not just the one menu item) and fixed costs are $60,000, the break-even figure would be $150,000 or:

$$\frac{\$60,000}{40\%} = \$150,000$$

This could also be calculated in terms of number of meals served instead of dollar sales. If the average meal is sold for $2 and the contribution per meal is 80 cents, then 75,000 meals would have to be served to break-even.

$$\text{Break-even volume in meals} = \frac{\text{Fixed expenses}}{\text{Contribution margin per unit}} = \frac{\$60,000}{\$.80} = \frac{75,000}{\text{meals}}$$

It is also possible, by using the contribution margin, to determine the sales necessary to produce a desired profit.

$$\text{Sales revenue required to produce a desired profit} = \frac{\text{Fixed costs plus desired profit}}{\text{Contribution margin expressed as a percentage of sales revenue}}$$

A $30,000 profit before taxes is desired. This would require $225,000 in sales or:

$$\frac{\$60,000 \text{ plus } \$30,000}{40\%} = \$225,000$$

The contribution margin concept can be helpful in planning. A restaurant, for example, is considering closing down for breakfast, since it appears that little profit is being produced. However, if the breakfast income is considered in relation to its contribution to fixed expenses and overhead, it may be desirable to keep open for breakfast, since it may not be possible to absorb the necessary off-setting increases in the contribution margin from the other meals. A type of contribution margin concept can be used in pricing menus, which is explored in Chapter 8.

In calculating the contribution margin, one variable cost such as food might be used, or the total of all variable costs can be used. It is sometimes difficult to differentiate realistically between some variable and fixed costs. What portion of the labor cost is fixed and what portion is variable, for example, may be hard to determine. It is usually best to consider a cost as either fixed or variable and to eliminate the semivariable category.

chapter 17

Cost Analysis of a Food Service Operation

The success and profit of a commercial food service operation depend on two factors: the volume of business serviced, and the control of costs in servicing this volume. When it is not possible to increase the volume of business, the only way to increase or maintain profits is by keeping costs in line. The goal of a nonprofit operation is to provide the best food service that its resources permit, and this can be accomplished only through strict cost control. All operations want to control costs, but too often operators give little careful systematic thought to the ways to achieve this goal. A management busy with day to day problems may not be aware of incipient cost-increasing tendencies. For all these reasons, an objective cost survey or analysis can be beneficial to an operation and can bring to light cost problems before they become too troublesome.

Quite often outside consultants are called in to examine an operation. The problems they locate may be rather specific, such as low profits or abnormally high cost areas. Also, an operation that appears to be satisfactory may want an objective evaluation and suggestions for improvement. A qualified cost survey expert may also be consulted by an operator who contemplates major changes, such as the large scale introduction of convenience foods.

Management should be constantly analyzing its operations. While it has the advantage of knowing its operation better than any outsider, this familiarity may blind it to possible changes and potential problems; or past procedures may be so deeply ingrained that new and different methods of accomplishing the organization's goals get overlooked or ignored. An outside person may be more aware of different approaches and new products than the management that has to spend most of its time on routine operating problems.

A survey or analysis may consist of a general operations review or may be designed for such specific purposes as a sales promotion, a remodeling, or a cost analysis. The following procedures are primarily concerned with cost analysis and provide a guide in doing such a survey. Considerably more detailed information on the various topics can be found in other chapters.

Part of the analysis can, and often should, be performed away from the establishment and before the first visit. Financial statements, payroll data, daily and cyclical menus, and sales and cost records should be secured first. By examining these, the analyst can spot potential cost problem areas and can also get a feel of the operation.

FINANCIAL STATEMENT ANALYSIS

This work entails primarily an analysis of the Profit and Loss Statement. Do the statements present an accurate picture of costs and profit? Are they prepared frequently enough to allow corrective action without substantial loss? Statements that are prepared infrequently, or are delivered far after the time they cover, cannot help recover any losses that may have occurred. Check if the statements follow the format suggested in the *Uniform System of Accounts for Restaurants*. If not, it may be necessary to rearrange them in this format for comparison purposes. Translate cost items and profit into percentages of sales if this has not already been done. Compare the cost percentages with those presented in Chapter 12. Any significant deviation should be investigated.

The results of the current fiscal period should be compared with the figures for the comparable period of the previous year, and significant percentage variations should be noted. Any trends in sales, profit, or major cost items should be brought to light by comparing the last three yearly statements. How does profit compare as a percentage of sales for the last three years? Are increases due to higher menu sales caused by inflationary price increase or are the increases real?

The most significant figures from a cost standpoint are the food cost percentages, the labor cost percentages, the inventory turnover, the average sales per cover, and the profits (if a commercial operation is being analyzed).

The consultant should investigate whatever food cost accounting system is in use and determine whether this system is adequately providing information to reveal any food cost discrepancies. Perhaps, for example, a standard cost type system would be more helpful for a particular operation than the strict percentage system it might be using.

PAYROLL DATA ANALYSIS

The ratio of payroll to sales will suggest whether or not payroll costs are excessive. Payroll calculations should be investigated. Are all the hours paid for actually worked? Check the productivity of the various jobs by work production standards such as covers served per man day. Check to see if scheduled work hours are appropriate for the levels of activity at various times. Is a forecast of volume prepared in advance and is scheduling done on the basis of the forecast? Bar charts may be very helpful in pinpointing where the number of labor hours is excessive. Calculate the hours and cost of overtime. Is this excessive for the size of the payroll? Calculating turnover and absenteeism ratios can suggest whether these factors are causing excessively high labor costs.

Do employees know what they should be doing and the best way of doing it? Job descriptions help eliminate the former problem; training programs, the latter. Check the worker's supervision. It may not be adequate. Also check to see if supervisors or the more highly paid employees are doing tasks that lower paid employees could be doing.

Is a job control list used to control the number of employees on the payroll and specifically to indicate the job each employee should be performing? Are employees hired for busy periods, then retained when business decreases?

Are progressive personnel management policies being followed? Are recruitment, hiring, orienting, and training performed in a haphazard manner, or is a real effort being made to do a competent job in these areas?

Are employees motivated to do the best job of which they are capable? This motivation can be effected by appreciation and praise or by material rewards, such as profit sharing.

MENU ANALYSIS

By carefully examining a typical menu, or several typical menus, a consultant can determine whether the price of each item is appropriate to its cost and whether the combined food costs and selling prices are advantageous to the operation. If the operation is an institution without direct sales, a consultant should determine if the daily food costs of the menus are within the food cost budget.

All the items on the menu should be considered. Are there more items than necessary? (Usually the more elaborate the menu, the harder it is to control costs and maintain quality.) Are there too many items that have to be prepared in advance? (These may be hard to utilize as left-overs. There is little profit in using leftover prime rib in beef pot pies.) Is there a plan for handling leftovers? (No item should be on the menu if there has been no prior thought on how to utilize it in leftover form.) Do the items on the menu provide balanced labor and equipment utilization? (If part of the kitchen is overworked and part underworked, inefficiency and higher costs will result.)

REVENUE CONTROL

Lower profits because of excess costs are bad enough; but even worse are sales where the operation does not receive the money paid by customers. A guest check system should be employed. The guest checks should be audited to see that all checks are accounted for. If not routinely, at least occasionally, the arithmetic on checks should be checked. The total sales from the guest checks should be reconciled with cash register sales figures and figures from the food checking system, if one is utilized. The cashier should not have access to a key that clears balances from the machine; and unannounced, the manager should take occasional daily readings. The cash turn-in should be in agreement with the total of guest checks and register readings. If one person makes up the cashier banks, reads the registers, keeps accounts receivable, and prepares the bank deposit, it is very important that the work be audited, preferably at unannounced times.

PURCHASING ANALYSIS

A consultant should determine the prices paid for merchandise and then compare these with the prices paid by other establishments or quoted by other purveyors. Prices can change from day to day so the prices must be correlated with the day of purchase. Is the purchasing of perishables being done on the basis of forecasted volume to cut down the chance of over purchasing? Standard purchase quantities and reorder points may be used for staples. Unless there are approved arrangements to the contrary, check to see if competitive bids have been secured. Do the purchasers have the time and knowledge to do a competent job? For best control, the person who purchases food should not also be responsible for receiving it or preparing it. (Of course, many operations are too small to spread their purchasing responsibilities.)

Has management provided a list of approved purveyors, or can the items be purchased from anyone? Have specifications been developed to provide the ideal purchase quantities, the best yield, the most consistent quality, and the fairest bids on equal quality merchandise? Is there an inventory or check to determine quantities on hand before order quantities are determined? Is there a means, such as the *Steward's Market Order Sheet*, to compare the quoted price with the invoice price? Would a contract purchasing system be desirable?

RECEIVING ANALYSIS

Is there real receiving control, or is merchandise delivered without checking? There should be a central receiving area, preferably with definite hours for accepting merchandise. Check to see that scales are accurate by using a known weight on them. See that incoming food is properly weighed and that allowance is made for packing. Is the receiving man competent to pass on food quality? Does he have the purchase specifications available to him? How are short weights or short counts handled? Is credit actually received for discrepancies or returned merchandise? Is a receiving report utilized, all items recorded, and the report signed? Are meat tags employed and, if not, should they be adopted? Management should make surprise visits to the receiving area to ensure that proper receiving techniques are actually being used and to uncover any unethical arrangements between receiving personnel and the purveyors or their deliverymen.

STORAGE ANALYSIS

The merchandise in storage represents money and should be handled accordingly. Is access to the storeroom limited only to the personnel who have to be there? (Establishing definite times to accept and fill requisitions is a wise practice.) Are sanitation and housekeeping practices adequate to prevent losses from insects and rodents? Is the food stored off the floor and not against exterior walls? Is FIFO (first in, first out) practiced? Are inventories taken periodically with a disinterested person involved? Are unused items in storage brought to the attention of management? Are sufficient inventory quantities on hand, without tying up an excessive amount of working capital and space?

Are perishables stored under proper temperature and humidity ranges? In refrigerated areas, is food stored to allow adequate air circulation? Are dates of receipt marked on items so that extended storage periods will be noticeable, and the oldest items will be used first?

It may not be feasible to keep a perpetual inventory on all items, but figures can be kept on items susceptible to loss such as coffee, butter, and steak. It is wise to check the amount of an item actually on hand against the amount that should be on hand, taking into consideration beginning inventory, new purchases, and issues for the period.

ISSUING ANALYSIS

Is there control over food leaving the storage areas? (This control is usually accomplished by requisitions.) Should the requisitions be signed or initiated by the person requisitioning the food, the person filling the requisition, and the person who receives the requisition? Would it be possible to install an ingredient room which, along with other benefits, could provide better issuing control?

If food items are provided for bars or for home employee consumption, there should be credit requisitions for full accountability.

PREPARATION ANALYSIS

A great deal of money can be lost in the preparation process. A consultant should determine whether standard recipes are available and are being used. Proper cooking temperatures are very important, especially in the roasting of meats, and it is helpful to see that the thermostats are accurate as well as being set for the proper temperature.

A look at the garbage may reveal excessive waste in pre-preparation. Excessive waste may also indicate simple overproduction.

Is a forecast made of anticipated consumption and definite production quantities? (Too often restaurants prepare the same amount of an item, despite fluctuations in volume.) Is there a form that shows how much of an item has been produced, how much has been consumed, how much was left over, and how the leftovers were utilized?

SERVING ANALYSIS

Irregular portioning can cause fluctuations in food costs and customer dissatisfaction. Check to see that portion sizes have been determined and publicized and are readily available. Are there means available to serve these standard portions—proper sized scoops, ladles, portion scales, dishware, and glassware? (It is most important that management check to see that the employees are actually serving the proper portions.)

LAYOUT AND EQUIPMENT ANALYSIS

While there are limits on the changes that are feasible in an already equipped kitchen, a consultant can often suggest improvements or changes that can be accomplished at a relatively small expense.

Faults that are common to many kitchens include an inadequate work table area, poorly installed equipment, seldom used equipment, equipment of the wrong size or capacity for the volume of the operation, and bottlenecks at soiled dish tables.

It is often possible to increase counter work area by rearranging facilities. Many operations have become more efficient with the added space gained from disposing of surplus equipment. If a piece of equipment is not the proper size, a study should be made to determine the costs involved in and the benefits gained by replacing it. Bottlenecks can often be alleviated or eliminated by studying alternative procedures. Perhaps installing overhead storage racks or having dishwashers work on scraping and stacking dishes before starting the actual washing could help solve a soiled dish table bottleneck.

The consultant should check to see that there are enough small utensils like ladles, pans, and knives. Often it is helpful to have these small utensils placed in several areas of the kitchen to eliminate the extra steps necessary to secure them from one central area. However, there should also be a definite station for these utensils so that time will not be lost trying to find them.

Placing some equipment, the slicer for example, on a coaster or a cart may provide efficiency by making it possible to bring the equipment to the materials, instead of having to transport the materials to the equipment.

A consultant should check to see that the equipment is in proper repair. (Not replacing a dull can opener blade or worn gaskets on refrigerators can become costly.)

MANAGEMENT ANALYSIS

Is management fulfilling its control responsibilities? Are management personnel spending a disproportionate amount of time in the front of the house and neglecting discrepancies in the back of the house? (Most control procedures become effective only when everyone knows that management is vitally interested in and concerned with them.) Besides demanding control records and reports, does management study them and then review them with the individuals involved?

Has management provided an organization where everyone knows what he is supposed to be doing, how to do it, to whom he reports, and who might report to him? (A consultant would check to see if there are job descriptions, an organization chart, and training routines.)

Control does not happen by itself. It occurs only with advanced planning and persistence on the part of management.

index